Universal Emancipation

UNIVERSAL EMANCIPATION

RACE BEYOND BADIOU

ELISABETH PAQUETTE

University of Minnesota Press

Minneapolis

London

Portions of this book were published in a different form in "Humanism at Its Limits: A Conversation between Alain Badiou and Sylvia Wynter," *Philosophy Today* 62, no. 4 (2018): 1069–88.

Published by the University of Minnesota Press
111 Third Avenue South, Suite 290
Minneapolis, MN 55401-2520
http://www.upress.umn.edu

Printed in the United States of America on acid-free paper

The University of Minnesota is an equal-opportunity educator and employer.

Library of Congress Cataloging-in-Publication Data
Names: Paquette, Elisabeth, author.
Title: Universal emancipation : race beyond Badiou / Elisabeth Paquette.
Description: Minneapolis : University of Minnesota Press, 2020. |
    Includes bibliographical references and index.
Identifiers: LCCN 2020020383 (print) | ISBN 978-1-5179-0943-7 (hc) |
    ISBN 978-1-5179-0944-4 (pb)
Subjects: LCSH: Badiou, Alain. | Liberty. | Equality.
Classification: LCC B2430.B274 P39 2020 (print) | DDC 320.092—dc23
LC record available at https://lccn.loc.gov/2020020383

UMP BmB 2020

Contents

Introduction   1

1   Indifference to Difference and
Badiou's Theory of Emancipation   13

2   Badiou on Race and the Fanon–Sartre Debate   41

3   A Critique of a Politics of Indifference   65

4   Politics Is to Culture as Class Is to Race   95

5   Sylvia Wynter's Theory of Emancipation   125

Conclusion   157

Acknowledgments   167

Appendix: A Timeline of the Haitian Revolution   169

Notes   173

Bibliography   185

Index   195

Introduction

What is required in order to end systemic forms of oppression, and in what ways should political theorists interpret systemic forms of oppression and their solutions? This book proposes two divergent responses to these questions through the works of Alain Badiou, a twentieth-century French political theorist, and Sylvia Wynter, a twentieth-century decolonial theorist. Badiou, who is influenced by authors such as Jean-Paul Sartre, Louis Althusser, Michel Foucault, Karl Marx, and Jacques Lacan, seeks to provide a new and innovative approach to the concept of political revolution. His project weaves together set theory (a "branch of mathematics that deals with the properties of well-defined collections of objects, which may or may not be of a mathematical nature, such as numbers or functions" [Enderton and Stoll 2016]), drawing from Georg Cantor, with a number of notable political events (such as the Maoist peasant revolt and the French Revolution) to theoretically engage the concept of revolution. Wynter, who is an Afro-Caribbean decolonial theorist, is influenced by such figures as Frantz Fanon, Aimé Césaire, and C. L. R. James. Both Badiou and Wynter are concerned with systemic forms of oppression that can take place through political bodies such as a nation-state or a colonial state. Similarly, both authors offer analyses of the correlations between the structures of oppressive institutions and the formation of who counts within a state (whether nation-state or colonial state). In this sense they agree that oppressive institutions and formations of who counts in a state are often instrumental in the maintenance of political bodies. Additionally, they both seek to address ways to remedy structural forms of oppression. However, this project argues that the means through which each author proceeds to bring about emancipation, and their respective conceptualizations of the political, are markedly distinct. Most importantly, their respective treatments of race distinguish their projects. Notably, for Badiou, without rejecting the concrete existence of a socially constructed notion of race, a politics of emancipation ought *not* center race. Race is furthermore excluded from his account of emancipation and the political. In contrast, Wynter maintains an important role for race in her theory of emancipation and the political. A comparative analysis of their respective theories of emancipation and the political in relation to their theorizations of race is important for understanding the (unintended) consequences of their respective projects. To each theorist, we might then ask, "For whom is emancipation possible?"

With increasing frequency, contemporary theorists are returning to texts in the history of Western philosophy in an attempt to investigate the role that race and gender play in a given theorist's overall project. The Penn State University Press series *Feminist Interpretations of X,* for instance, offers a rereading of various Western philosophical theorists, such as G. W. F. Hegel, Jacques Derrida, Plato, and Simone de Beauvoir, through the lens of feminist theory. Such engagements with the history of Western philosophy are becoming increasingly commonplace and important to critical philosophical inquiry.

The goal of the following project is to perform a similar kind of analysis regarding the role race plays in the work of Alain Badiou. To analyze the conception of race in his work, we ought first to consider how such an endeavor is possible and the kind of approach that would be desired for such a project. In what follows I outline three approaches that are employed in critical philosophical investigations of race, and I defend one such approach that is most suitable for my project.[1]

The first approach begins with the question of the moral character of a given theorist. For instance, in Barbara Hall's 2005 essay "Race and Hobbes," she begins with the following statement: "In this chapter I examine the question of whether Thomas Hobbes . . . was a racist" (43). This kind of investigation can take the form of looking at the actions of a theorist and then drawing a correlation between what that theorist did and what they said in their philosophical writings. For instance, it is now well-known that John Locke profited from the transatlantic slave trade. How then are we to make sense of his writings on slavery in his *Two Treatises of Government* and his conception of natural and inherent human rights (Bernasconi and Mann 2005)? The additional implication of Hall's question, whether Hobbes was a racist, extends beyond the analysis of his texts and actions during his lifetime to say something about his character. While there might be various reasons to support such a method, this method is not employed in the following project. The justification for declining such a method is, in part, because it might offer a strong prescriptivist stance on those texts that ought to be read and those that ought not to be read. This project is not concerned with providing an answer to the question: "Is Badiou a racist?"

A second approach focuses on the language or specific comments an author uses to discuss race and gender, or racialized and gendered subjects. This kind of investigation can also explicitly address a philosopher's method of theorizing marginalized subjects. For instance, we can think here of Hegel's *Lectures on the Philosophy of World History* (1822–28), in which he argues that Africa as a whole is a "state of innocence . . . [whereby] man is as yet unconscious of himself" (1997, 128). In addition, he writes, "Man is not truly a human being until he knows what goodness is, has experienced opposition, and become divided within himself" (128). As a result, as readers of Hegel have argued, he appears to propose that the peoples of Africa are not truly human beings. In a similar vein, Immanuel Kant's "On the Different Races of Man" (1775) describes what he believes are four distinct races, and in his "Observations on the Feeling of the Beautiful and the Sublime" (1764), he ascribes different moral and aesthetic sensibilities to these four distinct races (Eze 1997, 38–64). Such lines of critical philosophical investigation regarding race often shed light on texts that have been historically dismissed as peripheral writings. More often, such texts regarding race have been overlooked by a number of philosophers, seemingly for the purpose of absolving a given theorist from having made derogatory statements about groups of non-European peoples (see Eze 1997; Bernasconi and Lott 2000). This kind of investigation, however, is often times a more feasible approach for theorists in the history of Western philosophy as opposed to a method of critique aimed at a given present-day theorist. Badiou, like most present-day philosophers, is far less likely to write an ethnology or philosophical anthropology that characterizes particular groups of people.

A variation on this second line of investigation would be to provide an account of a given author's use of racialized language or racialized tropes. The purpose of such a method would be to come to an understanding of what a given theorist believes to be the case about race or racialized subjects. One could conceivably provide a critical analysis of Badiou's work on the basis of his statements regarding racialized or gendered subjects or regarding racial tropes and stereotypes. For instance, regarding his book titled *Black: The Brilliance of a Non-color* (2017), one could analyze Badiou's use of (a) the "dark continent" (25), (b) the "dark Phallus" (39), (c) his discussion of blackness as dirty (3), (d) blackness as subverting virginity (16), or (e) blackness as connoting an impurity when juxtaposed against whiteness (a color that connotes both purity and female virginity) (38). While each of these five examples introduced by Badiou are located in the first part of this book, which does not specifically discuss race but is instead focused on "color,"[2] his intentions in this instance can neither wholly dictate whether these concepts are imbued with racial significance nor whether they can be dissociated from race. For instance, the term "dark continent" used by Henry M. Stanley, a U.S. explorer, in his 1878 book *Through the Dark Continent* refers to the continent of Africa. According to Lucy Jarosz, "This metaphor identifies and incorporates an entire continent as Other in a way that reaffirms Western dominance and reveals hostile and racist valuations of Africa and Africans in travel accounts, news reports, and academic writing" (1992, 105). In addition, examples b through e provided above all have sexual overtones that invoke historically saturated symbolic representations of white women, Black men, and the absence of Black women, all of which cannot be disassociated from histories of race and processes of racialization. For example, as noted by Barbara Smith, "black and white women were defined as polar opposites, locked together within the social context of the Jim Crow South. . . . Whereas elite white women in particular were constructed as chaste and pious, the symbol of virtue and civilization, black women, within the oppositional logic of the race-gender contrasts, became depravity incarnate: unclean, promiscuous, savage" (1999, 22–23). The symbol of the white female virgin also served to reinforce the justification for the lynching of "the beastial black male rapist" (23), reinforcing the "symbolic power of the black male as a terrifying racial signifier, whose menace rested both on blackness and on masculinity [, and] conversely, the white woman stood alone in her 'pure' claim to femininity" (23).[3] Thus these connotations of blackness cannot be extricated from the racialized contexts of the U.S. South, for instance. That said, while I make note of Badiou's use of racialized tropes and note that such statements are worthy of additional analysis, this project is not wholly concerned with that particular aim either. Rather, as I argue below, I propose that his use of racialized tropes points to a larger and more systemic problem in his work. This second approach is thereby not entirely suitable for my project.

A third approach to philosophically studying race is to analyze the role of race in the overall *structure* of a theorist's project. This would mean focusing on how race might function as an implicit or explicit presence or notable absence in a theorist's work. In this vein, for instance, it may be useful to consider the unintended consequences a theory can have for marginalized subjectivities. One might ask, "How might the conception of freedom offered in this view impact someone living within a marginalized socio-political location?" or "What kind of freedom is being offered in this theorist's work and does that conception of freedom have any implications for marginalized subjects?" The following project adopts this third approach.

In the realm of Badiou scholarship, there is a growing field of literature that offers analyses of Badiou on the basis of gender, sexual difference, and race. On the topic of race, various theorists have considered the implications of Badiou's project for political movements in the Caribbean (see Wright 2009, 2013, 2018; Nesbitt 2008, 2013; Hallward 2001, 2007; Paquette 2018), Latin America (see Mentinis 2006; Cerdeiras 2003), and South Africa (see Farred 2018; Neoscomos 2012, 2016, 2018). Similarly, there are theorists who develop an analysis of Badiou's work on the basis of queer theory (see Menon 2015), and French feminism and psychoanalysis (see Paquette 2015; Burchill 2018; Jöttkandt 2010, 2018).[4]

My analysis of Badiou's work developed below is situated within the abovementioned literature by scholars working on race explicitly. My project will not offer a robust analysis of his project on the basis of sexual difference and gender. While an analysis of his account of sexual difference is surely important, and understanding the unintended consequences of these concepts is illuminating for his overall project, there are various reasons why I have not included a robust analysis of his use of sexual difference in this book. Generally speaking, Badiou's construction of sexual difference is based upon Lacanian psychoanalysis. In order to provide an analysis of sexual difference in Badiou's project, one would need to provide a treatment of Lacanian psychoanalysis *in addition* to offering an account of his theorization of race. While race and gender do importantly intersect as historical, social, philosophical, and embodied categories, there is insufficient space in this book to properly address both within the framework of Badiou's work. That said, throughout this project, my analysis will reference some of the analytical efforts of theorists working on sexual difference and Badiou. However, I do so only when a given scholar's theoretical efforts offer explicit connections to an analysis of race.

This third approach to a critical analysis on the basis of race in Badiou allows us to understand how he conceives of race and the role that race plays in his overall project. Specifically, this approach allows us to develop an analysis that extends beyond the author's explicit discussions of race and instead affords us the opportunity to explore other concepts that are relevantly linked to systems of oppression and emancipation. This approach thus allows us to ask questions such as: Is there an implicit notion of race operating within Badiou's conception of politics? And does his theory of emancipation employ a notion of emancipation for only a particular racial category? Through such questions I propose that we can come to a better understanding of the function of race within Badiou's overarching project, and it is to this task that I now turn.

A central goal of this book is to demonstrate that Badiou's theorization of emancipation and his political theory are limited because they cannot account for race or racial emancipation. For Badiou, all politics is emancipatory. Politics takes place when a collective of people are fighting for justice (or what he calls political emancipation) against an oppressive system. One might ask: What then is justice? Or how is it determined? Generally speaking, Badiou states that justice designates "the possible truth of a political orientation" (2005b, 53). Justice is the goal of a collective, but the content of that goal cannot be prescribed from within an oppressive system. The possible truth of politics always transcends a given oppressive framework. Justice is thus what is brought about by a collective of people against the oppressive logic of the state. Insofar as justice transcends the logic of the state, it cannot be beholden to particular interests that are inherent to the state. It is for this reason that Badiou invokes a conception of equality that refers solely to a "generic humanity"—that is, not a conception of humanity that is founded in any particular interest but one that is subtracted from all specific interests (53).

For Badiou—within his articulation of emancipation, truth, and generic humanity—race is conceptualized as particular and concrete. As a result, race is not included in his theorization of political emancipation premised on equality and justice. It follows that race must be overcome in order to attain universal emancipation—that is, universal justice and equality. Given that race is excluded from his theorization of emancipation, and all politics are emancipatory, it follows that race is also excluded from politics.

Race is conceptualized as particular and concrete because Badiou posits that race is solely a product of racism, and as a result, race is deemed unimportant for emancipation, politics, or thought. In an attempt to combat such an articulation of race, I demonstrate in a two-step process that Badiou portrays an inadequate and limited conception of race. First, I argue that race is not a particularity that needs to be overcome in order to achieve universal emancipation. To defend this view, I turn to various readings of the Négritude movement and also to historical and contemporary articulations of race in the United States. Second, I argue that race ought to be regarded as important for a politics of emancipation and by extension ought not to be excluded from politics. To clarify this claim, I turn to the Haitian Revolution as an example of a political emancipatory movement that centralizes race. The conclusion that I come to following this line of investigation is that there are structural issues with Badiou's conception of emancipation and thus politics in light of his articulation of race. Specifically, his project perpetuates a Eurocentric framework for politics that circulates around a conception of whiteness. For instance, if it is the case that the Haitian Revolution is only political (and emancipatory) if it exists in proximity to the French Revolution (a claim that is manifest in Badiou scholarship, which I demonstrate below), then the value that is attributed to the Haitian Revolution only exists to the extent that it coincides with a

European conception of liberty; all that is distinct about the Haitian Revolution becomes inoperative. Kimberlé Crenshaw offers a similar critique in her 1989 paper titled "Demarginalizing the Intersection of Race and Sex: A Black Feminist Critique of Antidiscrimination Doctrine, Feminist Theory and Antiracist Politics," whereby she locates a concern that, given the language of the definition of discrimination at that time, Black women could only be discriminated against (legally) when white women faced the same form of discrimination; all that was distinct about how Black women experience discrimination gets denied, except when it coincides with the experience of white women.

Returning to the question with which I began this book—for whom is emancipation possible in Badiou's political project?—I argue that Badiou does not offer a theory of emancipation that is universal but rather one that is Eurocentric. An issue that lies at the heart of Badiou's political project is how he conceptualizes the relation between particularity and universality. As I demonstrate below, he argues that particularity and universality operate at odds with each other, thus requiring the exclusion of particularity (such as race) from a properly universal (and political) project. However, I also aim to demonstrate that such an articulation of the relation between particularity and universality is misplaced. To defend this view, I turn to the work of Sylvia Wynter, or more specifically, I conclude this project by demonstrating that Wynter's decolonial theory provides a possible solution to the limitations of Badiou's project. Namely, she demonstrates that it is possible to construct a theory of political emancipation that maintains the importance of particularities (such as race) alongside universality. To demonstrate this point, I discuss Wynter's articulation of the Négritude movement, and therein her conception of race, as providing the foundation for a political theory of emancipation. Furthermore, I develop her analysis of James's "pluri-conceptual" framework for political emancipation in which she articulates "particularities" not at odds with universal emancipation but rather providing the content for it.

The remainder of this project is broken down in the following manner. Chapter 1 develops an analysis of Badiou's conception of race in relation to his political theory. For instance, in *Ethics* (2001) Badiou argues that an ethics of emancipation should be structured on the basis of what he calls an "indifference to difference." As I describe in greater detail below, an "indifference to difference" is a rejection of identity categories, such as race, in order to maintain an appeal to universality that exceeds what are considered to be problematic divisions. In order to develop this account of indifference to difference, I incorporate Madhavi Menon's book *Indifference to Difference* (2015), in which she develops Badiou's ethics for the purpose of developing what she calls a queer universalism. While Badiou admits that one might have the experience of being racialized, this experience cannot inform political truths. The juxtaposition of race and truth is premised on race being immanent to the oppressive state it seeks to upend and political truth transcending it. Furthermore, emancipation necessitates transcending the logic of the oppressive state. It is for this reason that Badiou argues that race cannot be central to political emancipation. In other words, this chapter describes Badiou's politics of indifference to difference and develops the unintended consequences of this politics for racialized subjects.

Regarding the role of race in politics, I suggest that the tension I highlight between Badiou and Wynter reflects a historical debate concerning the role of race in political emancipation that took place between Sartre and Fanon. As such, in chapter 2 I focus on the respective readings of Négritude by Sartre and Fanon to provide an analysis of the divergent roles they assign to race and race consciousness. This debate is further exemplified in chapter 3, wherein I turn to the work of Kathryn Sophia Belle, Lewis R. Gordon, and Robert Bernasconi to develop the implications of Fanon's critique. Drawing from the works of Kathryn Sophia Belle (Gines 2003), I propose that a positive conception of race/racial emancipation can be understood as maintaining (at least) the following three characteristics: (1) race is understood as something that maintains relevance in peoples' lived experiences and in family and cultural relationships, (2) race ought not be reduced to racism, and (3) race and racial emancipation ought not be construed as things that are politically deficient that subsequently need to be fulfilled by something other than themselves. While situating Sartre's "Black Orpheus" in relation to Badiou's own writings,[5] I argue (alongside Fanon) that Sartre's project is limited insofar as it fails to provide a positive conception of race. This chapter furthermore provides a robust account of Fanon's critique of Sartre, in relation to his own writings,[6] alongside an analysis of Césaire.[7] I thus offer a justification for the inclusion of race and race consciousness for theories of emancipation.

This point is echoed by Négritude poet Aimé Césaire, who stated that race should be a central (1972, 27) and a persistent question (31) for a theory of emancipation. Given the influence of Sartre on Badiou, and Fanon on Wynter, the Fanon–Sartre debate provides a fruitful opening for developing an analysis of Badiou and Wynter and provides an example that I return to throughout this project.

Chapter 4 addresses the distinction Badiou makes between "culture" and "politics." For instance, Badiou states that the Négritude movement emanating from Paris in the 1930s was "cultural" but not "political." Drawing upon the conception of the political developed in chapters 1 and 2 and the Fanon–Sartre debate developed in chapters 2 and 3, I examine why movements that centralize race are cultural for Badiou. In particular, chapter 4 discusses Colin Wright's *Badiou in Jamaica* (2013), which addresses the divergent roles of culture and politics. In response to this book, I argue in agreement with Linda Martín Alcoff, Kathryn Sophia Belle, Michael Monahan, and Frantz Fanon that there are various problematic implications that emanate from this distinction. Put briefly: First, it presupposes a conception of race that forecloses the importance of race consciousness and collective memory for political movements. Second, such a view runs the risk of falling into patterns of Eurocentrism whereby the knowledge that emanates from race consciousness becomes inconsequential for emancipation. I then offer the Haitian Revolution as a problem case for Badiou's theory of emancipation. Following present-day scholarship by such authors as David Geggus and George Ciccariello-Maher, I argue that if Badiou's theory cannot consider the Haitian slave revolt a political movement, then his theory is severely limited.

Chapter 5 introduces the work of decolonial theorist Sylvia Wynter. The chapter focuses on what she claims are problematic conceptions of the subject and the knowledge structures that serve to maintain hierarchical and oppressive structures of power. Furthermore, like Badiou, her goal is to develop a theory of emancipation that provides the conditions for overthrowing systems of oppression. However, unlike Badiou, she argues that particular identities, such as race, are central to a theory of emancipation. This point becomes evident in her discussion of Négritude, as a movement that is both political and centered on race. The conception of race that she offers is not merely a product of an oppressive system, as it is for Badiou.

Instead, she argues that the recognition and affirmation of marginalized positions are important for overturning oppressive systems. In this sense, while Badiou appeals to an indifference to difference, Wynter proposes instead that particular forms of liminality or marginal positionalities ought to maintain a pivotal role for a theory of emancipation.

1. Indifference to Difference and Badiou's Theory of Emancipation

In *Ethics: An Essay on the Understanding of Evil,* Alain Badiou claims that any theory of emancipation must be premised on an "indifference to difference" (2001, 27). The goal of this chapter is to provide an account of what this statement entails and its implications for a study of race. This chapter is divided into four sections. I begin with Badiou's conception of politics and the role of his conception of indifference to difference within that political theory. I describe his attempt to develop a political theory that moves away from a state-based model of the political—that is, a model that addresses representation. This section also provides an account of Badiou's theory of emancipation as well as various other concepts that are important for a fruitful understanding of his work (concepts such as event, truth, appearance, subtractive and additive political concepts, and materialist dialectic). More specifically, in the first section, I address Badiou's rejection of state-based politics. Namely, I examine why he proposes that state-based politics fail to be universal and thus fail to be emancipatory. Second, I discuss his broader sense of politics. By offering a move away from the state, he proposes that politics should be "subtractive." This conception of subtraction is his attempt to rectify a problem with state-based politics and his way of ensuring a kind of universality. Third, I describe what this universality looks like according to his view, and I examine the relationship between his view of universality and his conceptions of truth and event.

Following this broader analysis offered in the first three sections, the fourth section of this chapter examines how what Badiou means by indifference to difference is located within a "politics of indifference," a view that is opposed to "identity politics." This section describes how Badiou conceives of identity politics as inherently tied to oppressive state-based conceptions of identity. A politics of indifference, in contrast, provides the means to reject oppressive state-based structures of identity. This section draws extensively from the work of Madhavi Menon, whose book *Indifference to Difference: On Queer Universalism* (2015) offers a constructive and clear account of Badiou's conception of a politics of indifference.

This chapter serves to develop and situate Badiou's politics of emancipation. In the following chapters, I examine the implications of his politics of emancipation in conversation with the Fanon–Sartre debate developed in chapter 2, with the writings of Aimé Césaire and C. L. R. James in chapter 3, and in debates around the Haitian Revolution in chapter 4.

A REJECTION OF STATE-BASED POLITICS

In a 1998 interview with Peter Hallward, Badiou describes his relation to politics in the following manner:

> Up to the end of the 1970s, my friends and I defended the idea that an emancipatory politics presumed some kind of political party. Today we are developing a completely different idea, which we call "politics without party." This doesn't mean "unorganised politics." All politics is collective, and so organised one way or another. "Politics without party" means that politics does not spring from or originate in the party. It does not stem from that synthesis of theory and practice that represented, for Lenin, the Party. Politics springs from real situations, from what we can say and do in these situations. (Badiou and Hallward 1998, 113)

Badiou here articulates a turn in his own political thinking in which he no longer conceives of politics as found in localized state practices such as elections and political parties. This stance refers in part to his rejection of the Communist Party following the events of May '68 in France. Notably, he also refers to the Maoist Revolution as the last historical instance where party politics could have had a significant impact on the realization of a given set of political aims. However, as he argues, the Maoist Revolution ultimately rejected party politics as a means for progressive or emancipatory politics (Badiou 2011a, 292).

Much of Badiou's critique of party politics is premised on his conception of the state and the manner in which it operates, an understanding of which depends upon his conception of "world." According to Badiou, a world "is nothing but a logic of being-there, and it is identified with the singularity of this logic. A world articulates the cohesion of multiples around a structured operator (the transcendental)" (Badiou 2009, 102). At its most basic level, a world is defined as the way in which "objects" are organized or ordered in relation to one another, and furthermore, a world provides the conditions through which these objects can appear in virtue of this order. For instance, an example of a world might be a political demonstration. A political demonstration could be composed of union members who are on strike, and there may be police officers and bystanders present as well, two groups that are observing the strike. It might also be apparent to bystanders that the union members can be distinguished from the police officers. Within this example, it is possible to conceive of these groups (protestors, police officers, and bystanders) as objects that appear in the world of the political demonstration in different ways. Namely, the appearance of each group is dependent upon a certain logic. Badiou states "that every world possesses a singular transcendental organization means that, since the thinking of being cannot of its own account for the world's manifestations, the intelligibility of this manifestation must be made possible by immanent operations. 'Transcendental' is the name of these operations" (2011b, 101). The transcendental operator, or the logic of a particular world, is immanent to it, which means that a given logic would be, in our example above, specific to the given political demonstration (within a specific space and time). Thus for every world there is a transcendental operator that orders every network of relations and that provides the cohesion that is necessary for objects to appear at all.[1]

Additionally, for the participants in the demonstration mentioned above, it is not the experience of the political demonstration that determines the logic of this particular world. Badiou is clear that the organization of any particular world is not dependent upon human or transcendental subjective consciousness, and he draws a distinction between his conception of the transcendental and Kant's, for instance (Corcoran 2015, 363). Rather, for Badiou, there are ways in which "various groupings of elements appear more or less distinctly and more or less compatibly according to the criteria that come to govern the logic of this demonstration" (Hallward 2003, 299). Accordingly, we can ask, in what way does a given group appear, such as a group of union members who are on strike, and how is their appearance distinct from other groups? According to Badiou, a world is "a local site of the identification of beings" (Badiou 2009, 113). Appearance in a world is dependent upon two things: first, the transcendental index, as described above, provides the logic according to which objects appear; second, "(at least) one other being" (113). Appearances are thus dependent upon the relation between at least two objects in a world. Appearance and existence in this instance are thought of, or conceived through, the differences between objects that are always in relation. Identity too is dependent upon differences between at least two objects. Appearing "measures the identity of appearance of two beings in a world" (200). In this sense, identity is dependent not only upon the logic of a particular world but also on a given identity's relation to another identity.

Regarding the measuring of identity and differences of objects in a given world, we might consider how a union member, a police officer, and a bystander appear in the world of the political demonstration offered above. First, given what we have just outlined, Badiou might propose that there is a degree of identity or similarity in appearance between all the union members who are on strike. For instance, they might be collectively walking in a circle or forming a picket line. Similarly, there is likely to be a significant degree of difference in appearance between union members who are picketing and police officers who are observing the demonstration. Police officers, for instance, might be wearing police uniforms that would serve to mark them as having a different role in that world. For example, they might be wearing riot gear or be openly armed with firearms. In addition to modes of dress, the choices and actions of each particular group could also serve to differentiate these groups. The identities of, and differences between, bodies in the world of this political demonstration are organized according to the logic of this demonstration and appear in virtue of this logic.

Objects also appear in a world to different degrees, either maximally or minimally. For instance, police officers who are in full riot gear might appear *maximally,* demonstrating a show of force and power. Otherwise, if a police officer were to infiltrate the union workers collective acting as an undercover officer, then she might appear *minimally* as a police officer because she aims to dress and act like the picketers. Despite this relatively discreet presence, her choices and actions would be to subvert the efforts of the picketers.[2]

There are three additional implications for Badiou's conception of worlds that are particularly important to my analysis of his project. First, the invocation of the transcendental index means that the order of any given world is capable of change. In other words, there is nothing *necessary* about the transcendental index of any particular world; rather, the transcendental operator pertains only to the world that it orders. For instance, the world of the political demonstration takes place in a particular space and time. At another moment in time, the objects that appear, and the manner in which they appear, might be radically different. The contingency of the transcendental index has additional implications for Badiou's account of the state, which will be developed below.

Second, according to Badiou, there is no totality or universe—that is, there is no singular overarching world and no conception of wholeness. Rather, there are a multiplicity of worlds.[3] One can think of multiple worlds in the following way: As a woman, I exist in a world that determines my having a specific gender, and that conception of gender inscribes my body with a particular set or cluster of meanings. The logic or network of relations that inscribe my body with meaning may be differently constituted in some other world. For example, when I travel between countries, or between cities, my gendered body can appear differently in different spaces. More specifically, being a femme-identified queer woman, my gender appears very differently if I am in a straight bar or a gay bar. These are distinct worlds that are ordered according to different transcendental operators, the former of which is heteronormative and the latter of which is not (or at least not entirely).

Third, for Badiou worlds are not mutually exclusive. Consider the worlds of "Québec" and "Canada." There is a world that is Canada, and this world includes Québec if we are considering the nation of Canada and the provinces and territories that compose it. However, we can also distinguish between these worlds, because Québec can appear as distinct from the nation-world of Canada. For example, one need only to turn to language laws, structures of education and employment, or the sovereigntist movements of the 1990s to demonstrate how Québec is ordered by a different logic than Canada at large. The implication is *not* that there is a formed and static identity that is Québec. Rather, worlds can be sites of conflict and tension. For instance, we can say of Québec in the year 2016 that there are conflicts between proseparatist and antiseparatist groups, and these conflicts are pertinent to the political organizing principles that make up that world (Badiou 2009, 304).[4]

According to Badiou, the "state" is not equivalent to his conception of "worlds." Yet there exists a kind of consistency or continuum between them. One can think of the state as something like the reification of worlds. Similar to a world, a state is organized according to a particular logic; however, instead of a degree of *appearance* (which he also calls "presentation") in a world, the state determines what is *represented* in it. As noted above, an object appears in a world (that is organized by a particular logic—i.e., the transcendental operator) and is always in relation to other objects. This also means that objects cannot be thought of abstractly but are always situated in a particular location or context. Appearance is the situated existence of an object. That said, "the state does not present things, nor does it merely copy their presentation, but instead, 'through an entirely new counting operation, re-presents them,' and re-presents them in a way that groups them in relatively fixed, clearly identifiable, categories" (Hallward 2003, 96). The entirely new counting operation of the state serves a particular goal—namely, objects are fixed or regulated by the state to ensure a particular order that subsequently reinforces the position of a dominant group. Or, as described by Hallward, "the state is always the state of the ruling class [, which] means that it re-presents, or arranges, the existing elements [or parts of the state, grouping them] . . . in various ways to keep them [i.e., including but not limited to the ruling class], ultimately, in their proper, established places" (96). Furthermore, along with the state comes the force of law, or the imposition of power, that serves to maintain a particular order. To be represented within the state, as a result, is to be fixed by the logic or the law of the state, which is reinforced by state power.

Consider the following example: Julia has eight family members living with her in her house. Each person belongs to the family; within the family-world all members *appear* as a member of the family. At the same time, however, members of that family might be *represented* differently by the state. One can think here of the Canadian long-form census where all those who appear to belong to the family are counted, albeit in a different manner. For instance, if a family member living within Julia's house is undocumented—Uncle Juan, in this instance—then they might *appear* in the logic of the family or household but not be *represented* in the state (i.e., long-form census in this example). Insofar as an "object" is *present* or *appears* in a world, it need not be *represented* by the state. Furthermore, insofar as one can appear in a world, but at the same time not be counted by and represented by a state that contains that world (Julia's family living in Canada, for instance), it becomes evident that there is an incongruity between the operation of a world and that of a state.

The incongruity between the operations of world and state—and thus appearance and representation—lies at the heart of the problem regarding the state for Badiou. Specifically, as Jeff Love and Todd May claim, for Badiou, "whatever is not counted by the state . . . *does not exist*, in the sense that it cannot be recognized by those inhabiting the situation" (2008, 53, emphasis added). The operation of counting mentioned here is in reference to what is represented by the state—in other words, what is counted by the state is also what is represented by the state. Recalling the example above, even though Julia's Uncle Juan appears in the world of the family and thus exists in that world, because he is undocumented he is *not* represented by the state, and thus does *not* exist according to the state.[5]

It is important to recall that the state is the manifestation of a particular kind of order and, furthermore, that the state exerts power over its parts. For instance, the political nation-state is responsible for the enforcement of laws and the protection of rights. However, "the state defines itself by virtue of what it excludes while what is excluded is given no other recourse than the state for its protection" (Trott 2011, 82). Often, the protection of rights does not extend to those who do not exist, according to the state. Along these lines, Badiou considers the operation of the state problematic for the following reason:

> In a world structured by exploitation and oppression[,] masses of people have, strictly speaking, no existence. They count for nothing. In today's world nearly all Africans, for example, count for nothing. And even in our affluent lands the majority of the people, the mass of ordinary workers, basically decide absolutely nothing, have only a fictional voice in the matter of the decisions that decide their fate. . . . Let us call these people,

who are present in the world but absent from its meaning and decisions about its future, the *inexistent* of the world. (Badiou 2012b, 56)[6]

As a result, there are two specific problems with the operation of this state. First, drawing from Badiou's claim that "there is one world," Trott states the following:

> If the problem is that an uncounted is always at work within a community and the state works to close off the dispute over the count, the solution is not to institute a community that always counts all the uncounted, leaving itself open to similar critiques, but to develop a notion of politics that keeps this concern at the fore, a notion that Badiou develops in his account of the confrontation between the state and the politics of one world. (2011, 83)

There is always an excess that cannot be accounted for by the state. As noted by Hallward, "Like all states, the liberal-capitalist state defends itself against any attack on its way of arranging parts, that is, it is designed to foreclose the possibility of an uprising against property," insofar as property is an organizing principle of the liberal-capitalist state (2003, 98). For Badiou the state is thus organized in such a way as to foreclose the possibility that it could be ordered otherwise. This reinforces the mistaken assumption that the state as it is ordered is *necessary*, which serves to ensure that the state maintains the functioning of its power. An implication of this force of the law of the state is that there is always necessarily an excess of the state.[7]

Historically there have existed and continue to exist systems of disenfranchisement that take place through the operation of a state insofar as it determines who counts and who does not count, and by implication who exists and who does not exist. In addition, the inability of a state to represent all that are present in the state, and thus the existence of the excess or inexistent in every count, "explodes the liberal myth of an organic isomorphism between 'the people,' their 'representative' and the State" (Wright 2009, 80). Furthermore, part of the operation of the state is that it attempts to continually cover over the existence of any excess. The assumption here is thus that the state is both universal and totalizing. The state assumes that it can represent all that are present in the situation. However, the state is inattentive to its own structure to the extent that it fails to recognize that what/who it does not count is also inherent to its structure and its maintenance of power.

Given the inability of a state to represent all that are present within it, Badiou aims to transform the way in which emancipation and inclusion can be thought and performed at the political level (80). Specifically, Badiou proposes a theory of the event that is capable of doing such work. According to Trott, an event "performs the unity of the world as a disruption to the totalizing and excluding effort of the State" (2011, 83). The event, a concept that I describe in further detail below, provides the conditions for disrupting the operation of the state and also changing the way in which the state is ordered.

SUBTRACTION FROM STATE-BASED POLITICS

As a result of the dilemma inherent to state-based politics—whereby there is always an excess of which the state cannot account—Badiou offers what he calls a *subtractive* theory of politics. For him, politics means "subtracting truth from the communitarian grasp, be it that of a people, a city, an empire, a territory, or a social class" (Badiou 2003, 5). Put another way, he is concerned with a conception of politics that exists independent of the logic that organizes how objects are represented within a given state; rather, politics must turn to something that exists outside of the current logic or law of the state.

This subtractive theory of politics is juxtaposed with an additive theory of politics, the latter of which is consistent with state-based politics and can be thought of as "amenable to parliamentary ratification" (Wright 2009, 87). An additive conception of politics can take the form of an already existing state's recognition of a particular group identity or culture. For example, recent legislation in the United States (and elsewhere) ensures that same-sex couples can attain a legally recognized marriage throughout the nation-state. The right to be married has been extended to a group of people who had previously been denied this legal possibility. This is an example of an *additive* theory of politics because it maintains the power of the state (insofar as it determines who can be married) and extends its power to include more/other individuals.

A *subtractive* theory of politics, on the other hand, is distinct from the logic or law of the state and is not concerned with expanding state power. In order to facilitate this distinction from state-based politics, Badiou's subtractive politics is dependent upon principles that exceed the logic of the state and furthermore provide the conditions for a new or alternative logic or transcendental operator (Badiou 2003, 27). As noted by Wright:

> There is no sense here of pre-existing marginalized groups empowered to demand a greater slice of the social pie through the rhetoric of democracy. This would merely be to expand the parliamentary model beyond its institutional, bricks-and-mortar manifestations: *society* as parliament. Badiou utterly refuses this vision. True politics must be subtracted from the State and its debilitating parliamentarisation of social difference. (2009, 80)

True politics, therefore, are not located in the state. Rather one must turn to what exceeds the state in order to offer a politics that is universal—that is, a politics for all. According to Badiou, that which exceeds the state, and thus the foundation for his subtractive politics, is truth.

TRUTH PROCEDURES, TRUTH, AND POLITICS

In the *Second Manifesto for Philosophy*, Badiou states that he is foremost concerned with "'things,' endowed with a transworldly and universal value . . . [, or] what I [Badiou] name *truths*. The whole point . . . is that *truths exist* just as do bodies and languages" (2011b, 22). Bodies are objects that appear in a world, and their appearance is made possible through the transcendental operator. Likewise, languages belong to a world. As I demonstrate below, however, while truths exist like bodies and languages in a world, at the same time (and unlike bodies and languages) truths are transworldly (i.e., as that which does not *belong* to the situation or world) and are universal (i.e., what is for all and *subtracted* from a situation). He calls his theory a *materialist dialectic,* which can be summarized in the following manner: "There are only bodies and languages, *except that* there are truths" (Badiou 2009, 45). What then is involved in this exception by which truths become possible? Wright considers five central elements of a political truth procedure, each of which will be discussed below: (1) an event, (2) a truth unleashed by that event, (3) an evental name catalyzing the truth's transformative implications, (4) a faithful "subject-body" to force change onto the situation, and (5) a "subject-language" with which to articulate the truth *against* its situation (Wright 2009, 84–85). In addition,

I describe what Badiou calls the "evental site." Let us consider each of these aspects of a political truth procedure in turn.

Recalling the discussion of worlds above, objects (such as bodies and languages) appear in a world as ordered by a transcendental operator and always in a relation with other objects. In addition, there are degrees to which any object might appear (i.e., minimally or maximally). Regarding a state, it similarly organizes objects on the basis of what it represents. Furthermore, a state, through the process of representation and because of its rigid structure, will always fail to represent some objects. There are always objects that "inexist" in a state, a term that serves to designate (for instance) people that are not represented by a state and therefore whose existence is not recognized by the state. For instance, we can recall Julia's Uncle Juan who is undocumented and thus not represented by the state. He does not have access to some rights afforded to those who are represented by, and exist in, the state.

For Badiou an event is of particular importance for political emancipation because it provides the condition necessary to attend to the tension between the order or law of the state and what, or who, this order excludes—that is, the inexistent. An event itself is described as what surges forth and yet does not adhere to or belong in the transcendental index that orders the state in which it appears. Furthermore, "an event [is] something that doesn't enter into the immediate order of things" (Badiou 2012a, 28). An event is what exceeds the order or law of the state. As a result, given that events exist outside the law and the language of the state, events are initially unintelligible and illegal. However, it is this quality of not belonging to the law of the state that is necessary for the event to produce the conditions through which the inexistent can become apparent. The event exceeds the logic of the world (i.e., it is not produced out of a world) and instead is manifest as a radical break from the state. Furthermore, an event can reveal the way in which a state is ordered. Such a form of revealing can make it possible to reevaluate the foundations guiding that world or state. For example, during the Algerian Revolution, masses of people took to the streets to demand an overturning of the colonial state. In this act, among others, people who had previously been deemed inexistent by the Algerian state demanded that they be recognized and represented. Such political statements serve to demonstrate how the state is structured—that is, that it excluded a given group of people—in order for the state (and those who are represented) to change radically.

That an event has taken place is a necessary although insufficient condition for radical change. Rather, an event must also produce a truth. For Badiou, truths can only be produced from an event, and are therefore the product of an evental situation (Badiou 2001, 42). As noted above, truths are necessarily transworldly and universal. As a result, truths cannot arise from the logic or law of a particular state.

How then is it possible for a truth to appear in a state without having arisen from it? According to Badiou truths can appear in a state by way of an event because an event is an immanent break: "'Immanent' because a truth proceeds *in* the situation, and nowhere else—there is no heaven of truths. 'Break' because what enables the truth-process—the event—meant nothing according to the prevailing language and established knowledge of the situation" (42–43). There are two implications of this description of truth as a product of the event. First, truths exist in a world or a state, and for this reason they exist like bodies and languages. There is no other realm in which truths can exist for Badiou. And yet because truths are products of an event (i.e., that which breaks with the ordering of the state), the manner in which they appear will be very different from how objects are represented by the state.

One of the foremost examples of a political truth is justice.[8] One might ask, what is justice and in what way is it determined? Furthermore, to what extent is a particular state just? And on what basis can the justness of a state be determined? For Badiou the justification for whether a state can be deemed just ought not emanate from the organization of a state itself, nor its own conception of justice. Instead, justice, like all truths for Badiou, is necessarily transworldly and universal and thus must exceed the logic and power of any given state. At the same time, however, we might ask in what way a transworldly and universal truth like justice appears in a state. A truth can appear in a state given the following three features of a truth procedure: naming the event, the subject of the event, and language.

As noted by Wright, "No evental truth can get underway without a name: it is an element with the event itself" (2009, 86). As previously discussed, languages, like bodies, are organized by the logic of a state. Because an evental truth is that which exceeds the logic of a state, a truth cannot employ the language of an already existing state that it seeks to disrupt. Rather, an event must constitute its own language. Furthermore, an event requires the creation of a name that cannot be reduced to the logic or law of the state.

There are thus two kinds of naming being employed in this view. The first kind of naming serves to "generate a shared consciousness and militancy" (86). For instance, in Wright's articulation of the Rastafari movement in Jamaica, he describes "Haile Selassie" as the name that marks the Rastafari event. Haile Selassie is the proper name of an "anti-Fascist leader in exile [and once] quasi-dictator of Ethiopia" (86). However, for the political event of the Rastafari movement, this name takes on a significantly different meaning for those who utter it. Similarly, for Badiou the instantiation of "the people," enacted by way of masses of people taking to the streets demanding recognition, can also be construed as a kind of naming that generates a shared consciousness and militancy. Second, naming serves to demarcate when an event has taken place. For instance, the "French Revolution" is a name that refers to a series of moments (or points in time) that resulted in the overthrow of one state and, ultimately, the creation of a new state. For Badiou, the French Revolution is an example of a political event.

Who performs the act of naming? A "body," or more specifically a "subjectivated-body," can perform the act of naming. According to Badiou, "a body is really nothing but that which, bearing a subject form, confers upon a truth, in a world, a phenomenal status of its objectivity" (Badiou 2009, 36). Bearing in mind his conception of materialist dialectic provided above (that there are only bodies and languages, except that there are truths), certain bodies are situated in such a way as to perform a specific kind of function. He draws a correlation between certain bodies and truths in the following manner: "If a body avers itself capable of producing effects that exceed the bodies-languages system (and such effects are called truths), this body will be said to be subjectivated" (45). There are several implications in this statement regarding the difference between bodies generally and subjects, or the process of subjectivation. First, it should be noted that not all bodies, or individuals, are subjects. On the one hand, "bodies" are those objects that appear in a world. "Individuals," on the other hand, map onto a theory of consciousness or personhood. For instance, it is the individual that has a particular experience of the world, such as a gendered or a racialized experience. A "subject" is a body that has undergone the process of subjectivation—that is, a subject is the product of an event (45). A subject is "the local status of a procedure, a configuration in excess of the situation" or world (Badiou 2005a, 392). The subject of an event thus does not map onto an individual and their experiences. Rather, the subject of the event is militant and is also collective. For instance, the subject of the Algerian Revolution is the Algerian people.

Badiou's invocation of "the people" is not new and, to a certain extent, can be understood as an extension of a great deal of European political philosophy. For instance, as noted by Ernesto Laclau in *On Populist Reason*, "The political operation *par excellence* is always going to be the construction of a 'people'" (Laclau 2005, 153). Similarly, as noted by Bruno Bosteels, Jean-Jacques Rousseau "is the eighteenth-century philosopher who, no doubt more than anyone, has given center stage to the coming into being of a people as the modern political act par excellence" (Bosteels 2016, 4–5). In "Twenty-Four Notes on the Uses of the Word 'People,'" Badiou (2016b) provides various examples of his intended use of "the people" as well as several problematic uses of the term. Regarding his intended use of "the people," it is meant to signify a shared consciousness and a militant and collective organization that seeks to uphold principles that exceed the logic of the state. Regarding problematic uses of "the people," he states the following: "We distrust the word 'people' when it is accompanied by an adjective of identity or nationality" (Badiou 2016b, 22). In other words, the conception of the people (and similarly the subject of the event) must be divorced from any *particular* conception of a people. In this sense, the ability of a people to demarcate an event requires that all particularity be subtracted from that notion of "the people." The justification that Badiou provides for the scission between the people and particularity is thus an attempt to safeguard politics from fascist and exclusionary conceptions of the people, such as those used in Nazi Germany.

There is, however, an exception to this rule that "the people" ought not be accompanied by an adjective of identity. Namely, it is possible for "the people" to be accompanied by an adjective of identity or nationality (such as Algerian) when this particular name locates a position of revolt against a shared oppressive structure (such as colonial rule). In other words, when the name generates a shared consciousness and militancy around which a revolution is organized, a particular name can be used.

In this sense, "the people" is an example of the subject of a political event. However, there are three variations of subject positions in Badiou's political theory: "The faithful subject organizes its *production,* the reactive subject its *denial* (in the guise of its deletion) and the obscure subject its *occultation* (the passage under the bar)" (Badiou 2009, 62). The reactive subject "consists in the active denial of the event" (Hallward 2003, 146), for instance, by stating that the Algerian Revolution never took place. The obscure subject "refuses to recognize the possibility of a truth *en acte*" (146) and thus fails to recognize that an event is taking place by choosing to reinforce the previous order of the state in an attempt to maintain the law of the previous state. Both the obscure and the reactive subjects are produced from the event and thus have a kind of relation to the event; however, they both have a negative relation to the event. The third subject, the faithful subject, has a positive relation to the event. The faithful subject, "rather than existing solely by virtue of its linguistic position, instead 'in-exists,' thereby opening the space for it to construct a truth that necessarily evades knowledge" (Srnicek 2008, 111). In line with our previous discussion regarding the inexistent and the state, the faithful subject is what inexists in a state that is produced or appears through the event.

The faithful subject also enacts the truth of the event and produces this truth through a series of actions. In other words, truths exist only insofar as there are subjects to bring them about: "the 'except that' [invoked in the statement made by the materialist dialectic] *exists* qua subject" (Badiou 2003, 45). The faithful subject must force the truth against the power of the logic of the state that seeks to maintain itself.

Furthermore, the faithful subject is inaugurated in a particular location. Badiou describes it in the following manner:

> [The particular location is the] "aside from," the "except that," the "but for" . . . [, or] "what has no place to be" [taken in two possible senses]: as that which, according to the transcendental law of the world (or the appearing of beings), should not be; but also that which subtracts itself (out of place) from the worldly localization of multiplicities, from the place of being, in other words, from being-there. (2009, 45)

The two senses of "no place" can be thought of as follows. The particular location of the subject of the event cannot be located within an already-ordered logic or law of the state because the subject is the appearing of what inexists in a state, or what does not immediately enter into the order of the state. Likewise, what "distinguishes this [the event] from pure transcendence is the fact that an event *must* be localizable within a particular situation" or world (Srnicek 2008, 114). If an event is conceived as that which exceeds or inexists in a state, as something that cannot be determined by the logic of that state, then what binds it or localizes it in the state? In response, Srnicek states that an event for Badiou "must employ the local beings in a situation to give it its minimal embodiment" (114). An "eventual site" is thus the term used to designate when an event is localized, and for Badiou all events must be localized within a particular state.

The particular location of an event is not abstracted from the logic or order of the state; rather, an event is a militant action against the state. And yet an event transcends the state by creating new universal principles. For example, the truth of a political event can be justice, and justice is what "the people" (or the subject) of the event are attempting to bring about. However, the conception of justice that they employ (or are faithful to) is not the enactment of justice performed by the existing state. Rather they are faithful to a conception of justice that seeks to overthrow the existing logic of the state and institute a new logic that recognizes and represents those who had previously been excluded from the state. For example, the anti-apartheid struggle of South Africa (1950–94) can be construed as "the people" attempting to enact justice for all against the oppressive state of the white South Africans who determined the law. Here justice cannot be sought through the apartheid state but it must exceed the state and furthermore requires that the apartheid state be overthrown.[9]

In *The Rebirth of History,* Badiou describes this localization of the event as "people who rally in sites that have become impregnable—squares, universities, boulevards, factories, and so on" (2012b, 58). For example, one might here think of the people who rallied in a Cairene square in Egypt under the banner of Egyptian people (56–59). Similarly, he describes the localization of the event as "the necessity of constructing symbolically significant sites where people's capacity to dictate their own destiny is visible" (68). Elsewhere he describes this as "a particular popular market, an African workers' hostel, a factory, a tower block on some housing estate, and so on" (65). Regardless, it is particularly important to note that the localization of the event in a site serves to ground or make immanent Badiou's theory of the event. It is in this way that the event can be singular, in so far as it is taking place in a particular space and time.

The emergence of the event is predicated on the subject's fidelity of this event in the evental site. As previously discussed, the subject comes into existence out of the event. This means that the subject inexists prior to the event. Badiou states: "We shall then say that a *change of world* is real when an inexistent of the world starts to exist in this same world with maximum intensity" (56). An event is thus what makes possible the "restitution of the existence of the inexistent" (56). This is only possible through a proclamation—that is, a naming of the event.

Additionally, it is important to keep in mind "that the event is strictly *nothing* without its subsequent consequences" (Srnicek 2008, 115). Thus for Badiou an event is dependent not only on its universal and transcendental features—it must also be localized through the production of the subject of the event, the act of naming, and the creation of a new language. As noted by Srnicek:

> An event, therefore, is not transcendent to its situation, but is instead localizable within the immanence of the situation. There is no radical disjunction between truth and knowledge, but instead a subtle, *dialectical* interplay [is] carried out by the aleatory path of a truth procedure. . . . In this regard, Badiou has rightfully highlighted the continuance of the old within the new, and has developed an ontological theory capable of transversally crossing the division between the leftist wish for a pure flux of revolutionary change and the rightist affirmation of universal stasis and continuity. (116–17, emphasis added)

Srnicek has rightly pointed out in this instance that the universal and the singularity of the event—that it is both transcendent and immanent to the situation (i.e., the evental site)—carries with it the implication that there is a minimal continuity between the old situation and the new.

And yet in *The Rebirth of History,* Badiou states: "Localization is the idea of asserting in the world the visibility of universal justice in the form of restitution of the inexistent" (2012b, 69). Justice is thus necessarily universal. In fact, the structure of the event as rupturing with the state provides the conditions for this universal truth. It is the condition for universality by way of his politics of indifference that is the focus of the following section.

A POLITICS OF INDIFFERENCE

Importantly for Badiou, "Only a truth is . . . *indifferent to differences. . . .* [A] truth is *the same for all*" (2001, 27). Within the political context, "differences" can be synonymous with "identities." In this sense, there are two distinct yet overlapping conceptions of identity that operate in Badiou's political theory. In *St. Paul: The Foundation of Universalism* (2003) he provides an account of identity bound up with a capitalist system. In *Logics of Worlds* (2009) he offers one that is formed through state-sanctioned enforcement. While I describe these two conceptions of identity independently of each other for the purpose of clarity, it is important to note that, for Badiou, there is a strong connection between capitalism and the state. Accordingly, these two conceptions of identity are intertwined.

Regarding identity as bound up with a capitalist system, he states the following: "Each identification (the creation or cobbling together of identity) creates a figure that provides a material for its investment by the market" (Badiou 2003, 10). While his discussion of identity may change slightly depending on the text and the context to which he is referring, his text on St. Paul describes identity in a specifically political context. The kind of investment that he is here referring to is utilized for the purpose of "commercial investment" (10). For example, we can think about how Pride in Canada and the United States have become sites for capitalist expansion and, furthermore, have created new kinds of markets (gay cruises and gay bars, for example). Additionally, he states:

> [With each combination of predicative traits, such as] Black homosexuals, disabled Serbs, Catholic pedophiles, moderate Muslims, married priests, ecologist yuppies, the submissive unemployed, prematurely aged youth . . . a social image authorizes new products, specialized magazines, improved shopping malls, "free" radio stations, targeted advertising networks, and finally, heady "public debates" at peak viewing times. (10)

Interestingly, he claims that "the capitalist logic of the general equivalent and the identitarian and cultural logic of communities or minorities form an articulated whole" (11). There is thus some sort of symbiotic relation, it would seem, between the creation or formation of minority identities and capitalist structures.

How are we to understand the relation between identity and the state? Badiou writes: "The consideration of identitarian traits provides the basis for determination, be it the State's or the protestor's, and finally it is a matter of stipulating, through law or brute force, an authoritarian management of these traits (national, religious, sexual, and so on) considered as dominant political operators" (12–13). In the broadest sense, identity is organized by the logic of the state. For instance, the United States has attempted to regulate homosexuality either by suppressing it through medical or legal means or, more recently, through the incorporation, or addition, of same-sex marriage into its legal structure. Both suppression and incorporation/addition in this instance serve to recenter the power and logic of the state. Similarly, the position of a group of protesters can also reinforce the logic and power of the state if the protesters' demands are able to be recognized by the existing state.

That said, I am particularly interested in where Badiou asks whether racial or gender identities can operate progressively: "When I hear people say, 'We are oppressed as blacks, as women,' I have only one problem: what exactly is meant by 'black' or 'women'? . . . Can this identity, in itself, function in a progressive fashion, that is, other than as a property invented by the oppressors themselves?" (Badiou, cited by Hallward 2003, 229). In response to his self-imposed question, Badiou states that racial identities are *not* progressive, because they serve to resituate or recenter the logic of the state. In other words, to take up Black identity, for instance, is to reinforce or recenter the logic of a state (like white supremacy) since the process of racialization emanates from this state in the first place.

Along this line, Madhavi Menon, a Badiou scholar, defines identity in the following manner: "Identity is the demand made by power—tell us who you are so we can tell you what you can do" (2015, 2). Additionally, "by complying with that demand, by parsing endlessly the particulars that make our identity different from one another's, we are slotting into a power structure, not dismantling it" (2). According to both Badiou and Menon, identity is thought of in a manner that is similar to the description of "representation" offered above. Namely, identity is the manner in which the state can represent a particular group of people. However, as previously discussed, the state will always fail to represent all persons, and there is always an inexistent of a state. As noted by Wright, "Ultimately, the terms 'race,' 'class,' 'gender,' 'sexuality,' 'nationality,' 'religion' and their various cognates remain State-based ways of counting the elements of a situation [or organizing the parts of a state], and are consequently incompatible" with Badiou's goal for political emancipation (2013, 271). Identity generally operates as a category that has been created by the state itself that serves to represent "its people" according to a particular logic. For example, the Canadian long-form census as well as various job applications list a number of state-recognized "races" by which one can choose to identify. In Canada and the United States, these lists of "races" have changed over time. Of course, the purpose of including "races" on job applications could be an attempt to ensure that an institution that had previously been discriminatory becomes more "diverse" and "inclusive." However, diversity and inclusion are demonstrated within the terms of a current state logic. Badiou's rejection of identity is prefaced in part on how identities are constructed and organized by the state in order to maintain the power of the state. Recall the example above regarding the expansion of the power of the state to include same-sex couples within the category of those who have a right to marry.

Menon extends Badiou's critique of identity advanced in *Ethics* to queer theory. She states that her own project is "against the investment in difference that marks our current iterations of identity politics . . . [and takes] seriously the politics of indifference. Invested as it is with all the explosiveness of a signifier that lives in difference, indifference argues for a radical break with the identity that undergirds liberal and conservative politics alike" (2015, 1–2). Menon juxtaposes identity politics (i.e., difference) with a politics of indifference, the latter of which she argues possesses a capacity for true emancipation. The juxtaposition between these two positions does not exist along party lines (liberal and conservative politics, for example). Rather Menon claims that identity politics undergird both liberal and conservative politics alike. She states: "By investing in somatic difference as the *truth* of one's particularity, identity politics counterintuitively reifies the frame of oppression it claims to be undermining" (4).[10] With this description in mind, one should understand that identity is meant to signify something that operates within and perpetuates an oppressive state. On this view, a politics of identity, therefore, would serve to perpetuate systems of oppression rather than seek to resolve problematic systems of hierarchization. Dismantling these oppressive power structures thus requires an alternative method in order to seek emancipation. Emancipation requires a radical break with a politics of identity. For Menon, a politics of indifference offers such a radical break.

Menon provides us with an example of crossing the border of a nation-state in order to demonstrate how identity can operate in this problematic way. For some, what might seem like a casual conversation with a border guard upon entering a country that is not one's own can turn quickly to specific questions about one's area of work and, if one is an academic, one's specific area of research.[11] During one of these interchanges the border patrol guard questions why Menon, a woman of Indian descent, was studying Shakespeare as opposed to Indian literature. The frustration experienced by Menon following this line of questioning is that her Indian identity ought not prescribe for her a certain profession or field of study, a point with which I agree. As a result, Menon argues that identities can be imposing when they emanate from a power structure—power that, in this example, is manifest in the border patrol guard.

Contra Menon, Badiou's rejection of identity politics does not pertain to the inability of identities to account for the truth of who you are. Rather, he is concerned with the manner in which identities are constructed through state power. Emancipation does not come through the expansion of the power of the state (adding identities, and thus categories of representation); rather, emancipation is when the logic of the state is interrupted and overturned such that the inexistent can become apparent. Identity and emancipation, the former emanating from the state and the latter emanating from the dissolution of the state, are necessarily at odds with one another. For this reason, identity is of no interest to Badiou's conception of political emancipation. As Badiou states, "We must recognize . . . that these [identitarian or cultural] differences hold no interest for *thought*, that they amount to nothing more than the infinite and self-evident multiplicity of humankind, as obvious in the difference between me and my cousin from Lyon as it is between the Shi'ite 'community' of Iraq and the fat cowboys of Texas" (2001, 26). What then is a politics of indifference such that these kinds of difference are of no interest to it? And what reasons does Badiou offer, or could one offer, for such a politics of indifference?

Even though "Badiou . . . rejects identity as a real possibility" for politics, he recognizes that identities like race and gender do exist (Calcagno 2015, 186). Identities are, in some sense, real for him. He is not proposing a kind of rejection of identity tout court, nor would I argue that he is proposing a version of racial eliminativism. Linda Martín Alcoff describes racial eliminativism (or nominalism) in the following manner:

> Race is not real, meaning that racial terms do not refer to anything "really real," principally because recent science has invalidated race as a salient or even meaningful biological category. It is the biological meaning of racial concepts that have led to racism, but racial concepts are necessarily biological claims (as opposed to ethnic or cultural concepts, for example). Therefore, the use of racial concepts should be avoided in order to be metaphysically accurate as well as to further an antiracist agenda. (2006, 182)

Racial eliminativism, here described by Alcoff, assumes an inherent connection between biology and race, whereby if biology can demonstrate that there is no coherent conception of race that can be developed through biological terms, then it is impossible to say that there is a thing called "race" in the world. But, of course, this is not the conception of race Badiou is using. Instead, he draws from a social constructivist model of race. Notably, unless otherwise stated, all theorists discussed in this project generally adhere to what is considered a "social constructivist" model of race. Michael Monahan describes social constructivism in the following manner: "On this view, race exists as a real, though socially contingent and context dependent, category" (2006, 551). Within this model, race is described as a category that does exist; however, the rules of racial designation can change depending on the geopolitical context. For instance, a woman who is identified and identifies as "Black" in the United States might be identified as "colored" and not "Black" if she were to travel to South Africa. In the context of the United States, this is because there is a history of racialization that operates through "the one drop rule," meaning that the categories of race (specifically white and Black in this instance) are strictly marked and separate. However, in South Africa, and similarly in Haiti, a particular history of miscegenation has led to a distinct hierarchy whereby some people of African descent who are of mixed-race descent are racialized as "colored" and granted more rights or a higher social standing than those with darker skin tones who are racialized as "Black." Notably, the constructivist model of race is juxtaposed against a natural or biological conception of race in which it is presumed that there are biological features that determine race (such as genetics or phenotypical features). While most theorists I discuss in this project endorse a social constructivist conception of race (at least most of the time), there continues to be numerous distinctions between how each theorist interprets the implications of this model. That said, Badiou does problematize the role particularities like race can play in any progressive or emancipatory movement, and furthermore, whether race can be political.

A first point of justification that one can offer for Badiou's politics of indifference is that his politics calls for a revolutionary change as opposed to a reformist change, and it is for this reason that he argues that identity cannot be progressive and political. For him, identities are immanent to a particular logic and state, and thus identities can only result in change that reforms the existing state rather that actually calling for a new state on the basis of new ordering principles. For Badiou, the goal of politics is emancipation. Emancipation results when the inexistent in a state gains existence through a change in the logic of the state—that is, a revolutionary change. In order to achieve a revolutionary change, it becomes necessary to base revolutionary ideas on something that exceeds the logic of the state and thus is not determined by the state—that is, political truths.

As noted by Menon, Badiou's "universalism does not mandate sameness nor does it use difference as the basis for identity. Rather, it involves the recognition that difference itself is universal and therefore unremarkable" (2015, 14–15). It is on the basis of this conception of the political that Badiou states that "a truth procedure [cannot] take root in the element of identity. For it is true that every truth erupts as singular, its singularity is immediately universalizable. Universalizable singularity necessarily breaks with identitarian singularity" (2003, 11). Categorically, there is an inconsistency between truth—which is both universal (to the extent that all particularity is subtracted from it) and singular (to the extent that every truth is located in a particular eventual site)—and identity (that is immanent to a state logic). Notably, "a truth, political or otherwise, recognizes itself in [the] fact that the principle of which it is a particular instance does not, as far as the principle is concerned, have anything particular about it. It is something that holds absolutely, for whomever enters into the situation about which this instance is stated" (Badiou 2011a, 107). As a result, identity can never be the site or the source of truth or justice for his political theory, because the categories of identity and truth are categorically opposed. It is for this reason that he states the following: "It is a question of knowing what identitarian and communitarian categories have to do with truth procedures, with political procedures for example. We reply: these categories must be absented from the process, failing which no truth has the slightest chance of establishing its persistence and accruing its imma-nent infinity" (Badiou 2003, 11).

Likewise, drawing from Badiou's *St. Paul: The Foundation of Univer-salism* (2003), Menon states that "identity is no longer an additive pro-cess that increases its potency by adjectival enhancement. It becomes the minus one—that which has to be subtracted from all substance in order to qualify for the universal" (2015, 5). Here we see a semblance of Badiou's critique of state-based politics discussed above. What is required is no lon-ger adding new identities, an endless task that does not change the existing state of the situation but rather only amends it for the time being.

A second justification one could offer for Badiou's politics of indif-ference is that he attempts to move away from a method of abstraction— whereby abstract concepts become the foundation for a theory of politics—and instead offers a method that he calls "subtraction." The pri-mary difference between these two modes of approach is that subtraction is not wholly dissociated from actual singular events in space and time. Events are always both universal, and thus not reducible to a particular lo-cation, and singular, thus situated within the specific actions and choices of a collective of people—that is, in an evental site. The effect is then to universalize what takes place in a particular site or place and what occurs for a particular group of people.

A third justification one can offer for Badiou's politics of indiffer-ence is that it seems in part to suggest that the structure of a revolutionary change must be able to transcend any particular group of people and thus must be made on the basis of what he calls a "generic humanity." Generic humanity entails that all particularity is subtracted from humanity in order to offer a universal humanism. Therefore, contra racial eliminativism, it is not that race does not exist or that it is not real; rather, particularities such as race cannot serve as the foundation for political truths that exceed the logic of the state—given that racial particularities are determined by the state—and not a generic humanity (a position that subtracts particularities from its constitution). For example, as noted by Nesbitt, "The generic prescription of universal justice as equality, premised upon the destruction of slavery, appeared as fully formed as immanent critique from the first moments of the Haitian Revolution" (2013, 1). Similarly:

> From its very first iterations, Caribbean Critique appears concerned not with individuals or with classes but with a series of abstract universal concepts of relevance to *all human beings* and not to any specifically regional, racial, or gendered experience. Yet these universal concepts— rights, freedom, equality, justice—are formulated by enslaved, Caribbean subjects in ways that would have been unavailable or unimaginable for the white French subjects of 1789. (1, emphasis added)

All this is to say that in Badiou's politics of indifference, identity is not done away with altogether. But instead, identities do not aid in political movements toward emancipation. Identity is subtracted when it rises to the level of the universal or truth. Or, as Menon states: "The specific difference of negritude [a movement for Black liberation that I discuss at length in chapter 3] can rise to the level of the universal by demanding universal human rights for all. In doing so, negritude would tap into the disenfranchisement experienced by women, homosexuals, and other minorities, and *stand in for them all*" (2015, 5). Most obviously, the subtractive move is one that passes from a position of particularity to one of universality.

There are three implications that follow from the conception of generic humanity that Badiou claims are central aspects of his politics of indifference. First, the struggle for recognition of the inexistent is not particular to any space and time but is, rather, a universal struggle because of the function of states generally. Second, particularity cannot determine who can participate or benefit from a given political event. For instance, as a white person I can participate in the emancipation of people of color. Third, for the purpose of political emancipation, there is little to be gained from being epistemically situated within a particular identity. Badiou states that typology, identitarian or minoritarian logic (consistent with identity politics), becomes additionally problematic, for instance, when it "does not hesitate to posit that this culture's constitutive elements are only fully comprehensible on the condition that one belongs to the subset in question" (2003, 12). For instance, according to the identitarian or minoritarian logic, one can only *fully* understand what it means to be queer, racialized as Black in a U.S. context, or a woman unless one is queer, racialized as Black in a U.S. context, or a woman respectively. He considers such pronouncements "genuinely *barbaric*" because they are situated in a kind of singularity (homosexuality for instance) and fail to attain a kind of universal position. Such claims thus fail to rise to the level of truth (12).

At stake for this book in particular is the manner in which Badiou juxtaposes particularity and universality. Furthermore, it is important to examine the role he allocates to identity for political emancipation and the unintended consequences of his political theory. For instance, in "Twenty-Four Notes" he states that the subject of the event, or "the people," must abandon expressions like "the French people" that invoke a particular identity (2016b, 23). The justification for "the people" to abandon a particular identity, such as identifying as "French," is because in this case identity can serve to delimit who the designation of "the people" applies to (in this instance it applies to those who are French). Furthermore, this conception of "the people" also maintains a category of people who are excluded from that particular identity. As such, it fails to be universal.

There is one exception to his rule of the subtractive necessity of the subject (such as "the people") from predicates: "We will accept this yoking only in cases where that identity is in reality a political process under way, as with 'the Algerian people' during the French war in Algeria, or the 'Chinese people' when the expression is pronounced from the Communist base of Yan'an" (24). What distinguishes these two examples, the latter in which "the people" can be yoked with a predicate such as "Algerian," from the former whereby the "the French people" cannot? First, a predicate can be attributed to "the people" when "that identity is in reality a political process under way." The political process he is referring to in this instance is a political event, or a process toward political emancipation. For instance, during the Algerian Revolution, "the people" took to the street in revolt against a colonial regime that sought to oppress them. The implication in this instance is that the use of "the Algerian people" of the revolution is quite distinct from "the Algerian people" of the colonial state. In the case of the former, the people of the Algerian Revolution use the name "the Algerian people" to designate or name the rejection of the oppressive colonial logic and bring into existence the inexistent. In other words, in instances of war and "so-called national liberation," the predicate can take on political significance (24). However, in instances in which there is no so-called national liberation underway, it becomes problematic to use such particular names and designations.

An additional characteristic that designates when a political process is underway for Badiou is violence. For instance, in "Twenty-Four Notes," he states a reality of a political process refers to "violent opposition to another 'adjective + people'" (24). Badiou here seems to echo the words not only of Jean-Paul Sartre in the preface to Frantz Fanon's *Wretched of the Earth* (1961), but also Fanon's writings on violence in the same text. For instance, Sartre states that "it is through this mad rage, this bile and venom, their constant desire to kill us . . . that they become men. It is *through* the *colonist,* who wants to turn them into beasts of burden, and against him" (2004b, lii). Fanon, however, has written significantly more on the topic of violence, a topic that is often a point of contention in Fanon scholarship. In *The Wretched of the Earth,* Fanon states that "decolonization is always a violent event" (2004, 1).[12] What he means, according to Lewis R. Gordon, is the following: "Colonialism's victory would be continued violence; the colonized's victory would be, to the colonial forces, violence incarnate. . . . No side of the equation is without it" (2015, 118). As such, what Fanon is drawing our attention to is that colonialism is a violent process. Simultaneously, acts on the part of the colonized, especially the overturning of colonization, will appear as violent to the colonizers. Fanon's articulation is not an attempt to valorize violence (118) but rather a reflection of the ways in which violence is enacted and perceived within a colonial context, and also a reflection of the presumed illegitimacy of the actions and existence of colonized people (114).

Second, for a predicate to be attributed to "the people," the people must not only *be* the people (rather than *represent* the people) but also be *"what the official people, in the guise of the state, regards as nonexistent"*

(Badiou 2016b, 28, emphasis in original). Thus the people must name those who are refused legal status or legal recognition, and those who are not represented within the state. Third, "It is *in the retrospective effect of the nonexistence of a state* that the 'people' can be part of the naming of a political process and thus become a political category" (25). For example, the Algerian people sought the dissolution of the French colonial Algerian state through the Algerian Revolution. This articulation of national liberation requires the dissolution of the previous state such that a new state that is based upon different principles and is organized according to a different logic eventually becomes possible. As soon as a state, like the Algerian state, is established by the people who sought national liberation, then "Algerian people" can no longer be a political category, in the sense invoked by Badiou above. In other words, if "the people" are no longer seeking national liberation then "the people" no longer designates a political subject but rather is representative of the logic of the state. In a sense, during the revolution or national liberation, the people designate what exceeds the logic of the oppressive state and thus what transcends the logic of the state. As a result, "we see that 'people' here takes on a meaning that implies the disappearance of the existing state" (27). The validation of whether "the people" are a true political entity is confirmed through the disappearance of the existing state. However, following national liberation "the people" becomes imminent to the logic of the state.

In summation, this chapter has attempted to demonstrate the logical argument and motivations for Badiou's theory of emancipation located in his politics of indifference. In chapters 2 and 3, these arguments and motivations, as well as their implications, are developed in reference to the Fanon–Sartre debate about Négritude as well as through the writings of Aimé Césaire and in relation to prominent debates central to the Négritude movement.

2. Badiou on Race and the Fanon–Sartre Debate

The following three chapters comprise an engagement with, and critique of, the political project of Alain Badiou. In many ways, the critique that I offer in these next chapters is not new. Rather, it can be traced back to various debates in philosophy, critical race theory, and decolonial theory. For the purpose of this project, however, I turn to what is one of the most prominent articulations of the kind of critique I offer against Badiou in order to help demonstrate my argument. Namely, I focus on the debate between Jean-Paul Sartre (1905–80) and Frantz Fanon (1925–61). As noted by Lewis R. Gordon, "Jean-Paul Sartre has explored racial concerns in some of his work of the 1940s and early 1950s, such as *Anti-Semite and Jew*, *Notebooks for an Ethics*, *The Respectful Prostitute*, 'Black Orpheus,' and 'Black Presence'" (1995, 3). The debate discussed below is located most explicitly between Sartre's "Black Orpheus" (1948) and Fanon's "The Lived Experience of the Black Man," chapter 5 of *Black Skin, White Masks* (1952). As Gordon states, in "Black Orpheus," "Sartre makes an effort to understand black particularity *from the inside*. He regards his project in that work as an attempt to explain the specificity of black writers to white readers under the concept of negritude" (1995, 3, emphasis in original). Fanon's fifth chapter in *Black Skin, White Masks* responds to "Black Orpheus." While acknowledging that some aspects of Sartre's critique of Négritude are not without their merits, Fanon is also critical of the role Sartre allocates to race in his theory of emancipation.[1] He also offers an alternative conception of race to Sartre in that text.

The Fanon–Sartre debate focuses on their respective conceptions of the function of Négritude. Generally speaking, "Négritude" is a term coined by the Martinican poet and politician Aimé Césaire (1913–2008) in "Notebook of a Return to the Native Land" (1939). According to Nick Nesbitt, there are two competing conceptions of Négritude, one originating from the work of Césaire and the other from Léopold Sédar Senghor (1906–2001), a Senegalese poet, politician, and cultural theorist. Nesbitt writes, "Césaire's original conception sees the specificity and unity of black existence as a historically developing phenomenon that arose through the highly contingent events of the African slave trade and the New World plantation system. [While, by contrast, Senghor] argues for an unchanging core or essence to black existence" (2005, 193), the latter of whom has ultimately been critiqued for proposing a kind of Black essentialism. However, contra Nesbitt, Clevis B. Headley states that "in misconstruing Senghor's philosophical project as, among other things, . . . a vulgar biological essentialism . . . critics dismally fail to acknowledge the philosophical impetus by Senghor to capture the basic ontological orientation of an African mode of existence" (2019, 91). Headley offers an articulation of Senghor's Négritude as "among other things, a critique of colonial and scientific reason, and the imperialistic designs of modern scientific rationality" (100), which are informed by Senghor's concern with epistemology, ontology, and his reading of Henri Bergson.

While I attend to Senghor's work in some places, my project pays particular attention to Césaire's working out of Négritude. As noted by Nesbitt, Césaire "postulates Négritude as self-estrangement, a fact or quality that confronts the black subject as an object. Such a gesture initiates a movement in Césaire's poem toward a self-consciousness that breaks the bonds of subjugation through a grappling with negativity in the form of self-alienation. Négritude is not the lifeless object society has reduced it to. . . . Instead, it is active, creative, and liberatory" (Nesbitt 2005, 196–97). Central to Césaire's project is not only the negation of racial stereotypes constructed within an anti-Black society but additionally raising consciousness of the imposition of these stereotypes. In addition, his project seeks to understand how the negation of negative stereotypes can be liberatory. Négritude is thus an example of how a racially marginalized group in society both recognizes their marginalization and seeks to affirm an active, creative, and liberatory conception of race. Additionally, following Nesbitt, "Négritude is thus for Césaire the self-created object that negates the very objectivity of black existence itself—where humans are reduced to pure animal-objects (slaves)—in a becoming-human. . . . In the concept of Négritude, Aimé Césaire produced the material, textual objectification of black self-consciousness, a program for self-understanding and liberation" (197).

IDENTITY POLITICS AND UNIVERSALITY

Before I expand upon the particulars of the Fanon–Sartre debate, I would like to offer an analysis of Badiou's use, and conceptualization, of Négritude. Badiou invokes racialized religious subjectivities in various texts. For instance, in "'Anti-Semitism Everywhere' in France Today" (2013), Badiou and Eric Hazen make reference to Jews by way of various constructions of anti-Semitism that exist in France and globally. Similarly, in "La frustration d'un désir d'Occident ouvre un espace à l'instinct de mort" (2016), an interview that can be roughly translated as "The frustration with Western desire opens up space for the instinct towards death," Badiou discusses what he conceives of as the conditions that serve to produce "jihadists." However, in these texts, it is not clear how Badiou conceives of race in particular—that is, race as distinct from religion.[2] It is for this reason that I turn my attention to Badiou's most recent book, *Black* (2017), in which he provides a more explicit discussion of race.

First, invoking the question Jean Genet poses in *The Blacks*—"What is a Black? And first of all, what color is he?"—Badiou provides his conceptualization of race and a discussion of the Négritude movement (2017, 91). He states the following: "We so-called Whites of Western Europe had to invent the fact that the majority of Africa's inhabitants clearly constituted an inferior 'race,' condemned to slavery and then to forced labor of colonial occupation simply because this enormous population was 'black'" (91). First and foremost, it seems that for Badiou race is socially constructed, and that it is constructed by "so-called Whites of Western Europe." Generally, the presumption in this case is that race was created for the purpose of racism—that is, that race was an invention that served to benefit one group of people at the peril of another. This statement can be understood in two ways. The stronger claim presupposes that race can solely be thought of as being imposed through a hierarchical power structure by the dominant group for the purpose of the continued oppression of the marginalized group. The weaker claim assumes that while race was originally created for the purpose of subordination, it need not continue to be conceptualized that way. Which of these two claims best exemplifies Badiou's articulation of race? Recalling my previous discussion of Badiou's statement that race cannot function in a progressive fashion, it would seem that he is proposing the stronger claim of the social construction of race, namely that race can *only* be thought of as *emanating* from systems of hierarchy of oppression.

Second, in *Black,* Badiou intimates that there is no true or real "black." This point, which is made evident in a chapter titled "Confusion" (Badiou 2017, 22–24), is made in reference to the color black as it might be applied to a black cloud or a black pencil. These statements taken by themselves might appear meaningless; however, they take on significant meaning within his discussion of humanity as a whole. For instance, in answer to the question proposed by Genet (mentioned above), he answers, "As far as humanity as a whole is concerned, there are actually no colors" (102). Additionally, in *Black* he states, "Try to *really* decide what someone's color is" (102). This is unlike the black panther (the animal not the activist) which is "*really* black, because his fur, which covers his body from head to toe, is black" (103, emphasis in original).

Grant Farred sheds some light on why Badiou would say that "as far as humanity as a whole is concerned, there are actually no colors." In "Wretchedness" (2011), a Badiouian analysis of Fanon's *Wretched of the Earth,* Farred attempts to deal with what he calls a "hesitation, equivocation, about how race functions as an element of the political . . . [and a] distrust about how race is deployed as an essentialist political category" (161). This quick account of Fanon by Farred already provides a clear account of the intended relation between race and the political. According to Farred, for Badiou race might appear within a given situation but it cannot be a uniting feature of a revolution. Similarly, Farred draws upon what he called the anticolonial/decolonial dialectic in Fanon's *Wretched of the Earth.* Farred states, "The political allure—and power—of the [Black versus white, Arab versus Infidel] binary must be dispensed with in order to map the trajectory of the peoples through from popular, racially specific (or, indiscriminate) opposition to finer, ideologically rather than racially based political distinctions" (169). The claim that he makes here reasserts the juxtaposition of racially specific political movements on the one hand, and the "finer" ideological movements, subtracted from racially based identifications, on the other. In other words, the implication is that Fanon is calling for a rejection of the role of a group identity for Black people and Black racial consciousness in anticolonial or decolonial struggles in favor of a movement that maintains ideological unifying features, such as liberty, equality, and brotherhood ("for all," as in the French Revolution). Toward this end, Farred makes a compelling argument by presenting the following statement by Fanon in order to support his point:

> The people who in the early days of the struggle had adopted the primitive Manicheanism of the colonizer—Black versus White, Arab versus Infidel—realize en route that some blacks can be whiter than whites, and the prospect of a national flag of independence does not automatically result in certain segments of the population giving up their privileges and their interests. (Fanon 2004, 93)

It would thus seem as though, alongside Farred's analysis, that Fanon is demonstrating a shift that ought to take place regarding the role race can play in the struggle for Algerian independence. Specifically, insofar as "some blacks can be whiter than whites" in the Algerian Revolution, perhaps one ought to question the role that race can actually play in such an instance. However, the Fanon quote offered above is quickly followed up with the following statement: "The people discover that the iniquitous phenomenon of exploitation can assume a black or an Arab face" (94). The point that Fanon is drawing our attention to is that within any group identity there can be the need for self-critique, and much of *The Wretched of the Earth* provides a critique of the Black bourgeoisie and the role they play in the anticolonial struggle (or lack of a role, one might say). Similarly, one might also state that just because one is Black and/or a woman does not mean that they cannot perpetuate racist and sexist oppression. Intersectional feminism is one area of research that attempts to make evident that one's inclusion within a marginalized group does not preclude one from perpetuating any number of forms of prejudice (see hooks 2015; Crenshaw 1993). With that said, the presence of such critique need not negate the relevance or importance of racialized group identities for political movements.

Given Badiou's conception of race offered above, in which race is a product of white supremacy, one might ask what role race plays in processes of emancipation. There are three points to consider in responding to such a question. First, in *Black,* Badiou states that in both the Négritude movement and the Black Panther Party, "blacks, vis-à-vis whites, assume total pride in their blackness and can lay claim to their natural superiority" (98–99). But why is it that pride in being Black comes only in relation to whites? The reason, for Badiou, is because racialized identity is thought within a structure of hierarchy and within a dialectic. In this same book, he utilizes two notions of dialectic. In a section of *Black* titled "The Dialectics of Black," he states that (a) "black *connotes impurity*"; (b) "through negation of the negation . . . white connotes purity, including in its most physical form, namely female virginity"; and (c) whiteness is "secondary to the blackness of which it is the conspicuous negation" (38). While in this instance he is referring explicitly to what he claims is the "blackness" of the soul where dark and fatal feelings reside, it ought not be lost that there is already a dialectic between black (impure) and white (pure) whereby black is the negation. The negation of this dialectic results not only in whiteness, but also in purity.[3]

This structure of the dialectic is useful for understanding Badiou's discussion of racial identities drawing upon Négritude and the Black Panther Party. Regarding the reclaiming of Black identity in a colonial context by the Négritude movement, Badiou states the following:

> Since the whites have called us blacks, why shouldn't we turn this name against their power? The dialectic of colors is very dense here. Black, a stigmatized category internal to white domination, is reappropriated by its victims as the banner of their revolt. The blacks are thus between two whites: the whites who invented the blacks in order to enslave and segregate them, and the whites who are the target of the blacks' insurgent independence. (99)

Of importance to note here is that Négritude is thus forever located in relation to whites.

This brings us to the second point, which is comprised of the "gradual dissolution of the whole black-white dialectic . . . in favor of political universalism" (100). Of course, it comes as no surprise that Badiou is offering a political universalism as the solution to political emancipation. That said, it is the structure for universal emancipation, as well as his conception of universality, that is of concern. Badiou summarizes the transition as follows: "The first revolutionary approach, proud negritude, prepared the ground for the second, namely that, while there are of course different communities, and the black community in particular, they must all have strictly the same rights" (101). In other words, Black power and Black liberation movements were necessary for universal emancipation. That said, we must consider the justification for such a claim.

At this point, Badiou offers a maxim: "We need to establish once and for all that a politics of emancipation has nothing to do with colors—in terms of norms and hierarchies, of course, but also in terms of objectivity" (102). This move to universality is to take cultural differences "one step further" (101). Badiou claims that race does exist and that it impacts people's lived experiences. However, race has no political import for Badiou. Rather, emancipation requires an indifference to difference, such that particularity is subtracted from the situation in favor of what is universal. Thus race is a moment in the dialectic or the process toward emancipation, but a moment that will ultimately fail to provide the conditions to achieve emancipation. Instead, we must take *one step further* toward the universal in order to achieve emancipation.

ON SARTRE AND NÉGRITUDE

As noted in the introduction of this book, Sartre had a significant influence on Badiou's work. How then does Sartre conceive of race and the Négritude movement? The secondary literature on Sartre provides a possible framework to understand Sartre's conception of race across various works. For instance, in "Sartre and the Social Construction of Race" (2003), Donna-Dale L. Marcano proposes that there are two models of racialized group membership operating in Sartre's work, located specifically in *Anti-Semite and Jew* (1946) and *Critique of Dialectical Reason*, volume 1 (1960). The first model, located in *Anti-Semite and Jew*, is described as a model that "bases group constitution and identity on the gaze of the dominant Other, and the second [located in *Critique of Dialectical Reason*] . . . places the group as a prominent facilitator of history that produces itself in the domain of the Other" (Marcano 2003, 214).[4] To be clear, in both of these instances, Sartre is proposing a kind of social constructionist model of race. However, Marcano makes evident that between Sartre's earlier and later work there is a shift in terms of the agential capacity allocated to marginalized groups.

In *Anti-Semite and Jew*, Marcano notes that "what we have . . . is a socially constructed idea of the group called the Jews, and the construction of the idea of the Jew occurs through the efforts and gaze of a community, the French community [in postwar France], which sees these 'others' as outside its bond of history and nationality" (218). The anti-Semite conceives of an idea of "Jew" and imposes it upon the Jewish people she/he/they meet(s). In such instances, the idea of the Jew is not something that the Jew can escape or refute, instead he/she/they are said to be trapped (218). This position is nicely juxtaposed against what Marcano calls the "'democrat,' who rejects the idea of the Jew and recognizes only 'man' with universal traits, rebuking any assertion of identity that may persist beyond the individual . . . [furthermore asserting that] there is no Jewish consciousness, no class consciousness, no Negro consciousness" (218). Through the work of Marcano, contra the democrat position that seeks to do away with any particular consciousness altogether, it becomes evident that Sartre maintains a role for identity and consciousness within his political theory.

According to Marcano, Sartre's earlier conception of racial identity "neglects the ways that groups play a part in the formation of their own identities as well as their agency, in some part, in constituting the group" (220). Doing so also neglects a long and vibrant history of resistance movements against other imposed racial identities. Perhaps for this reason, in *Critique of Dialectical Reason*, Sartre extends the conception of group identity he advanced in his earlier work to include the ability for groups to not be solely constituted by the gaze of an external and dominant group but by group members themselves (222). Group members are thus portrayed as able to construct their own self-image over and against a dominant group's construction of the negative group identity.

In Sartre's 1961 preface to Fanon's *The Wretched of the Earth*, the author seems to portray a conception of identity that corresponds with the second model articulated by Marcano. In this essay, Sartre describes the conditions that produced the dehumanization of Algerians under French colonial rule (2004b, xlix). French colonialism is the cause of racial inequality in Algeria. At the same time, colonialism also produces the white French identity (xlix). He thus speaks of the various forms of dialectical movement that seem to be operating in the relation between the colonizer and the colonized. For instance, he states that he has written the preface to *The Wretched of the Earth* "to carry the dialectic through to its conclusion: we, too, peoples of Europe, we are being decolonized: meaning the colonist inside every one of us is surgically extracted in a bloody operation" (lvii). Of the dialectical relation between the colonizer and the colonized, it seems that the last stage of the dialectic is for the colonizer to recognize and renounce (or be removed from) positions of power and dominance over the colonized. He writes: "This last stage of the dialectic [is where] you [white Europeans] condemn this war but you don't yet dare declare your support for the Algerian fighters" (lxii). The last stage is subsequently sublated into a new history, which he calls the history of man, once white Europeans join the rank of those who are fighting against the colonialists.

One of the implications of the distinction between the two forms of identity Sartre develops pertains to how one ought to think about race as a political identity. In his earlier writings, it would seem that race is an inherently problematic conception. The argument that follows from this point is that because race is socially constructed and solely formed on the basis of the gaze of the dominant subject, race cannot be politically fruitful for the purpose of ending racial oppression. To this end, as Marcano states, "identities are negatively and predominantly determined from the outside and are, as such, unstable and worth dissolving" (2003, 216). However, the second model for group membership draws a different conclusion from Sartre's reformulation of the construction of identity—that "there is a necessity for group formation and identification, the foundation of which is the basic need of the individual to interact with the environment and with others" (224). In other words, if particularized group identities are formed not merely on the basis of external and oppressive factors then it can be argued that there is something worth preserving in social constructivist conceptions of race.

"Black Orpheus" seems to be situated between these two models of group-identity formation. This text was written for a poetry anthology that was edited by Leopold Sédar-Senghor, titled *Anthologie de la nouvelle poésie nègre et la malgache de langue Française* (1948), translated as *Anthology of New Black and Malagasy Poetry in the French Language*. Throughout his essay, Sartre describes Négritude as being beholden to something like a substance that is homogenous and interior to the black man (1948, 47), something akin to a black soul (20). Black poetry thus is an attempt to "*reveal* the black soul" (20) that serves to awaken the consciousness of the Black man (16). It would thus seem that the goal of Négritude is to promote the raising of consciousness of Black men as racialized subjects. For instance, he states: "The black man is a victim of [the capitalist structure of our society] *because he is a black man* and insofar as he is a colonized native or a deported African. And since he is oppressed within the confines of his race and because of it, he must first of all become conscious of his race" (18). Négritude becomes a means of resisting and rejecting the kinds of harms that are forced upon Black men because they are Black, the recognition of which is central to the abolishment of racism. Furthermore, he states, "black poetry in the French language is, in our time, the only great revolutionary poetry" and is particularly well situated to do the work of raising consciousness of Black men to the horrors they face (16).

There are two important features of Sartre's conception of Négritude just described. First, he states that "Négritude is, in essence, poetry" (52), insofar as it "is a shimmer of being and of needing-to-be; it makes you and you make it" (48). There is thus a kind of co-constitution between the creation of Black poetry and the creation of race-conscious Black men. But this is true only through the process of writing itself. For instance, he states: "Césaire's words do not describe negritude, they do not designate it, they do not copy it from the outside like a painter with a model: they *create* it; they compose it under our very eyes: henceforth it is a thing that can be observed and learned. . . . He ejects the black soul from himself at the very moment when others are trying to interiorize it" (35). The kind of operation that Sartre is here describing combines a subjective and an objective method. This method is objective to the extent that it pertains to the situation or circumstances that can be determined. For example, one can think of "the objective situation of the proletariat, which can be determined by the circumstances of production or of redistribution of property" (17) and what he elsewhere refers to as "the sociological" situation (17). At the same time, however, he claims "poetry . . . must in some way remain subjective" (17).

Sartre provides a further claim regarding what he calls the subjective–objective method as it pertains to Négritude. He states:

> There are only two ways to go about forming racial concepts: either one causes certain subjective characteristics to become objective, or else one tries to interiorize objectively revealed manners of conduct; thus the black man who asserts his negritude by means of a revolutionary movement immediately places himself in the position of having to mediate, either because he wishes to recognize in himself certain objectively established traits of the African civilizations, or because he hopes to discover the Essence of blackness in the well of his heart. (19).

It seems that the conception of "black consciousness" central to the Négritude movement, according to Sartre, presupposes the interiorization (read: subjectivity) of objectively revealed manners of conduct (read: objectivity), or the enactment of revealing (and thus making objective) what is inherently subjective. Objective Négritude is "expressed by the mores, arts, chants and dances of the African populaces" (29)—that is, the "established traits of the African civilizations" (19)—or what otherwise are construed as sociological features or features determined by circumstance. Subjective Négritude comes from finding oneself, from discovering the "Essence of blackness in the well" of the heart (19)—that is, it is a "relation of the self with the self" (20). To exemplify the subjective→objective movement, we can think of Sartre's description of the creative poetic writing of Césaire as the act of revealing to the world his Black soul in order that others might "find themselves" and accordingly recognize their subjectivity as racialized. Alternatively, exemplifying the objective→subjective movement is the interiorization of Césaire's Black soul by others. In light of the relation between the subjective and the objective, Sartre calls Négritude "objective poetry" (30) insofar as it fuses together the subjective and objective method outlined above.[5] In other words, the objective poetry of the Négritude movement provides the conditions not only for Black subjectivity to be affirmed in objective characteristics but also for objective characteristics to be internalized as Black subjectivity. It is the interplay between self and world and the affirmation of Black identity as subjective and objective that marks this movement as important to Black self-consciousness.

Before we move on to the justifications Sartre provides for why this realization of Black consciousness is necessary, one ought to keep in mind what is implied in Sartre's discussion of the Black soul. As noted above, there is a kind of homogeneity implicit in his discussion of Négritude. Most especially, he presupposes homogeneity in his description of *the* essence of Blackness, and *the* Black soul, as though it is a particular thing that is interior to, or true for all, Black people. Along these same lines, he provides his readers with an account of why the figures of the Négritude movement chose to write in the French language, stating that "having been dispersed to the four corners of the earth by the slave trade, black men have no common language" and thus they must write in French, even if they reject French culture, if they are to gain a large audience (23). However, we should be reminded that all Black men, or all Black people for that matter, did not speak the same language prior to the transatlantic slave trade. As a result, there continues to be a presumption of the homogeneity of all Black people without any recognition of the different languages, cultures, religions, and histories existing in Africa prior to slavery.

For the purpose of this book, there are two features of Négritude that Sartre outlines in "Black Orpheus" to which we should turn our attention. I would like to first draw attention to the manner in which he juxtaposes Négritude and the proletariat. The Black man, he claims, should shake off his Négritude and assume "his objective condition" as the proletariat in order to become part of the revolution (52). Despite the interplay between the subjective and the objective described above, ultimately he describes Négritude as "subjective, existential, [and] ethnic" when compared with the "objective, positive, and precise" position of the proletariat (48). Négritude is thus still too particular insofar as it is premised on an ethnicity and what he calls "comprehension" as opposed to the "intellection" of the proletariat position (49). Négritude can thus have a semblance of objectivity, but the proletariat is the *truly* objective position. The basis of this juxtaposition between the objective proletariat position and the particular/subjective position of Négritude is that the notion of the proletariat alone is capable of ensuring the solidarity of all oppressed persons (49).

Second, Sartre describes Négritude as an "anti-racist racism" (18). This turn of phrase is meant to imply that while, on the one hand, the Négritude movement sought the emancipation of Black people through the realization of Black consciousness, on the other hand, it was still mired in a conception of race that continued to be bound up with racism.[6] The dilemma surrounding racism is not merely the manner in which race is used to oppress, but the categorization of race itself in this line of thinking serves to demarcate and differentiate where there ought not be any differentiation. In other words, within this conception of the social constructivist model of race, since race was created for the purpose of oppression, the only way in which to eliminate racism is to do away with race altogether. Or similarly, Négritude remains far too subjective or too particular for the purpose of emancipation. It is for this reason that Sartre turns to "the one who is walking on this ridge between past particularism—which he has just climbed—and future universalism, which will be the twilight of his negritude; he is the one who looks to the end of particularism in order to find the dawn of the universal" (51). Sartre is quick to agree that it is important to abolish racism; however, it is only for the purpose of providing the conditions for the unity of class struggle. As noted by Kathryn Sophia Belle in her critique of "Black Orpheus," "Once black consciousness is realized, a total rejection of race follows" (Gines 2003, 61). In other words, it is only through the erasure of racial differences that a unity of struggle and revolution becomes possible. Race serves as an obstacle for class struggle.

Sartre thus claims that "Negritude is dialectical . . . it represents 'going beyond' a situation defined by free consciences" (1948, 51). Regarding the Black man, "He wishes in no way to dominate the world: he desires the abolition of *all* kinds of ethnic privileges; he asserts his solidarity with the oppressed of every color. After that, the subjective, existential, ethnic notion of *negritude* 'passes,' as Hegel says, into that which one has of the proletariat: objective, positive, and precise" (48). A "moment of separation or negativity" *precedes* the moment in which all oppressed peoples can unite in the same struggle toward universal emancipation. Négritude marks this moment of negativity. Similarly, he states:

> The notion of race does not mix with the notion of class: the former is concrete and particular; the latter, universal and abstract. . . . In fact, Negritude appears like the up-beat (un-accented beat) of a dialectical progression: the theoretical and practical affirmation of white supremacy is the thesis; the position of Negritude as an antithetical value is the moment of negativity. But this negative moment is not sufficient in itself

and these black men who use it know this perfectly well; they know that it aims at preparing the synthesis or realization of the human being in a raceless society. Thus Negritude is for destroying itself, it is a "crossing to" and not an "arrival at," a means and not an end. (49)

In relation to my previous discussion, Négritude is subjective to the extent that it is dependent upon a notion of race that is concrete and particular. Class struggle is objective to the extent that class is conceived as an abstract and universal category—that is, concerned with the suffering of all. Furthermore, Négritude is constituted on the basis of a negation of white supremacy. While Négritude is antithetical to the affirmation of white supremacy, it too must be negated in order to cross over into universal emancipation. Négritude is thus a moment that precedes the revolution—that is, a moment that is required in order to provide the conditions for it. The implication that follows here is that Négritude is not valued as a movement in and of itself but valued only because of the role that it plays for the proletariat revolution.

Already we can see the ways in which Badiou's conception of race echoes the work of Sartre. Most notably, for both Sartre and Badiou, race is a product of a social context, but more importantly is limited to this social context. The implication of such an articulation of race, which is situated in their discussion of race and the dialectic, is that the means of overcoming racial oppression is located in the overturning, or sublation, of that particular context. If you want to get rid of racism, then you must get rid of the context in which racism is produced—that is, white supremacy. In addition to this supposition for both Sartre and Badiou is that race itself is insufficient in providing the conditions for a move toward emancipation. Race belongs to the realm of particularity, and only universal conditions can provide the necessary conditions for emancipation. For Sartre, universality takes the form of the proletariat revolution, and for Badiou it takes the form of the event (as discussed in the previous chapter).

FANON'S RESPONSE TO SARTRE

Fanon's critique of Sartre's conception of racialized group identity is located primarily in chapter 5 of *Black Skin, White Masks*, translated as "The Lived Experience of the Black Man" in the 2008 Philcox translation.[7] In "Identity and Agency in Frantz Fanon" (2004), Robert Bernasconi states, "One of Fanon's objections was that Sartre in 'Black Orpheus' had attempted to locate the negritude movement within a dialectic whose ultimate end was a raceless and classless society" (106). Fanon's critique was not an outright rejection of Sartre's work. Instead, in various places one can see how Fanon upholds Sartre's work as a site of reference and positive influence.[8] Additionally, one might claim, as Bernasconi does, that Fanon advocates for a kind of raceless society at the end of *Black Skin, White Masks*. That said, there continues to exist a sizable distinction between the proposed projects and methods employed by each of these figures. Bernasconi suggests that the raceless society Fanon advocates for is "not of the same kind or arrived at in the same way as that proposed by Sartre" (106).

In the midst of his discussion of Sartre's "Black Orpheus," Fanon states the following: "So they were countering my irrationality with rationality, my rationality with the 'true rationality.' I couldn't hope to win" (2008, 111). This statement sheds light upon two particularly important moments in his discussion of the lived experience of the Black man. The first juxtaposition, between irrationality and rationality, is made in reference to the negative racialized identity imposed upon the Black man in an anti-Black social context. The second juxtaposition, between rationality and "true" rationality, is made in explicit reference to Sartre's critique of Négritude as "anti-racist racism" (Sartre 1948, 18). Fanon provides critiques of both of these "countering" moves while affirming the fact of Blackness. Let's consider each in turn.

First, there are at least two manifestations of the juxtaposition between irrationality and rationality in *Black Skin, White Masks*. On the most general level, the chapter begins with an account of how a Black man in France is fixed as an object by the white gaze (Fanon 2008, 89), whereby he comes to "experience his being for others" (89): "For not only must the black man be black; he must be black in relation to the white man" (90). The white gaze imposes various negative stereotypes upon the racialized person that are meant to dehumanize him through a process of racialization. In line with the previous discussion regarding racialized identities, the idea here too is that race is constructed by the white gaze. This experience of being "an object among other objects" that Fanon so carefully describes is the process of dehumanization that occurs *through* the white gaze. One can also see the implications of this in Fanon's description of what he calls his body schema, the dialectical relation between his body and the world such that he exists as a lived body in the world (90–91). And yet the white gaze imposes upon his body schema a historical–racial schema (91), or an epidermal racial schema (92), that serves to limit and significantly alter how his body's movements are perceived in an anti-Black world.

In a certain sense, one can see that Fanon's articulation of the experience of the Black man corresponds to the subject/object dichotomy not uncommon to existentialists like Simone de Beauvoir and Sartre. At the same time, however, Fanon draws a further implication from the juxtaposition of the subject (who gazes) and the object (who is gazed upon). One can here think of Fanon's invocation of "*Rhythm!*" as a basic element that defines Blackness under the white gaze, or perhaps the "magical black culture" that lies on the other side of rational white culture (102). Herein, the reference to irrationality as juxtaposed against rationality also represents a "phase" of human development (108). The negative identity of irrationality imposed upon the Black man presumes that he is closer to nature, that the Black man by way of the essence of Blackness is stronger or has better rhythm. This "natural essence" of Black people is problematic for two reasons. First and foremost, Fanon has positioned himself against theorists who might equate Blackness with qualities such as rhythm. The emphasis in this instance is that to praise Black people for having good rhythm is to uphold the dichotomy of irrational and rational and to operate toward the exclusion of Black people from the category of those who have rationality and subsequently humanness. With this in mind, Fanon states, "Beware of rhythm, the Mother Earth bond, and that mystic, carnal marriage between man and the cosmos" (104). At the same time, he is quite explicit to state that "what is called the black soul is a construction by white folk" (xvii). Second, this presupposition maintained in the juxtaposition of irrationality (and the natural caricature of the Black man) and rationality fails to recognize the rich history of Black peoples (109).

The second juxtaposition mentioned by Fanon in the above quote—of rationality and *true* rationality—is of particular importance for understanding Fanon's critique of Sartre. Regarding this juxtaposition, Fanon states the following: "When I tried to claim my negritude intellectually as a concept, they snatched it away from me. They proved to me that my reasoning was nothing but a phase in the dialectic" (111). His description of Négritude as "my negritude" is not meant to denote that Fanon has developed a robust articulation of Négritude that is distinct from the writings of Césaire or Senghor. Rather, his use of the possessive in this instance is meant to demonstrate his relation to this movement and to themes quite common to Négritude theorists. For instance, in "Notebook of a Return to the Native Land," Césaire states the following:

> My negritude is not a stone, its deafness hurled against the clamor of day
> my negritude is not an opaque spot of dead water over the dead eye of
>   the earth
> my negritude is neither a tower nor a cathedral. (2001, 35)[9]

Here Césaire affirms his possession of Négritude but for the purposes of rejecting previous conceptions of Blackness. Likewise, Fanon has a personal stake in Négritude, and thus also a personal relation to it as a Black man, given that this movement is concerned with the affirmation of the existence of Black peoples. However, perhaps more importantly, he recognizes and emphasizes in this instance that the Négritude movement serves to place him as a Black man in an agential capacity in relation to history.

It is perhaps in this way that we can understand the distinction between Fanon's and Sartre's articulation of Négritude. For Sartre, the Négritude movement is subjective and particular, and serves to replicate and reinforce racism through its use of racialized identity (as evidenced in his description of it as "anti-racist racism"). In order to achieve universal emancipation, Négritude must be sublated in favor of a more rational or more objective class-consciousness. For Fanon, on the other hand, Négritude is not lacking rationality or objectivity. Recalling a quote above, he states: "They were countering my irrationality with rationality, my rationality with the 'true rationality'" (2008, 111). He makes explicit that Sartre's juxtaposition of race consciousness as particular and class-consciousness as universal prioritizes class over race. In this sense, only class-consciousness can be truly rational.[10]

At issue for Fanon is the manner in which Négritude is situated within a dialectic by Sartre. On this point, Bernasconi states the following: "By locating negritude within a dialectic, he [Sartre] had attempted to render the absolute density of black consciousness relative to the historical role assigned to them" (2004, 107). The conscious awareness of being Black in an anti-Black society is pivotal for both Sartre and Fanon, both of whom discuss the importance of this realization. According to Sartre, however, Black consciousness is one moment in a historical progression that will ultimately be overcome. Fanon rejects the idea that Black consciousness and Négritude "is nothing but a weak stage" that must be negated on the path to a more universal emancipation (Fanon 2008, 116). On this point he states:

> The dialectic that introduces necessity as a support for my freedom expels me from myself. It shatters my impulsive position. Still regarding consciousness, black consciousness is immanent in itself. I am not a potentiality of something; I am fully what I am. I do not have to look for the universal. . . . My black consciousness does not claim to be a loss. It *is.* It merges with itself. (114)

There are various ways in which Fanon affirms Black consciousness throughout this text: "In terms of consciousness, black consciousness claims to be an absolute density, full of itself, a state pre-existent to any opening, to any abolition of the self by desire" (113). Thus Black consciousness is not dependent upon any other kind of consciousness in order to achieve a kind of fulfillment. Rather, Black consciousness offers a new relationality to history and to a people, and not a move away from Blackness itself. In addition, it emphasizes the nature and value of racial identity for continued political resistance to oppression but also in virtue of a long and vibrant history of resistance movements. Accordingly, the thickness, or the density, of this identity and history ought not be collapsed into or erased from any other form of resistance movement. The description of the fullness of Black consciousness offered above comprises some of the positive content of affirming Blackness. As noted by Belle, the presumption that class should be prioritized above race ought to invoke the following question: "Why must the black man strip himself of his blackness for the sake of 'joining' the class struggle?" (Gines 2003, 61). Furthermore, why ought we believe that "unity within the class struggle is not possible without erasing racial differences" (61)?

Contra Sartre, Fanon argues that the sublation of Black consciousness in order to achieve true rationality or universality reinforces the presumption that Négritude is irrational, or insufficiently rational, and unable to become universalizable. However, he also claims that the denigration of Black consciousness and Négritude fails to adequately understand the Négritude movement and race consciousness. In reference to Césaire in *Toward the African Revolution*, Fanon states the following: Césaire, "the faithful bard, would repeat that 'paint the tree trunk white as you will, the roots below remain black.' Then it became real that not only the color black was invested with value but black fiction, ideal black, black in the absolute, primitive black, the Negro" (1967, 24).[11] Fanon's reference to Césaire invokes a sense that an erasure of Blackness, or a covering over of Blackness with whiteness, will ultimately fail to get rid of Blackness. Rather, for Fanon, Blackness is imbued with value. One ought not be inattentive to the value that is allocated to Blackness and more so, the goal for Fanon and Césaire is to affirm a positive value associated with Blackness and have that positive value be recognized. The erasure of racial differences fails to recognize and imbue Blackness with that value.

DEBATES IN NÉGRITUDE STUDIES

There continues to be debate about the Négritude movement in present-day scholarship that in many ways extends from the work of Fanon and Sartre. In what follows I briefly introduce some of the major figures and contentions surrounding this debate. It should also be noted that the manner in which I have portrayed Négritude in this project is not the dominant interpretation of this movement and, therefore, in this section I briefly situate the texts and figures that are most prominent in my work.

Regarding prominent debates internal to Négritude scholarship, there are those who claim that Négritude is necessarily essentialist. As noted by Headley, "Most if not all criticisms of Négritude in one way or another chastise Négritude for an alleged embrace of essentialism" (2019). The argument that Négritude is essentializing presupposes that the conception of race that operates within this movement can be, in a certain sense, totalizing—that is, that one's way of being in the world (one's politics, culture, for instance) is wholly determined by one's race. An extension of this essentialist argument is the claim that Négritude is merely reactive to a dominant oppressive structure and therefore it cannot be useful for a theory of emancipation. For instance, according to Benetta Jules-Rosette in *Black Paris* (1998):

> Antinégritude negates the essentialist theses of négritude. Taking négri-
> tude as its point of departure, antinègritude acknowledges racism and
> oppression as the roots of a universal problem but denounces négritude
> as its solution. This antidiscourse contrasts with the complementary
> discourse of revolutionary writing and contradictory discourses of non-
> négritude. (244)

In this reading, an anti-Négritude position can, on the one hand, maintain
the importance of Négritude for the purpose of recognizing that racism
does exist and yet, on the other hand, claim that Négritude does not have
the tools necessary in order to upend an oppressive nation-state. Négritude
is thus presented as reacting to the dominant oppressive structure but not
able to get outside of it. Of the scholars that I discuss in this project, several adhere to this anti-Négritude position, including Badiou's reading of
Négritude (developed in chapters 2 through 4), and, of course, my discussion of Sartre above resonates with this interpretation of Négritude as well.

Furthermore, several scholars also locate Fanon's interpretation
of Négritude as essentialist. For instance, in *Creolizing Political Theory*
(2014), Jane Gordon, on the one hand, conceives of Fanon as quite dependent upon Négritude in developing his political theory. For instances,
she states, "Fanon emphasizes how much he needed Negritude; that as he
groped after a reason that kept eluding him, it hailed him, offering a bath
in the irrational" (71–72). On the other hand, Gordon argues that Fanon's
call for Négritude was momentary, that it was necessary only to the extent
that "he had to move through it to face his situation" (93). She notes here
the dialectical nature or relationality of Négritude to the conditions of oppression that it sought to upend (72). Similarly, drawing on the work of
Pramond Nayar in *Frantz Fanon* (2013), Headley states:

> Fanon famously denounced Négritude as engaged in the worship of an-
> cient African history, and as encouraging the folly of worshipping a mys-
> tical African past. Fanon considered this obsessive interest in ancient
> African history as politically, economically, and culturally misdirected
> in that this concern was not grounded in the various political, economic,
> and cultural exigencies of the present. . . . It is clear, however, that Fanon's
> reading of Négritude depended upon the act of treating Négritude as a
> static doctrine in search of a mysterious or nonexistent entity. (2019,
> 95)

This line of reasoning is distinct from my analysis of Fanon through the works of Bernasconi and Belle. For instance, according to Bernasconi, while "Fanon is widely identified as a critic of the negritude movement, . . . this impression is at best the result of an oversimplification of his rich and complex argument" (2002, 79). It should be noted, however, that Gordon maintains, like Belle and Bernasconi, that Fanon is critiquing Sartre's analysis of Négritude in "Black Orpheus" insofar as Sartre fails to understand the necessity inherent to Négritude, and yet she also argues that Négritude is a kind of "negation that must ultimately be surpassed" (2014, 93).

According to Headley and Bernasconi, however, the argument that Négritude endorses or presupposes an essentialist platform is often given for the purpose of dismissing it as an area of research or analysis. That said, the essentialist critique of Négritude results from a failure to recognize the conceptions of pluralism, dynamism, and universality that operate in the work of Césaire. My concern here is to demonstrate that Négritude should not be dismissed for these reasons. There are thus various scholars that offer critiques of these anti-Négritude arguments and, furthermore, who claim that there is more to Négritude than is being developed in these anti-Négritude arguments.

The vein of Négritude scholarship that I have introduced in this chapter can be understood as emerging from the desire to further develop an analysis of Négritude. In addition, it often adheres to at least one of the following positions: (1) Négritude is anti-essentialist and pluralistic rather than essentialist and totalizing, or (2) Négritude is a creative practice rather than a merely reactive process.

Regarding the anti-essentialist portrayal of Négritude, one can turn to Donna V. Jones's *The Racial Discourses of Life Philosophy: Négritude, Vitalism, and Modernity* (2010) in which she argues the following: "That Césaire insists on the plural form of black (*negre*) suggests already the distance from an essentialist and reductionist idea of blackness" (164). Similarly, one could turn to Souleymane Bachir Diagne's *African Art as Philosophy: Senghor, Bergson and the Idea of Negritude* (2011) and his description of Senghor, stating: "Everyone must be mixed in their own way" (186). Gregson Davis's *Aimé Césaire* (1997) also offers a study of Césaire's *Notebook* whereby Black identity is described both as an activity and as plural.

Regarding the portrayal of Négritude as a creative process, Jones states, "While negation and critique imply the determinate negation of given or inherited identities, they proceeded for Césaire only upon a prior affirmation of fundamental African selves . . . fundamental in terms of the retrieval of real, living heritage against a false tradition in which social roles are given as things, and fundamentally true to lived experience beneath concepts and reason" (2010, 170). Jones is emphasizing that one of the goals of Négritude is to recenter blackness, emphasizing the importance of the affirmation of positive difference first and foremost, before negative determination (171).

Jones, Diagne, and Davis represent just some of the present-day Négritude scholars who coincide with my analysis of Négritude that is developed through the works of Belle and Bernasconi above.

The debate between Fanon and Sartre is important for this project for several reasons. First, as noted above, Badiou's theorization of race closely maps on to Sartre's view. Namely, I argue that Badiou proposes a theory of emancipation that attempts to sublate particular identities such as race for the purpose of universal emancipation. This correlation is evident in Badiou's discussion of Négritude. Moreover, I propose that this connection is evident in the first chapter of this book—through a discussion of Badiou's politics formulated as an "indifference to difference"—and by way of his rejection of race as a political category, a claim that I develop in chapter 4. As a result of his logic of political emancipation and the continual disavowal of categories of difference, for Badiou, race is not a legitimate site for political emancipation.

The conception of race articulated by Wynter that I defend at the close of this book is an extension of the positive conception of race offered in the Belle/Bernasconi interpretation of Fanon. Specifically, in "Ethno and Socio Poetics" (1976), Wynter draws a distinction between race as a negative category that needs to be negated and rejected, on the one hand, and assertions that this method of overcoming negative conceptions of racial categorizations is only possible by way of a positive conception of race that is dynamic and self-constituting, on the other. She demonstrates this theorization of race in conversation with Césaire and through an articulation of the Négritude movement. Furthermore, like Césaire, she argues for a pluralistic theory of emancipation that reflects the view wherein race and class function alongside each other.

A central concern for me at this juncture is the role that the valuation of Blackness plays in these series of debates between Fanon and Sartre, within Négritude scholarship generally, and between Sartre and Badiou. While this chapter has, in one sense, served to set the stage for what will be my more explicit critique of Badiou in the following chapter, there is also a sense in which my critique of Badiou is infused in the sections above. For instance, I have argued that, like Sartre and against Fanon, Badiou locates race consciousness within a dialectic, a position that must be negated. As a result, universal emancipation is dependent upon the overcoming of race consciousness, and furthermore of the category of race itself, because of its inherent tie to white supremacy. I have also argued that for Badiou there is a tension between race and emancipation, wherein the former places a limit upon the latter.

That said, in order to complete this part of my argument, it is imperative that I make evident two particular moves. First, given Marx's influence on several figures in this book (notably, Badiou, Sartre, Fanon, and Césaire), it is important to locate my argument in relation to not only scholarship on Marx but also scholarship that addresses the relation between race and class. Doing so will allow me to expand upon the juxtaposition that Sartre, and Badiou, mark between these two categories. Second, it is also important to make evident some of the ways that Blackness is valued, and the implications of these valuations. For this reason, in the chapter that follows, I address these kinds of valuations in my discussion of positive and negative conceptions of race, which is situated in relation to critical race theory in the United States. As a result of this extended argument, chapters 2 and 3 can, and should, be read as inherently linked, while also doing the necessary work of situating my argument in a series of already contested debates.

3. A Critique of a Politics of Indifference

"I would like to say that I too am a Marxist" (Badiou 2012b, 8). His foray into mathematics and psychoanalysis notwithstanding, Alain Badiou is unequivocally a Marxist. As I have attempted to make evident in the previous chapters, Badiou's later political theory in particular makes evident his political leanings. For instance, his articulation of what is required in order to achieve universal emancipation—specifically an indifference to difference and a generic humanity—is not unlike what Karl Marx calls for in his articulation of a proletariat revolution. While Badiou is less likely to invoke the language of class, there is still a clear overlap to which Badiou himself admits. Much of Badiou's political project has been to move Marxism forward, by addressing the various crises he locates therein.[1] His turn to subtractive politics is one way in which he has attempted to address possible shortcomings within Marxism.

What is surprising, however, is Badiou's inattention to race-based critiques of Marxism that have circulated since well before his time. The inability of (certain) Marxist traditions to address colonialism and white supremacy, and thus the exclusion and erasure of race from theories of political emancipation and universal emancipation, is a crisis for Marxism. Badiou should have been well aware of such crises since, as I made evident in the previous chapter, the question regarding the relation between Marxism and race was explicitly debated by Frantz Fanon and Jean-Paul Sartre.

In what is essentially an extension of the Fanon–Sartre debate from the previous chapter, I begin this third chapter by first situating Badiou's politics of indifference in relation to various Marxist critiques that have addressed this crisis in Marxism. Second, drawing from historic and current debates regarding the "conservation of races," I argue that the conception of race and identity utilized by Badiou does not allow for what Kathryn Sophia Belle calls a positive account of racial identity. In addition, drawing from Lucius T. Outlaw Jr.'s *On Race and Philosophy* (1996), I argue that a positive conception of race is necessary for a theory of emancipation that does not fall into patterns of Eurocentrism within philosophy. Third, within Badiou's politics of indifference, I argue that he frames identities such as race as unnecessary categories that need to be negated in order to create a more emancipatory political sphere. Drawing a parallel to the Fanon–Sartre debate introduced in chapter 2, I propose that Badiou's conception of identity and his politics of indifference can be problematic for racialized subjects.

ON BADIOU, MARX(ISM), AND RACE

Badiou's exclusion and erasure of race from his political theory of emancipation is not a new problem.[2] Rather, the inclination to distinguish identities or particularities (such as race) from a conception of emancipatory politics that is necessarily universal was similarly proposed by Marx. For instance, as noted by Nick Nesbitt, Marx "famously concludes that a universal class must become the agent of this process, one whose 'sufferings are universal,' one that has experienced not particular wrongs (against a class, gender, or race) but the denial of humanity itself, a class whose emancipation necessarily implies the emancipation of humanity as a whole" (2013, 7). Or as noted by Marx:

> From the relationship of estranged labour to private property it further follows that the emancipation of society from private property, etc., from servitude, is expressed in the *political* form of the *emancipation of the workers*; not that *their* emancipation alone was at stake but because the emancipation of the workers contains universal human emancipation— and it contains this, because the whole of human servitude is involved in the relation of the worker to production, and every relation of servitude is but a modification and consequence of this relation. (Marx and Engels 1978, 80)

Marx places an emphasis on suffering that exists as a result of one being denied humanity, which is universal, rather than on the basis of a particular identity. Marx's concern is thus a general process of dehumanization rather than particular structures of dehumanization (colonialism, white supremacy, or patriarchy, for instance). Similarly, in "Badiou's Axiomatic Democracy against Cultural Politics," Colin Wright argues that, for Badiou, a political truth (such as justice and equality) "is ultimately reducible to no particular constituency, not even the working class or the proletariat" (2009, 79). Consistent with my description of Badiou's politics of indifference in chapter 1, the political truth of an event cannot be grounded in any particularity (such as class, race, or gender) but instead must appeal to what is universal or intelligible to all and furthermore is that which exceeds the logic of the oppressive state.

In "The Political Critique of Identity," Linda Martín Alcoff offers an analysis of post-Marxist theorists who critique identity politics (specifically Todd Gitlin and Nancy Fraser) on the basis of identity serving to fracture the universality required for emancipation. For example, she states that Gitlin's "main worry is that the focus on identities and thus differences inhibits the possibility of creating a *progressive* political majority based on class" (Alcoff 2016, n.p., emphasis added). According to Alcoff, Gitlin emphasizes the importance of removing race and other identities from the political realm in order to instigate a progressive and genuine social revolution. That said, she critiques him in the following manner:

> Gitlin's account thus returns us to an outdated view of class as an essentially homogenous entity rather than a cluster concept with internal contradictions. By separating class demands from identity struggles he implies that there are generic class demands rather than the demands of skilled or unskilled workers, of the trades of the service professions, of minority workers, of women workers, of immigrant workers, and so on, that is, of groups whose interests sometimes coincide and at other times collide. Gitlin implies that the labor movement can only maintain a united form if it ignores internal differences. (n.p.)

The presumption for Gitlin is that identity serves to detract from universal emancipation, as does any particularity. As a result, some other kind of universal category needs to supplant this particularism. In Gitlin's case, class comes to denote a universal category. The critique that Alcoff brings against Gitlin is that his conception of universal emancipation seems to require a kind of homogeneity, and that any kind of particular identity would only serve to fracture and diminish such a move toward emancipation.

In a similar manner, Alcoff describes Fraser's rejection of identity politics as follows: Fraser calls identity politics a "'culturalist' struggle that aims at self-realization" (n.p.). Struggles for self-realization (or recognition) "tend toward promoting 'group differentiation' while struggles for [what she calls] redistribution tend to 'promote group de-differentiation.' In other words, gays and lesbians, for example, are fighting for the very right to exist free of violence and discrimination, while the poor would rather eradicate their identity as poor" (n.p.).

According to Alcoff, Fraser distinguishes identity politics from other forms of struggle insofar as the former, she claims, are cultural and framed as a movement that is concerned solely with the realization of that particular group to the exclusion of other identities. Her prescribed conception of emancipation seeks to eradicate identities that are construed as problematic.

Alcoff draws a correlation between the works of Fraser, Gitlin, and Sartre in the following manner: "This solution [of the rejection of identity politics] is no different from the liberal approach Sartre excoriated in *Anti-Semite and Jew* when he said, the liberal wants to save the man by leaving the Jew behind" (n.p.). In a manner similar to my discussion in chapter 2, Alcoff is drawing her readers' attention to Sartre's claim that the emancipation of the Jewish man is possible when he gives up the particularity of his Jewishness. This tension between emancipation and one's particularity is also noted by Belle in her description of the manner in which Sartre uplifts Négritude only to the extent that "it serves to prepare blacks to become socialists. He [Sartre] states [in "Black Orpheus"]: 'before black peasants can discover that socialism is the answer to their immediate local claims . . . they must think of themselves as blacks'" (Gines 2003, 59). Furthermore, consistent with my discussion of Sartre in chapter 2, Négritude is construed as necessary only to the extent that it is subordinated to a conception of universal emancipation. There is a tendency in Marxist and post-Marxist thought to distinguish between movements that are considered "properly" universal and those that incorporate particular identities. Furthermore, there seems to be an inherent tension between these conceptions of universality and particularity.

How might one conceive of the relation between these various authors and Badiou? As noted in chapter 1, Badiou's politics of indifference similarly proposes a distinction between universal emancipation and identity politics, the latter of which he explicitly critiques in a manner that is similar to the critiques that are offered in this section (especially the critique directed against Sartre). However, Badiou also attempts to distinguish his project from the problems attributed to Giltin, Fraser, and Sartre—a distinction that is located in the pairing between Badiou's universal emancipation and what he calls an evental site. If we recall chapter 1, the evental site is intended to provide a local framework where universal emancipation takes place. An event is not conceived in *abstraction*; rather, it can be situated within a particular historical and geographical context. At the same time, however, the process through which this universal truth is intelligible for all, and through which emancipation is possible, requires that identity is *subtracted* from it. Recalling the reference to Marx at the start of this section, it is thus dehumanization itself, and not the dehumanization of a particular group of people, that is at issue for Badiou. It is then this conception of the inexistent that seeks incorporation into his conception of generic humanity.

STRETCHING MARX

Marx's refusal to defend emancipation on the basis of any particularity has been subject to critique.[3] For instance, Cedric J. Robinson begins *Black Marxism* (1983) with the following statement: "This work is about our people's struggle, the historical Black struggle. It takes as a first premise that for a people to survive in struggle, it must be on its own terms: the collective wisdom which is a synthesis of culture and the experience of that struggle" (2000, xxxv). Robinson's goal for *Black Marxism* is twofold: (1) he seeks to determine whether the Black Radical tradition is compatible with the Marxist tradition, and (2) he seeks to demonstrate that Marxism presupposes a Western framework (e.g., history and experience) to the exclusion of alternative frameworks. Robinson emphasizes the importance of developing a nuanced and rich account of race for a theory of emancipation. Similarly, one could also note Fanon and Césaire and discussions of attempting to "stretch" or "complete Marx." Regarding Césaire, for example, an attempt to stretch Communism entails a need to respond to what he calls "the Negro question" (1972, 27).

A central concern for many theorists within Black Marxist traditions is the way in which race is portrayed and the kind of location it is allocated in Marxist formulations of the political and of emancipation. As noted by Charles W. Mills, "The Marxist claim . . . is that this whole spectrum of phenomena [the problem of race and culture in the Caribbean] can only properly be understood in their relation to classes and class struggle" (1987, 92). The issue that Mills makes evident here is that within a Marxist tradition it is important to be attentive to the manner in which race and class operate. If race is only operative to the extent that it corresponds to class, what then are the implications? We might also ask, in what way *should* race circulate within a Marxist tradition?

There are various scholars who claim that the way in which class-based movements operate in Communist movements might not be equivalent to the way in which race-based movements work. For instance, a recurring theme throughout this project is the system of representation that exists within an (oppressive) nation-state that serves to count those who exist (and furthermore those who do not exist) within that nation-state. Following the politically emancipatory movement whereby the oppressive count of the nation-state is upended, then the representations (which include identities) will no longer exist, and furthermore, cannot exist if the political movement is to be designated as emancipatory. The absolution of identities is a necessary condition of emancipation in this view.

This framework for what counts as emancipation makes sense when one is thinking about a narrow articulation of Communist revolutions. For instance, part of the goal of a Communist revolution is that the proletariat (as a category that is produced in relation to the bourgeoisie) no longer exists following the revolution. The reason being, in this case, is that both of these categories operate through a particular ordering of the nation-state (a procapitalist one), and if that particular state order is upended (the goal of the revolution) then there will be no more proletariat or bourgeoisie. However, a pertinent question that resonates both in this book and for the scholars I have noted above (Robinson, Alcoff, and Césaire) is whether race operates in the same way as class. The response that is consistent between these three theorists is that race is different from class, partly because there may be good reasons to preserve race or racial group identities as a mode of existence after a revolutionary change. For this reason, Marxist analysis needs to find a way to account for the differences between race and class if it is to offer a theory of emancipation that is inclusive of all persons. Given Badiou's situatedness with Marxism, this line of critique equally applies to Badiou's politics of indifference.

In 1987 Mills offered an articulation of what is needed to "construct a Marxist theory of race and culture in the Caribbean": "In racially structured class societies like those of the Caribbean . . . the stigmata of putatively in-nate inferiority are phenotypically visible. Thus a racial interpretation of the class structure was the most natural ideological outcome" (1987, 95). The implication that Mills is making apparent in this instance is that, in the Caribbean, Marxism must be able to address the particular forms of hierar-chies that construct those spaces. Marxism must be attentive to historical processes of colonialism and slavery if it is to be applicable to construc-tions of race and the geopolitical contexts of the Caribbean.

Similarly, Césaire's 1955 essay "Discours sur le colonialisme" (trans-lated as "Discourse on Colonialism") begins with the following statement: "The fact is that the so-called European civilization—'Western' civiliza-tion—as it has been shaped by two centuries of bourgeois rule, is incapable of solving the two major problems to which its existence has given rise: the problem of the proletariat and the colonial problem" (1972, 1). He begins this essay by marking a distinction between the proletariat in a global capi-talist system and the racialized subject in a colonial system. Furthermore, in an interview he gave with René Depestre in 1967, Césaire makes a distinc-tion between "Communists" and his conception of Négritude. According to him, a problem that existed at the center of the Communist movement is that French Communists "were not attempting disalienation" and in-stead bore the marks of assimilation (27).[4] In conversation with Depestre, Césaire makes evident that the Communist movement was becoming assimilationist because it was becoming more and more abstract as a result of its failure to address the Negro question. On this point Césaire states the following:

> QUESTION [DEPESTRE]: At bottom what separated you from the Communist Martinican students at that time was the Negro question.
> RESPONSE [CÉSAIRE]: Yes, the Negro question. At that time I criticized the Communists for forgetting our Negro characteristics. They acted like Communists, which was all right, but they acted like abstract Communists. I maintained that the political question would not do away with our condition as Negroes. (27).

In effect, Césaire already notes that the Communist movement ought not forget the lived experiences of the Black man—doing so would do away with material and concrete experiences in favor of abstract conceptions of the subject. Moreover, class struggle overlooks the importance of Black history and culture for universal emancipation. Contra Sartre, who states that race and class do not mix, Césaire argues that it is important to maintain race alongside class. He thus calls for the "need to complete Marx" (27)—a claim that is similarly made by Fanon, who states, "Marxist analysis should always be slightly stretched when it comes to addressing the colonial issue" (2004, 5)—and to particularize Communism (Césaire 1972, 27). For Sartre, Négritude denotes a kind of racism, albeit an antiracist racism, because of its incorporation of "the Negro question," a critique that was similarly brought against Césaire (27). However, for Césaire and for Fanon, it is necessary to situate emancipation in the concrete and the particular and to assert that Blackness ought not be relegated to a secondary position (30).

One might also consider the writings of Leon Trotsky on the role of race in Marxism. In November 1928 the American Communist Party declared the slogan "The Communists Are for a Black Republic" (Trotsky 1978, 14). Many Marxists critiqued such a stance, declaring it reactionary and divisive for the Communist Party (not unlike the arguments offered above). According to Trotsky, however, "The argument that the slogan for self-determination [of Black peoples] leads away from the class point of view is an adaptation to the ideology of the white workers" (29). In other words, arguments against the self-determination of Black peoples as a central tenant for the Communist Party serves to recenter white workers, and white workers alone, in the proletariat revolution. In response, he states that "the white worker must meet the Negroes halfway and say to them: 'If you want to separate you will have our support'" (29).

Alongside Césaire's attempt to mark the importance of keeping in mind the Negro question for the Communist movement, he is also explicit about the role and importance of maintaining race consciousness. For instance, he states:

> I have always thought that the black man was searching for his identity. And it has seemed to me that if what we want is to establish this identity, then we must have a concrete consciousness of what we are—that is of the fact of our lives: that we are black; that we were black and have a history, a history that contains certain cultural elements of great value; and that Negroes were not, as you put it, born yesterday, because there have been beautiful and important black civilizations. (1972, 30)

In this quote Césaire emphasizes the value of Black histories for world history, and he proposes that there is a continuity between Black race consciousness and Black histories that are not wholly determined by the white gaze and white supremacy. In addition and against Sartre, it is not that the Négritude movement presupposes a singular or essential identity, nor a singular history. For instance, according to Césaire, "Everyone has his own Négritude" (30). There is no singular or homogenous identity that pertains to all Black persons. Recalling Sartre's discussion of the singular Black soul and his implication that all Black people spoke the same language, it becomes apparent that Sartre is inconsistent with Césaire's conception of Négritude.

In an essay titled "Fanon and Sartre 50 Years Later: To Retain or Reject the Concept of Race" (2003), Belle takes up the tension between Sartre and Fanon (and, by extension, Césaire, as described above) surrounding the issue of whether each author wants to reject or conserve race consciousness. Alongside Fanon, she challenges "Sartre's claim that we should reject the concept of race once an 'authentic race consciousness' is attained" (Gines 2003, 55) and she seeks to conserve Black racial consciousness. Central to this preservation of race consciousness is the idea that combating and eliminating racism does not require the elimination of racial identities altogether (55). The implication of this statement is that one should come to think of race in (at least) two distinct ways. On the one hand, race is conceived as a negative category that was constructed and used for the purpose of oppressing a particular group.[5] Race thought of in this way takes the form of stereotypes used for the purpose of discrimination and various forms of harm. Within this framework, ending racism would require that race must also be abolished. This view is consistent with Sartre's articulation of race consciousness and group-identity developed in "Black Orpheus." On the other hand, race can also be thought in a positive sense, as a "more positive category that encompasses a sense of membership or belonging, remembrance of struggle and overcoming, and the motivation to press forward and endeavor towards new ideals and achievements" (56). For Belle, Bernasconi, and Fanon, while it is important to abolish negative conceptions of race, this does not mean that we also need to get rid of race as a positive category. This project addresses reasons why race (and identity generally) should be thought of as more than just a negative category and how the positive conceptions of identity and race articulated by Belle and Fanon offer other ways to think about race. The conception of the positive affirmation of race has been provided throughout this chapter via the works of Fanon, Bernasconi, Césaire, and Belle. According to these authors, race is negative if it is something that needs to be overcome for the purpose of a greater struggle or more universal emancipation. If race can be affirmed in and of itself, then it is positive and bears with it its own historical and existential import. In addition, this positive conception of race presupposes that race exceeds the colonial gaze, both historically and in terms of its content.

NEGATIVE AND POSITIVE CONCEPTIONS OF IDENTITY

My analysis of Badiou's conception of race and identity centers on the differentiation of, and the implications for, what is often referred to as positive and negative conceptions of race. These seemingly divergent conceptions of race are firmly situated in historical discourses. Namely, W. E. B. Du Bois's "The Conservation of Races" (1897) gestured toward the distinction between positive and negative conceptions of race, and his work continues to be relevant for present-day research in critical race theory. Let's consider each conception of race in turn.

First, what is a negative conception of race? In *Race: A Philosophical Introduction,* Paul C. Taylor describes race as follows:

Our Western races are social constructs. They are things that we humans create in the transactions that define social life. Specifically, they are the probabilistically defined populations that result from the white supremacist determination to link appearance and ancestry to social location and life chances. (2004, 86)

Similarly, in Mills's *The Racial Contract* (1997), he states that the goal of the creation of racial categories should be understood as "creating not merely racial exploitation, but race itself as a group identity" (63). Within a social constructivist model of race, it is generally accepted that the origin of the process of racialization was for the purpose of the creation of a social hierarchy that benefited some populations and dehumanized others.

The conception of race offered by Badiou fits squarely within this (negative) conception of race. For instance, we might recall the following question posed by Badiou: "Can this identity [Black or women], in itself, function in a progressive fashion, that is, *other than as a property invented by the oppressors themselves*?" (Hallward 2003, 229, emphasis added). The implication that we can draw from his statement is that racial identities are a product, and property, of an oppressive structure that was invented for the purpose of maintaining racial hierarchies.

It is not my intention to argue against the existence of negative conceptions of race. I take it as evident that there are negative conceptions of race through which the dehumanization of racialized peoples takes place that result in social and political hierarchies. My concern is rather whether the definition offered above is sufficient to the extent that it incorporates all the various facets of race. In "Fanon and Sartre 50 Years Later," Belle raises a similar concern:

Race is not just a negative category used for the purpose of oppression and exploitation or for the purpose of establishing a sense of supremacy over others. Race has also come to represent a more positive category that encompasses a sense of membership or belonging, remembrance of struggle and overcoming, and the motivation to press forward and endeavor towards new ideas and achievement. (Gines 2003, 56)

As such, the question that should follow statements regarding negative conceptions of race is as follows: Is a negative conception of race *all* that there is? In other words, is it possible to conceive of race in a way that exceeds, or is distinct from, this negative conception? These questions are in no way new, nor am I unique in offering them for consideration. Most notably, W. E. B. Du Bois in "The Conservation of Race" engages with these questions. He asks, "What then is race? It is a vast family of human beings, generally of common blood and language, always common history, traditions and impulses, who are both voluntarily and involuntarily striving together for the accomplishment of certain more or less vividly conceived ideals of life" (2000, 110). Du Bois is well known for engaging in a critique of systemic oppression on the basis of race, and thus a negative conception of race. However, as demonstrated above, he also offers a conception of race that is not limited to systemic oppression but indeed seeks its foundation elsewhere. In other words, while Du Bois engages in a project that aims to end racism, he also argues for the continuation of race categories, as the title of his essay suggests.

Anthony Appiah, in "The Uncompleted Argument: Du Bois and the Illusion of Race," critiques Du Bois's argument for a positive conception of race. He argues the following: "The truth is that there are no races: there is nothing in the world that can do all we ask 'race' to do for us" (2000, 134). Appiah's argument falls within an antirealist or eliminativist approach to race (defined in chapter 1) whereby he argues that race is not real because there is no unifying trait or essence that can be attributed to it. I would not go so far as to argue that Badiou's description of race overlaps with Appiah's, given that previously I have suggested that Badiou's is more akin to a social constructivist model. However, as developed above, Badiou does not suggest that there is anything more to race than this negative conception, nor does he seek to conserve a place for a more positive conception of race within his political theory of emancipation.

What then is the positive conception of race indicated by Du Bois? And what purpose does a positive conception of race serve for a theory of emancipation? Drawing from the work of Du Bois, various authors have argued for the conservation of race categories as important for dismantling racism. For instance, in the inaugural issue of *Critical Philosophy of Race*, Bernasconi, Belle, and Taylor state, "Critical philosophy of race is a critical enterprise in three respects: it opposes racism in all its forms; it rejects the pseudoscience of old-fashioned biological realism; and it denies that antiracism and anti-racialism summarily eliminate race as a meaningful category of analysis" (2013, iv). According to Bernasconi, Belle, and Taylor, the preservation of race is so important that it qualifies as one of the three main characteristics of critical race theory, stressing the importance of maintaining race as a meaningful category of analysis. That said, while they express the importance of a positive conception of race, it becomes much more difficult to define it. Chike Jeffers articulates a positive conception of race as follows:

> What it means to be a black person, for many of us, including myself, can never be exhausted through reference to problems of stigmatization, discrimination, marginalization, and disadvantage, as real and as large-looming as these factors are in the racial landscape as we know it. There is also joy in blackness, a joy shaped by culturally distinctive situations, expressions, and interactions, by stylizations of the distinctive features of the black body, by forms of linguistic and extralinguistic communication, by artistic traditions, by religious and secular rituals, and by any other number of modes of cultural existence. There is also pride in the way black people have helped shape Western culture, not merely by means of the free labor and extraction of resources that economically supported this culture but also directly through cultural contributions, most prominently in music and dance. These contributions are racial in character—that is to say, they are cultural contributions whose significance can only be fully understood when they are placed in proper context as emerging from a racialized people. It does not seem necessary, however, to assume that the oppressive nature of this process of racialization must necessarily problematize the continued existence of the culture that emerged from it. There is, in fact, reason to think that the historical memory of creating beauty in the midst of struggling to survive oppression can and should persist as a thing of value in black culture long after that oppression has truly and finally been relegated to the past. (2013, 422)

This passage begins with Jeffers drawing a distinction between problems of stigmatization, for example, that accompany being racialized, and the joy and pride that is associated with being a particular race. It is important to note that for Jeffers, even though race may have emanated from white supremacy, race in its entirety need not be limited to this problematic structure. It is thus possible to dissociate a negative conception of race (that emanates from hierarchical structures) from a positive conception of race (black culture as a thing of value, in and of itself). Within this same essay, drawing from Du Bois's "Conservation," Jeffers emphasizes the importance of a sociohistorical racial identity that is additionally expressed in various cultures. Alongside Du Bois, Jeffers thus argues for the conservation not only of cultures but also of historical memory (426).

At the same time, however, I would argue that a positive conception of race is more than the joy that accompanies being a particular race; that is, that alongside cultural (and positive) conceptions of race offered by Jeffers, there are political (and positive) conceptions of race as well. In both instances, part of the justification for these conceptions of race is that if one focuses merely on a negative conception of race, then one fails to adequately respond to the requirements of emancipation. Furthermore, as I discuss below, the conservation of races is important for avoiding patterns of Eurocentrism. Most notably, a method for avoiding patterns of Eurocentrism is to maintain political resistance to conceptions of sameness by affirming both universality and equality, on the one hand, and difference, on the other. By way of his theory of political resistance, Lucius T. Outlaw Jr. offers a political (and positive) conception of race. Each of these points is considered in turn below.

In "The Cultural Theory of Race," Jeffers states "that racism works and must be addressed both in terms of the way it creates difference and the way it suppresses difference" (419). There are two modes of racism at work in his statement. First, one ought to address the manner in which racism is enacted through the creation of race for the purpose of oppression and discrimination. This is what I have previously called the negative conception of race. Second, there is that form of racism that works through the suppression of differences. What does this second enactment look like? According to Jeffers, "Insofar as racist discourse sets up the ways and values of white people as the standard by which black people are judged to be deficient, thus degrading black cultural traditions and creativity, black people ought to resist the pressure for sameness" (419). It becomes important to recognize that racism can exist in more ways that I have suggested at the start of this chapter. To reiterate this position once again, this original conception of race presupposes that race is (merely) a product of white supremacy. A result of this formulation of racism (and presumably part of its solution) is to say that in order to do away with racism, one must also do away with categories of race. However, this second conception of racism poses a problem for the aforementioned solution to racism. In other words, if patterns of Eurocentrism are manifest through an assumption of sameness or through assimilation, then the dissolution of race as a meaningful category (and distinct from white supremacy) would itself be problematic. This argument is further bolstered by Du Bois's and Jeffers's arguments regarding the existence of a positive conception of race.

Jeffers's argument echoes Du Bois, who states that "as a race, we must strive by race organization, by race solidarity, by race unity to the realization of that broader humanity which freely recognizes differences in men, but sternly deprecates inequality in their opportunities of development" (2000, 114). The imposition that Jeffers draws in his reading of Du Bois's "Conservation" is the importance of unity *and* diversity. Namely, "What Du Bois articulates in 'Conservation,' then, is a sharp critique of Eurocentrism: he claims that the liberation of black people requires that they demand equal rights and fair treatment but that they simultaneously affirm that 'their destiny is not a servile imitation of Anglo-Saxon culture, but a stalwart originality which shall unswervingly follow Negro ideals'" (Jeffers 2013, 419).

In *On Race And Philosophy*, Outlaw provides an account of a (positive) conception of race that exceeds cultural dimensions and serves as a political category. He states: "I argue the need to conserve 'race' and 'ethnie' (and 'ethnicity') as vital components of a philosophical anthropology, and of a social and political philosophy, [is] more adequate in the present and near future to the exigencies of life in racially and ethnically complex societies" (1996, 136). Outlaw returns to Du Bois's "Conservation of Races" in order to develop what he calls a politics of differences that emphasizes the role of race and ethnicity for addressing the problems of modernity. According to Outlaw:

> Du Bois' reconsideration of "race," then, is not simply an effort in taxonomy. Rather, it is part of a decidedly *political* project that involves prescribing norms for the social construction of reality and identity, for self-appropriation and world making. In his [Du Bois] words, "the history of the world is the history, not of individuals, but of groups, not of nations, but of races." (154)

Outlaw is here citing Du Bois. The entirety of Du Bois's statement is as follows:

> At all times, however, they have divided human beings into races, which, while they perhaps transcend scientific definition, nevertheless, are clearly defined to the eye of the Historian and Sociologist. If this be true, then the history of the world is the history not of individuals, but of groups, not of nations, but of races, and he who ignores or seeks to override the race idea in human history ignores and overrides the central thought of all history. (Du Bois 2000, 110)

Two points in particular should be evident from Outlaw's reading of Du Bois. First, Outlaw is concerned with race as a political category, and as a category that should remain politically salient. In other words, race is not simply a means of classification of people into groups. Instead, race belongs to the fabric of how political spaces are constructed. Failing to incorporate a conception of race into political discourses results in the inability to accurately portray the history of the world. Second, Outlaw is not primarily concerned with individuals and nations, but instead with the relation between race and history. In this sense, he emphasizes the importance of race for the *thought* of all historical change.

Similarly, "'Difference,' rather than similarity, has become a significant basis of political mobilization. But, not for the purposes of exclusion. Rather, 'difference' is now a highly valued preference that many persons and groups would have accommodated and recognized as the basis for their participation in civic, political, and economic life" (Outlaw 1996, 140). Outlaw is pointing out that the reason one might become involved in political life is because of the differences that mark that person. A nuanced understanding of the political would thus need to address the differences that are politically meaningful for individuals. As observed by Jeffers:

> People like Outlaw . . . have rightfully drawn our attention to the prescriptive, political dimension of Du Bois's project, that is, the sense in which he sets out not merely to define race for the sake of conceptual or empirical accuracy but, rather or also, to promote a conception of race that will ground and encourage collective action among his people in the face of their oppression. (2013, 412).

Perhaps one of the most telling moves employed by Jeffers and Outlaw, and indeed even Belle, is the conservation of race even in a postracial society. In other words, even if a postracial society were possible (whereby racism no longer existence) it need not be that there is (as a result) no conception of race in this postracial world. The reason being is that the continued battle against patterns of Eurocentrism is located in an emphasis in the universal equality of all persons *while also simultaneously* emphasizing the importance of differences like race (as positively conceived).

RETURNING TO FANON, SARTRE, AND CÉSAIRE

Regardless of the similarities between the writings of Sartre and Fanon, Fanon's critique of Sartre's "Black Orpheus" in *Black Skin, White Masks* is well documented.[6] Without dismissing these tangible and significant connections entirely, our task becomes to discern what it is about this debate in particular that is important for my current analysis of Badiou.

Recalling the discussion above, for Belle, this debate makes apparent the difference between what she calls a positive and a negative conception of race. Belle's description of a positive conception of race "encompasses a sense of membership or belonging, remembrance of struggle and overcoming, and the motivation to press" forward for communities of color (Gines 2003, 56). For the purpose of this argument, however, I would like to extend Belle's description in the following way. I propose that a positive conception of race/racial emancipation can be understood as maintaining (at least) the following three characteristics: (a) race is something that maintains relevance in peoples' lived experiences and in family and cultural relationships, (b) race ought *not* be reduced to racism, and (c) race and racial emancipation ought *not* be construed as something that is politically deficient and that subsequently needs to be fulfilled by something other than itself. This first point, that race is something that matters, is implicit in the second and third points listed above; however, it warrants an explicit statement because, in a sense, the second and third points are an attempt to provide a clarification on what it means for race to matter. The second point, that a concept of race ought not be wholly reduced to racism, is proposed because the assumption that race is a category that is reducible to racism implies a loss of efficacy for and meaningful solidarity within race-based movements. Furthermore, this assumption then results in the view that race-based emancipatory movements are lacking and thus require something (or someone) else in order to achieve a more justified or more total form of political fulfillment.

As previously noted in my discussion of Sartre's "Black Orpheus," while it might be the case that one *could* argue that Sartre would agree that (a) race matters, it is not the case that he would argue that (b) race ought not be reduced to racism. Furthermore, it is quite evident that Sartre would claim, contra (c), that racial emancipation is lacking and needs to be overcome in order to attain a more universal form of emancipation that is located in the figure of the proletariat. For instance, we can recall Sartre's articulation of Négritude, and Black race consciousness, as the "up-beat . . . of a dialectical progression" (1948, 49) whereby it becomes "a means and not an end" (49) towards the truly "objective" (48) and "universal" (49) position. Therefore, Sartre does not develop a positive conception of race given the characteristics I have outlined above.

However, I have been attempting to demonstrate that within Fanon's critique of Sartre we see Fanon's adherence to these characteristics of a positive conception of race. Most explicitly, it seems that for Fanon, and in line with (c), racial emancipation and race ought not be considered lacking and thus requiring something else in order to be fulfilled. My presupposition of such a position is based on my discussion of Fanon above. More explicitly, drawing upon these discussions, we need only to turn to Fanon's statements regarding black consciousness—wherein he states, "I am not a potentiality of something; I am fully what I am. I do not have to look for the universal" (Fanon 2008, 114), and similarly, "My black consciousness does not claim to be a loss. It *is*. It merges with itself" (114)—in order to recall that for him Black racial consciousness, and Négritude as well, ought not be construed as lacking. Given these statements, it thus follows that he does not think it ought to be the case that (b) race and racial emancipation be reduced to racism. Furthermore, given these premises, it could also follow that, for Fanon, (a) race and racial emancipation is something that maintains relevance. It should also be noted that the manner in which these issues matter to Fanon and Sartre are quite distinct (given the two other characteristics located in this argument). On the basis of this description of a positive conception of race and Fanon's critique of Sartre offered above, it is thus conceivable that Fanon *could* uphold a positive conception of race.

An additional consideration for this argument might be to address the relation between Fanon and Négritude. Namely, it is important to note that Négritude is not wholly equivalent to a positive conception of race, and therefore a rejection of Négritude does not necessarily amount to a rejection of a positive conception of race.[7] My aim has rather been to demonstrate that Fanon's affirmation of race through this positive conception of race coincides with my reading of the Négritude movement's affirmation of race. For instance, one might recall my discussion of Césaire above on the role of "the Negro question" for the purpose of Communist movements. Similarly, one can turn to Césaire's use of "acceptance" in "Notebook of a Return to the Native Land"—whereby he utters "I accept . . . I accept . . . totally, without reservation" (1983, 73) and "I accept, I accept it all" (77)—as similar to the affirmation held by Fanon (i.e., "I am fully what I am" [2008, 114]). Regarding Césaire's affirmation, his statements "I accept . . . my race that no ablution of hyssop mixed with lilies could purify" and "I accept . . . my race pitted with blemishes" (1983, 73) are meant to be an avowal and acceptance of his racial embodiment even though white supremacy attempts to assert his ugliness. Therein, according to Donna V. Jones, "Césaire accepts his physical inheritance against colonial somatic prejudice, he accepts the ignominy of blacks' present condition against attempts to escape to a mythic past or transcendent future, and he accepts the childlike violence and fecundity of the natural world of which he rightfully understands himself an evanescent and fragile expression" (2010, 176). In other words, he accepts that the colonial world proposes a standard of beauty that inherently excludes him, and through such an acceptance does not react to it through an outright rejection, and furthermore, he affirms his embodiment irrespective of that standard.

We might also consider Césaire's "Letter to Maurice Thorez," originally published in 1956, eight years following Sartre's "Black Orpheus." In this essay, Césaire offers various critiques of Communist and socialist movements, not unlike the critique offered in his interview with Depestre discussed above. Therein, he emphasizes the singularity of the situation of men of color in the world. He states the following:

> Suffice it to say that we [men of color] are convinced that our question (or, if you prefer, the colonial question) cannot be treated as a part of a more important whole, a part over which others can negotiate or come to whatever compromise seems appropriate in light of a general situation, of which they alone have the right to take stock. . . . In any case, it is clear that our struggle—the struggle of colonial peoples against

colonialism, the struggle of peoples of color against racism—is more complex, or better yet, of a completely different nature than the fight of the French worker against French capitalism, and it cannot in any way be considered a part, a fragment, of that struggle. (2010, 147)

In this statement it becomes apparent that Césaire is very much offering a critique of Sartre's formulation of universal emancipation through the subordination of race consciousness to class consciousness. Such a formulation, Césaire argues, fails to account for the complexity and the difference in nature of colonial and racial struggles.

Césaire's critique mirrors the critique offered by Fanon, as discussed above. Once again, in line with my argument above, we see that for Césaire that (a) race matters, (b) that race ought to be affirmed and not reduced to racism, and (c) racial emancipation ought not be found lacking and in need of something else. It thus follows, given the criteria for a positive conception of race offered above, that Césaire would argue for what I, alongside Belle, have called a positive conception of race.

As such, while I utilize various nontraditional articulations of Négritude to further my argument, Négritude serves as an example of what I argue is a positive conception of race. Even if one rejects Négritude as a viable final option (as many argue Fanon does at the end of *Black Skin, White Masks*), this does not imply that one also fully rejects the role of a positive conception of race. Furthermore, the central claim of my argument in this project is not the misrepresentation of Négritude by Sartre or Badiou, rather I am concerned with the importance of a positive conception of race for a theory of emancipation. Lastly, there are various other scholars who emphasize the importance of a positive conception of race for their respective theories of politics and emancipation without depending on an account of Négritude. For instance, above I discuss W. E. B. Du Bois's argument for the conservation of races, as well as present-day discourses that have emerged from Du Bois's arguments, including the work of Lucius T. Outlaw Jr. and Chike Jeffers. The most important point to glean from this discussion is whether Badiou maintains a positive conception of race, and, as I elaborate below, this book argues that he does not.

For Césaire, political emancipation should not come in the form of the subordination of a part for a common goal or collective ends. Rather, as noted above, racial and colonial emancipation is more complex and of a different nature, therefore such emancipation may require different strategies than other forms of emancipatory processes. Additionally, he states the following:

> What I want is that Marxism and communism be placed in the service of black peoples, and not black peoples in the service of Marxism and communism. That the doctrine and the movement would be made to fit men, not men to fit the doctrine or the movement. (2010, 150)

Césaire warns against centering whiteness (for instance) in political emancipatory movements under the guise of universality. Contra the argument offered by Sartre (regarding the relationship between racial emancipation and class-based emancipation), Césaire argues that the Communist Party ought to be concerned with the needs of Black peoples. In other words, the center around which the Communist Party rotates need not be emptied of substance but instead filled with the particularity of those who are most marginalized.

To be clear, by outlining the importance of particularity for emancipatory movements one must not assume a position of pure particularity (or cultural relativism) against universalism. Similarly, this position does not presume a purity that cannot be altered by any other. In fact, in response to the former of these two claims, Césaire states the following:

> I am not burying myself in a narrow particularism. But neither do I want to lose myself in an emaciated universalism. There are two ways to lose oneself: walled segregation in the particular or dilution in the "universal." My conception of the universal is that of a universal enriched by all that is particular, a universal enriched by every particular: the deepening and coexistence of all particulars. . . . So we need to have patience to take up the task anew; the strength to redo that which has been undone; the strength to invent instead of follow; the strength to "invent" our path and to clear it of ready-made forms, those petrified forms that obstruct it. (152).[8]

In what follows in chapter 5, I outline the way in which a (new) form of universalism becomes possible through the affirmation of particularities, thus preserving the importance of a positive conception of race. Such a framework avoids the trappings of not only a narrow (or pure) particularity but also a Eurocentric conception of universality.[9]

It is also important to keep in mind that Négritude does not describe a positive content that cannot be altered by engaging with seemingly disparate discourses. As previously argued, the conception of race offered by Césaire in particular, and Négritude in general (while recognizing that this is not the dominant interpretation), does not propose that race is something static and unchanging. Rather, in these examples, race is better understood as dynamic and continually changing. The dynamism of racial identity is thematized in Césaire's "Notebook of a Return to the Native Land" as follows: "The great black hole where a moon ago I wanted to drown it is there I will now fish the malevolent tongue of the night in its motionless veerition!" (1983, 85). According to Jones, "the black hole [trou] . . . may be read as an internal cross-reference, signifying, among other things, the spiritual space uncovered by the poet's persistent probing of the depths of plural black identity" (2010, 165). Or, similarly, Gregson Davis describes this theme as follows:

> Negritude is positively defined not by predicate nouns . . . but by verbs. . . . The shift to verbs strongly indicates that Negritude is not to be regarded as a state, but an activity—an activity of self-exploration, of "delving" into the psycho-social unconscious. Negritude is nothing less than the ongoing process itself, the subterranean interior journey. (1997, 50–51)

Thus, Césaire offers a conception of race that is plural and dynamic rather than static, pure, totalizing, or unchanging. These points serve to reinforce the argument I provide above regarding debates in Négritude studies and they coincide with the various articulations of a positive conception of race offered by Jeffers, Outlaw, and Du Bois. It is on these grounds that the conception of Négritude that I advance through Césaire is distinct from Badiou's conception of universal emancipation.

RETURNING TO BADIOU

A question that might arise at this point is the following: If Black pride or racial identity is needed in order to achieve universal emancipation, then does this not mean that Badiou is in fact offering us a positive conception of race? In response to such a critique, I maintain that Badiou has not offered a positive conception of race. Insofar as he delimits race as a means toward another end—namely, universal emancipation—it follows that he has subjugated race to a secondary position. Such an act of subjugation fails to promote a positive conception of race. In addition, his emphasis on universality (over and against difference) fails to address the political prescriptive aspect of Outlaw's positive conception of race. If the function or goal of a positive conception of race is to maintain the importance of race for thought and to ground political action, and furthermore to maintain difference in order to avoid patterns of Eurocentrism, Badiou has not succeeded in offering a notion that does so. I argue that he does not, in fact, offer a positive conception of race as described above, insofar as, contra (b), he does not wholly distinguish between racial identity and racism and, contra (c), he argues that racial emancipation is found lacking.[10]

In *Creolizing Political Theory* (2014), Jane Gordon offers an alternative method for political theory that not only advocates for a kind of universalism but also emphasizes the importance of marginalized positions, the latter of which (presumably) allows her to avoid patterns of Eurocentrism. Gordon defines "creolization" in two ways. First, the concept "creole" is indebted to historically, geographically, and linguistically situated groups of people emerging in the sixteenth century (J. Gordon 2014, 2). Yet her use of "creolization" is distinct from these groups of people. Second, her working definition of "creolization" concerns a "particular approach to politics and to the engagement and construction of political ideas" (2) whereby "opposed, unequal groups forged mutually instantiating practices in contexts of historical rupture" (3). Most pointedly, this approach (a) "focuses on collective ends beyond those of basic coexistence and toleration [and] draws attention to the mutual transformation involved in molding that which emerges as politically shared" (3) (b) by offering "noncanonical interpretations of a canonical figure" (Gordon and Roberts 2015, 2–3).

It is on the basis of the two last points, regarding collective ends and the canonical figure, that I locate some of the differences between my project and that of Gordon's and Badiou's. First, Gordon's use of "collective ends" as an aspect of creolization for the purpose of universal emancipation might be construed as somewhat problematic, insofar as it does not acknowledge that struggles for emancipation may be more complicated and difficult to negotiate. Gordon's statement could be construed as presupposing that there is always a common goal, or a collective end, which can be located between various disparate disenfranchised communities. However, according to Alcoff, "group interests sometimes coincide and at other times collide" (n.p., 2016). Although sometimes various groups can come together and work toward a common goal, to presume that a politics of emancipation *only* takes place in these circumstances is to offer a very narrow conception of politics and emancipation.

Second, Gordon's process of creolization is located between non-canonical and canonical figures, and thus seemingly situated in relation to Western European theory. For instance, Gordon's and Neil Roberts's 2015 edited collection titled *Creolizing Rousseau* engages in the political practice of creolizing Rousseau (as the title of this book suggests). Similarly, her 2014 monograph titled *Creolizing Political Theory* engages in creolizing Rousseau by way of a relation to Fanon.[11] This analysis may reinforce the idea that it is only by placing the dominant figure in relation with a nondominant or marginal theorist that the political practice of creolization is possible. Such a pairing should raise questions regarding the extent to which Rousseau and, by extension, Western philosophical theory, is necessary for theories of emancipation. Furthermore, one might ask the degree to which creolization is a process that is demanded of all theorists or merely those for whom creolization (or proximity to that which is creole, or marginal) is not yet attained. As a result, it could seem as though the political process of creolization implicitly recenters (albeit unintentionally) an already dominant position. Or, to put it in different terms, one might inquire into whether marginal theorists are important in and of themselves or only to the degree that they are in conversation with dominant theorists.[12]

One might also read Gordon's articulation of creolization in conversation with Monahan's use of this same term. Monahan states, "My understanding of the creolizing subject seeks to disrupt the norms of purity at its roots by placing at the forefront that emphasis on *becoming*" (2011, 188), as well as an emphasis on ambiguity (2017, 3). As such, Monahan is quite careful to assuage the concern that creolization necessarily implies putting marginalized figures in the service of dominant figures in this history of philosophy. In "What Is Rational Is Creolizing," Monahan explicitly states that the goal of creolizing Hegel is "neither an uncomfortable imposition of 'marginal' texts, figures, and methods on Hegel's intellectual legacy (adding a splash of 'color' and 'spice' to an otherwise austere palette) on the one hand, nor the unwelcome colonization of marginalized thinkers by a paradigmatic 'great white theorist' on the other" (1). Rather, he calls for the developing of a cultural/linguistic model of creolization that offers an opportunity to see "hybridity and ambiguity as a strength rather than a weakness, and to conceive of a unity born of openness to others, rather than conquest (both real and metaphorical)" (4), whereby "unpredictable and new hybridities relatively quickly develop to the point that they can no longer be reduced to the sum of their original 'parts'" (2).

My use of Jane Gordon's conception of creolizing is helpful for this project in order to demonstrate various differences between the motivations for her work and Badiou's work. However, it should be noted that there are also significant similarities between their respective projects. In what follows, I outline a few of the most important connections and differences between these two authors.

First, unlike some of the theorists I have discussed thus far (Belle, Bernasconi), Gordon does not seem to advocate for a positive conception of race through Négritude and in fact offers a critique of Négritude in her discussion of Fanon. Gordon's reading of Négritude and Fanon positions her political project somewhat closer to Badiou and against various other theorists I discuss throughout this project, namely Outlaw, Jeffers, and Du Bois, specifically their articulations of the importance of the conservation of races (something which I also attribute to Fanon in my alternative reading of him in chapter 2). While Monahan is critical of a particular articulation of a positive racial identity that is founded in ontology and is aimed at a color-blind ideal (2011, 197), he is also careful to avoid an outright rejection of race (198). More specifically, he states that "Creolizing subjectivity . . . calls upon an agent to recognize the ways in which the person is raced in particular ways . . . and the ways in which the person is both more and less his or her race" (199).

Second, we can also locate a similarity between Gordon and Badiou in her articulation of the "general will" and revolutionary politics that she develops through Rousseau and Fanon. For instance, she states:

> The boundaries of the emergent nation, as I have emphasized, are not based on racial, ethnic, or religious membership but on a particular brand of committed, decisive, and divisive action in which anyone could in theory engage. (Indeed, Fanon emphasizes that there are French men

and women who join the anticolonial cause while there are Algerians who resist it bitterly). (2014, 134)

Or, similarly:

> For Fanon, doing justice to the risks taken and lives lost in revolutionary battle required ongoing, dialectical constructive work of cultivating a unique scope of political identity, that of the nation, which could alone mediate among class, regional, tribal, ethnic, and racial differences, by articulating a past and future in which all were mutually implicated (132).

Using the language that is offered to us by Badiou, and that I have been developing throughout, one could note here a similarity between what Gordon calls a national political identity that is not determined by class or racial differences and instead mediates between them, and Badiou's articulation of the political subject in the form of "the people" that is not beholden to any particular identity (such as race and class) as its determining feature. Furthermore, like Badiou's political project as outlined above—whereby a political event takes place in a particular location, and, presumably, the truth of the political event takes on a meaning in that local site—Gordon claims the following: "Any abstract rule, however noble, must be made locally meaningful or indigenous in ways that reflect the changing makeup of the polity" (167).

Despite these similarities that exist between Badiou and Gordon, there are significant differences that ought to be noted. One such difference is that Gordon is offering a method for changing the ways in which political theory and philosophy are done. Her "approach to politics" (3) is mindful of the manner in which Third World writings are positioned in academia and also the manner in which they are used in relation to First World theory. For instance, "To creolize political theory necessarily expands who is involved in the theoretical dimensions of such discussion and as such the structure of what functions as evidential" (15). Similarly, according to Monahan, "creolizing the canon calls for the decentering of canonical texts, figures, and traditions from the normative hegemony that they tend to enjoy" (2017, 7–8). Furthermore, Monahan requires that one also acknowledge that "the intellectual canon as a whole has never been a pure, self-contained, and discrete entity, nor have the individual key figures that comprise it" (7).

Toward this end, Gordon calls for the explicit recentering of marginalized theorists for any creolized political project. For instance, she draws upon Paget Henry's *Caliban's Reason* (2000), in which he discusses the work of Frantz Fanon, C. L. R. James, and Sylvia Wynter. According to Gordon, Henry argues the following:

> Intellectuals needed to undertake a project of reenfranchising African and Afro-Caribbean philosophies, recentering long-concealed areas of the imagination and re-establishing their ability to accumulate authority. Rejecting "negative evaluations that block African and European elements from creatively coming together," creolization, in this context, involved the act of deliberately indigenizing theoretical endeavors, of drawing on local resources of reason and reflection to illuminate local aspirations and assuming that the fruit of these particular endeavors could, as had proved true of their European counterparts, be valuable in themselves and to projects elsewhere. (12–13)

As such, for Gordon it becomes imperative to be conscientious of how theories are constituted and by whom theories are constituted. However, as discussed above, Badiou seeks to be able to designate whether something counts as political, or whether it counts as emancipation and, by correlation, when something does not count as emancipation or politics. Furthermore, Badiou neglects to incorporate the work of critical theorists of race and decolonial theorists, thus failing to expand who is involved in the formation of political theory. Contra this position, Gordon attempts to be mindful of the manner in which her political theory is enacted, offering a methodological analysis of the task of doing political theory itself. Badiou, instead, seems more concerned with being able to determine the conditions through which one could name something "political" or "emancipatory." As such, it is Badiou's position that is problematic, because he assumes that a political theory can incorporate or discern what is true of all political emancipatory movements, while being firmly couched within a specific discipline (namely European philosophy). In other words, Badiou does not offer such a recentering of his own political theory through African, Afro-Caribbean, Latinx, or Indigenous theory, for instance.

Moreover, Gordon states that there are at least four preliminary components for creolizing political theory (13). First, it requires "a particular orientation toward historical work in political thought . . . in which we repeatedly ask if we are paying due attention to the geographies within which we situate our subjects" (13). A genuine attempt at creolizing political theory requires that one attempt to properly portray the subjects of politics, attempting to avoid negative and harmful characterizations. In addition, it also requires due recognition of historic moments that is often dependent upon "a different way of narrating the situations" (13). Second, "Creolizing political theory ... involves conceptualizing the task of theorizing in such a way that we create conversations among thinkers and ideas that may at first appear incapable of actually taking place" (14). For instance, Gordon develops a conversation between Rousseau and Fanon, both of whom are developed as having a significant impact upon her reading of the other. Third, she cautions against a political theory that proposes what is called a conception of the "native informant," whereby the experiences of intellectuals in the Global South are used solely to further the theories of Western European theorists and theories. Intellectuals of the Global South are appropriated for their experiences and incorporated into an already existing theoretical framework. In other words, "to creolize political theory necessarily expands who is involved in the theoretical dimensions of such discussion and as such the structure of what functions as evidential" (15). Fourth, she states that "the implications of creolization extend beyond political theory to political science more generally" (15).

Badiou's analysis of Black emancipatory movements does not seem to adhere to the four components of creolizing political theory outlined by Gordon. In particular, at issue is, like Sartre, his emphasis on the role of racial emancipation as a moment that is subsumed into a more universal emancipation, one that seems to foreclose a space for mutual transformation. As such, while one might attempt to bring the political projects of Gordon and Badiou into proximity, to do so would be to misunderstand what is at stake in Gordon's project of creolization.

As this project moves forward, it is helpful to keep in mind the kinds of identities that are possible as well as the kinds of identities that are desirable for a discussion of race and emancipation. Badiou maintains a negative conception of identity, whereas Belle, Jeffers, Du Bois, and Outlaw emphasize the importance of positive racial identities. It is important to remember, however, that a positive conception of race need not be essentializing. In fact, there is a body of literature in critical race theory that addresses this critique. Second, Belle argues that positive conceptions of identity are important for the formulation of collective memory (Gines 2003, 58) and collective memory is "a source of heritage and even resistance and empowerment" (66). Specifically, I have addressed the correlation between identity (and the Négritude movement), politics, and emancipation. In addition to the critiques that I have offered above in this section, I hold that Badiou's politics of indifference has further implications. Namely, it serves to demarcate what counts as politically efficacious in bringing about emancipation. Thus I propose that drawing a correlation between his rejection of identity in his politics of indifference and his rejection of certain historical movements as political or emancipatory serves to illustrate the limitations of his project for understanding race. The crux of my argument, as developed in the next chapter, rests on how Badiou conceives of culture and the relation between culture and politics.

4. Politics Is to Culture as Class Is to Race

Alain Badiou's use and description of culture and politics has garnered increased attention in the past few years. In *Conditions* (2008) Badiou describes cultural politics in the following manner: "Comic, purely comic, is the theme of cultural politics, as is the theme of a political culture" (175). Given Badiou's outright rejection of merging culture and politics, what then is at stake in his conceptions of and distinction between culture and politics? In order to understand his conception of politics, consider Antonio Calcagno's description of Badiou's notion of a political event, which he describes as follows:

> The political event arises when three specific conditions have been met: 1) the state has to exert incredible pressure on a situation in order to preserve a certain *status quo*—one can measure the power of the state in relation to the force of the event; 2) political events are collective; 3) political events bring about the destruction of an old form of politics and launch a new regime or form of politics. Here, we are not talking about a routine change of government or leadership; rather, we are talking about a new way of thinking and doing politics. (2015, 183)

As demonstrated in chapter 1, politics, as conceived by Badiou, is bound up with an event—that is, a rupture with the immediate logic or law (that is structured by the transcendental index). An event brings about the appearing of what inexists. By revealing what inexists or what has minimal existence within a state, a political event can not only demonstrate the structure and function of a state (and what it excludes) but also provide conditions for the emergence of truth. Such truths include justice and equality for a political event, and they provide some of the conditions for new ways of thinking. As previously discussed, this process also requires the naming of the event, the subject who both names the event and is a product of the event, and a new language from which to articulate a new politics.

"Politics" thus refers to a sequence of actions that emanate from an event, guided by a subject and principles or truths (i.e., justice and equality) that *transcend* the logic of an oppressive or problematic state. By contrast, and as I develop throughout the rest of this chapter, "culture" refers to practices that are *immanent* to the logic of a state.

The juxtaposition between politics and culture is not uncommon in political philosophy. There already exists significant literature that (a) utilizes this distinction, and (b) critiques this distinction, both of which I address below. That said, it is not the distinction alone that is of concern for my reading of Badiou's political theory. Rather, a culture/politics division has implications for the representation of real-world activist movements. My interest is in what gets lost in Badiou's exclusion of "cultural movements" from politics. In particular, I am concerned with the manner in which "cultural" designates movements that address race-based liberation and the idea that for a movement to be political it must subtract particularities such as race from its organization and founding principles.

An example of a cultural movement for Badiou that focuses on race-based liberation is the Négritude movement (1930s–1970s). As I demonstrate below, he describes Négritude as failing to be political insofar as it fails to become universal or "intelligible for all," a failure that (presumably) the Négritude movement could rectify if race was no longer an organizing principle of its operation. Similarly, Nick Nesbitt, in an extension of Badiou's work, describes how the principles of the Haitian Revolution (1791–1804) are rooted in universal principles (such as justice and equality) and not focused on race. As a result, the Haitian Revolution counts as a political movement rather than a cultural one. While Badiou's reference to the Haitian Revolution is minimal, Nesbitt's *Caribbean Critique: Antillean Critical Theory from Toussaint to Glissant* (2013) and *Universal Emancipation: The Haitian Revolution and the Radical Enlightenment* (2008) apply Badiou's conception of the political to the Haitian Revolution and Caribbean literary theory in order to productively extend Badiou's project to the

Caribbean. However, as I argue below, the distinction that Badiou draws between culture and politics actually limits his ability to be applied to the Caribbean context, and non-European contexts broadly speaking.

The following sections each address these concerns in various ways. To begin I address Badiou's juxtaposition between the universal and the particular enacted through his politics/culture distinction. In particular, I demonstrate that his distinction between the universal and the particular operates within a post-Marxist political vein. As such, I turn to Linda Martín Alcoff's essay "The Political Critique of Identity" (2016), which offers a critique of a number of post-Marxist theorists who discuss race as an identity category but who also uphold a conception of universality that forecloses any political role for race. Furthermore, I demonstrate how the Haitian Revolution can be understood as a problem case for Badiou, to the extent that it makes evident the limitations of his political theory of emancipation and politics of indifference. In short, if we accept Badiou's distinction between politics and culture, and subsequently the division between politics and race, then either it is the case that the Haitian Revolution is not about race or it is the case that the Haitian Revolution is not political. I argue that because neither of these positions can be considered true, we cannot accept Badiou's culture/politics division, which is central to his politics of emancipation and indifference. This chapter concludes with a discussion of the connection between politics and emancipation, in response to which I propose that Badiou's political theory is simply too narrow to interpret versions of political emancipation prefaced on race categories such as Blackness, and thus his theory fails to be universal.

NÉGRITUDE AND CULTURAL MOVEMENTS

Putting aside the work of Négritude scholars for the moment, the primary concern in this section is Badiou's conceptualization of the Négritude movement. In his 1998 interview with Peter Hallward, Badiou states the following:

> "Négritude," for example, as incarnated by Césaire and Senghor, consisted essentially of reworking . . . traditional predicates once used to designate black people: as intuitive, as natural, as primitive, as living by rhythm rather than by concepts, etc. It's no accident that it was a

primarily poetic operation, a matter of turning these predicates upside down, of claiming them as affirmative and liberating. I understand why this kind of movement took place, why it was necessary. It was a strong and beautiful, and very necessary movement. But having said that, *it is not something that can be inscribed as such in politics.* I think it is a matter of poetics, *of culture,* of turning the subjective situation upside down. It doesn't provide a possible framework for political initiative (Badiou and Hallward 1998, 118, emphasis added).

There are two discreet points regarding Négritude made in this statement. First, Badiou describes part of this movement as involving a reshaping or reappropriation of language. As previously noted, Badiou conceives of race as negative identities that were imposed upon colonial racialized subjects, for instance. Négritude, according to this view, aims to invert these negative identities, turning these predicates upside down.

In its generality, this is in part an accurate way of describing the Négritude movement. This description is similar to Kathryn Sophia Belle's discussion of Jean-Paul Sartre's *Anti-Semite and Jew,* who "in the spirit of Negritude . . . is taking traits that were considered negative for Blacks and rethinking them as positive attributes" (Gines 2003, 59). In this way, Négritude was in part an attempt to affirm Black identity. The writings of Aimé Césaire, for instance, celebrate Black culture and furthermore provide some of the conditions for what became the "Black is Beautiful" campaign in the 1970s in the United States. At the same time, however, Badiou's conceptualization of Négritude is markedly distinct, because while he recognizes the importance of the rearticulation of what it means to be Black as something that is affirming and liberating, he also contends that the Négritude movement is not political and is instead a cultural movement. The second point that I want to highlight from this quote is that for Badiou Négritude fails to be political because of its emphasis on the rearticulation of what it means to be Black. The designation of cultural in this instance assumes that the attempt to rearticulate or reappropriate Blackness from something that is negative into something positive is still implicated in the logic through which its negativity was first instantiated. In a sense, then, Négritude fails to transcend the logic of racial oppression and instead offers merely an alteration.

Badiou's most recent elaboration of the Négritude movement is located in his book *Black* (2017). In this book he states that "the revolt against the hierarchical stigmatization of part of humanity on account of its so-called color—black, in this instance—can take two forms" (95). He describes the first form of revolt against racialized oppression as follows:

> [It] consists in confirming the role of colors. It will be said that part of humanity is indeed black, but the hierarchy of values will be eliminated, or even reversed: blacks are strictly equal to whites, or anyone else, or even: blacks are more attractive, stronger, smarter, more in tune with nature, sexier, have more rhythm, are more graceful, more ancient, have a more complex symbolic order, are more poetic, more this or more that, than white. In a nutshell: 'Black is beautiful.' (95–96)

The first form of revolt against racialized oppression takes the form of an affirmation of Blackness. The affirmation of Blackness entails what he calls a confirmation of the role of colors, which means that "colors" continue to serve a role of designation, whether it be a positive or a negative one. According to Badiou the more radical form of this approach is manifest in the Négritude movement. He states that the movement highlighted "the positive assertion of blackness, which was considered the soul of both African humanity and the portion of it that had been deported to America" (96–97).[1]

It is important to note the implications of his description of the Négritude movement. First, for Badiou, Négritude represents that affirmation of "part of humanity" which he goes on to specify as an "African humanity." In other words, because of its emphasis on race (or its confirmation of "colors") Négritude is limited insofar as it only applies to, or is concerned with, part of humanity. Second, and by extension, to the extent that the Négritude movement is confined to the realm of "color confirmation," it seems to exist as only a reaction to the hierarchical structure that it is attempting to address.

What, then, does he mean by "culture," and in what way are we to understand the Négritude movement as cultural? Colin Wright, a prominent Badiou scholar, describes Badiou's use of culture in the following way: "Culture is ordinary for Badiou [, and] . . . the 'ordinariness' of culture for Badiou is simply a pejorative condemning its inert fixity. Evental novelty must be fiercely acultural if culture is understood in this reductive way, as simply an honorific name for 'what is'" (2013, 270). There are a number of characterizations of culture offered by Wright in the above quote. For instance, culture becomes synonymous with a kind of fixity or immanence. In my discussion of the transcendental index in the first chapter, I noted how the logic or law determines the way objects *appear* in a world as well as the manner the state *represents* objects in the state. Similarly, one might recall my example about same-sex marriage. For Badiou, same-sex marriage would be construed as a cultural movement because it operates as an extension of state power. Whereby a state already recognizes opposite-sex marriage, it merely extends that recognition to include (or add) same-sex marriage. It is immanent to the extent that the structures of power remain and merely extend its power. In other words, same-sex marriage is not something that transcends the logic of the state but instead is immanent to it.

Within this framework, culture exists in accordance with a given transcendental index; culture is immanent to the transcendental index and in a certain sense, it perpetuates the logic of the state, thereby reifying the authority of the state. He juxtaposes this characterization of culture as immanent (or additive) with his conception of politics as transcendent (or subtractive). Unlike culture, he defines politics by its ability to transcend the logic of a particular state. Politics must subtract particularity from its truth, thus distancing itself from the logic ordering a given state.

Returning to the example of the Négritude movement, the affirmation or reappropriation of Blackness—a central feature of this movement—maintains the authority of the logic of the state that created the concept of race in the first place. In other words, central to his argument is that racial division or categories continue to exist, they have simply been codified in a different way. As a result, for him, Négritude fails to transcend the logic of the state and instead it merely adds Blackness as a category that is recognized by the state. Négritude serves to alter the logic of the state, and extend the authority of the state, rather than offering any radical change to the way in which the state is structured.

A further extension of Badiou's argument is that the very structure of identity as particular—keeping in mind the correlation between Négritude and "part" of humanity—forecloses humanity from being shared, open, or intelligible to all persons. Recall, for instance, my discussion regarding

Badiou's indifference to differences, whereby Madhavi Menon states the following:

> The specific thrust of indifference for Badiou is that identity cannot be used as the basis on which to formulate universalism. Rather than elevating one's particular difference as the one that matters, indifference treats as infinitely transversable the boundaries among peoples, places, and things, and does not prescribe which belongs to whom or what. (2015, 14)

There is thus an incongruity between identity (as particular) and universality for Menon and Badiou. Given his description of Négritude, this movement fails to encapsulate the kind of universality that is required of a political movement.[2]

As noted in chapter 1, something can be political only if it fulfills the following conditions: (a) it transcends the logic of the state, thus bringing about a radical change; (b) it is universal or has "a meaning that is intelligible to all" (Badiou and Hallward 1998, 119); and (c) it is based upon (political) truths. Given that Négritude is a mere alteration of racial categorization, it fails to transcend the logic of the state and bring about radical change. Second, given that the Négritude movement is only for "part of humanity," it fails to be intelligible for all, or universal. Third, by extension of the immanence and particularity of Négritude, it fails to encapsulate a universal truth that transcends the logic of the state. It is for these reasons that Badiou claims Négritude fails to take on a progressive meaning and thus fails to be political.

Badiou develops a second form of revolt against racialized oppression as the solution to what he considers the failure of Négritude (and thus the first form of revolt). While the first form of revolt seeks the reappropriation of negative identities thereby confirming the role of "colors," the second form of revolt seeks to eliminate the role of "colors" altogether.

Like the first form of revolt, Badiou describes the second form in both a moderate and a radical fashion. The moderate position "consists in denying that color has any relationship whatsoever with any system of valorization or disparagement. This means that any overall judgment, whether positive or negative, of a supposed 'community' of color is rationally impossible. Color is of course an objective determination, but it *must* have no symbolic extension" (Badiou 2017, 96, emphasis added). While objectively people's skin color can have different pigmentation, there ought to be a dissociation of pigmentation from any system of valorization, regardless of whether it is a positive or negative valorization. As previously noted, this position exemplifies the juxtaposition between identities, racial identity for instance, and his universal politics that requires the denial of any role of particularity, such as the symbolic value associated with "color." At the same time, this "moderate" position is insufficient, and instead he offers the following position that is more "radical":

> Naturally, I accept its [the moderate version] universalist consequences, but I go further: there is not even any *objectivity* to the judgment of color. In reality no color can be assigned to a given human being, not black, of course, but not white or yellow of any color identity whatsoever either. An individual can be predicated as black and classified in the "Black people" category only through the use of a very rough and pointless approximation. (96, emphasis added)

Consistent with my discussion of truth as indifferent to difference in chapter 1, Badiou is here asserting that no color can be objectively applied to any human being. In this instance he seems to be saying that there is no objective method through which a person could be classified as Black, whether biological or any other "objective" standard. Furthermore, this denial of valorization based on what he calls "colors," it seems, is the only (or most) rational possibility. In *Black,* he claims that this second form of revolt is consistent with his political theory.

In chapter 1 I describe Badiou's conception of race as constructionist. However, in *Black* (2017) his conception of race seems to shift rather significantly. Recalling my discussion in chapter 3 of W. E. B. Du Bois's "The Conservation of Races" and Anthony Appiah's nonrealist conception of race, Appiah claims that, given that there is no biological or genetic foundation for race, there is no "thing" that race is that ought to be conserved. Notably, Badiou's requirement for objectivity to the judgment of "color" seems to be leaning toward Appiah's nonrealist conception of race. For Badiou the implication that follows from the lack of objective determination is that there is no thing that race is that ought to be conserved in a political movement. He discusses a similar point in *Polemics*:

The only problem concerning these "cultural differences" and these "communities" is certainly not their social existence, habitat, work, family life, or school. It's that their names are vain as soon as what is in question is a truth, be it artistic, scientific, amorous, or, especially, political. That one's life as a human animal is forged from particularities, well, such is a law of things. When the categories of this particularity profess to be universal, thereby taking upon themselves the seriousness of the subject, then things regularly become disastrous. What matters is a *separation of predicates*. (2011a, 107)

Once again we see the juxtaposition between truth (which is universal) and identity and culture (which are particular). For Badiou one must subtract the truth of politics from cultural differences and identities. The disastrousness he is referring to here is something like the Holocaust, whereby the Aryan race professed their particular culture as universal, which resulted in the massacre of Jews, Gypsies, and homosexuals during World War II. It would thus seem that Badiou has the best intentions when he proposes the importance of a universal principle such as justice and equality as the basis of a political movement. However, I would argue that one need not take an all-or-nothing approach and that his rejection of any role of identity or particularity for a political and emancipatory movement actually poses another kind of problem for him. For example, consider the following statement Badiou makes in *Black*:

I can do mathematics in yellow underwear, and I can actively pursue a politics subtracted from electoral "democracy" with rasta dreadlocks. This does not mean that the theorem is yellow (or not yellow) any more than it says that the directive under which we convene is dreadlocked. Nor, for that matter, does it lack dreadlocks. (2017, 107)

The presumption here is that the particularity, namely yellow underwear and rasta dreadlocks, ought not determine the thing that has taken place, namely the theorem and the directive. These cultural particularities are contingent and thus we ought not consider them important to or imposing upon the thing that has taken place. Predicates, cultural particularities, it would seem, are merely incidental for Badiou, and while they might seem important within a particular state, their importance is only attributable to the logic of that state. In other words, there is nothing essential, transcendent, or enduring about these particularities or identities, and furthermore they ought not be the basis for an emancipatory political theory that aims to change the logic of a state. As a result, cultural identities (such as race, gender, or religion) ought not impose upon nor inform a political truth and a political process, and such identities do not inform universal emancipation.[3]

This brings us back to the distinction Donna-Dale L. Marcano makes in the writings of Sartre, namely between *Anti-Semite and Jew* (1946) and *Critique of Dialectical Reason* (1960) discussed in chapter 2. Briefly, she states that Sartre's earlier conception of race developed in *Anti-Semite and Jew* proposes that "race" only emanates from the dominant gaze and furthermore is limited to what Belle describes as a negative identity. In his later work, however, Sartre attempts to provide a space for the self-naming practices of groups in a political sphere. That said, Badiou seems to favor Sartre's earlier conception of race, rather than the latter one outlined by Marcano, to the extent that he claims that his aim is to "put an end to any use of so-called colors in all forms of deliberation and collective action" (Badiou 2017, 102). Consistent with my description of his politics of indifference in chapter 1, this second form of revolt, and in particular its radical formulation, must preclude any reference to race and any other form of particularity insofar as particularity is bound up with the logic of the state toward which any emancipatory politics is attempting to upend. For Badiou, race is in no way political.

Badiou also portrays the first and second forms of revolt as being in a dialectical relation. The first form of revolt holds a position of importance if only for the purpose of the role it plays for the second form of revolt, the latter of which must sublate the former in order to attain a universal form of emancipation. This line of argument is consistent with Sartre's description of Négritude in relation to universal emancipation, as developed in chapter 2 of this book, whereby Négritude must be overcome for the purpose of universal emancipation. Furthermore, it is also consistent with my articulation of Badiou's conception of Négritude. We continue to see that Négritude is held in a kind of tension with universal emancipation, whereby the affirmation of identities in the Négritude movement is juxtaposed with the subtraction of identity for a movement to achieve universal emancipation. As previously noted, Négritude could have achieved universal emancipation only if it had substituted its affirmation and reappropriation of race for a principle that could be extended to all. Within Badiou scholarship, an example of a movement that does achieve universal emancipation and thus corresponds to the second form of revolt outlined above is the Haitian Revolution.

THE HAITIAN REVOLUTION AND POLITICAL MOVEMENTS

The Haitian Revolution has garnered considerable interest by Badiou scholars in recent years (e.g., Nesbitt 2013, 2008, and Hallward 2007). My interest in Nesbitt in particular stems from his portrayal of the Haitian Revolution through a Badiouian framework in order to illustrate further what is at stake in Badiou's political theory. The pertinent question for my project is: What is it about the Haitian Revolution that makes it political within a Badiouian framework? Consider the following very brief summary of the Haitian Revolution, as it applies to Badiou scholarship.[4]

According to Nesbitt, "On January 1, 1804, . . . the former slaves of the French colony of Saint Domingue took the decisive step of universally abolishing slavery unconditionally and immediately upon achieving independence as the new nation of Haiti" (2008, 1). Prior to the revolution, in the late eighteenth century, Saint Domingue was a colony of France and had "the Americas' strongest export economy" in cotton, cacao, and indigo, and had an important French military base (Geggus 2014, xi). As noted by the historian David Geggus:

> By the late 1780s Saint Domingue had become the single main destination of the Atlantic slave trade. Its enslaved population was almost as large as that of the United States south of the Potomac. . . . When the French Revolution broke out, Saint Domingue was home to about 30,000 white colonists,[5] a roughly equal number of free people of color, and almost half a million slaves. (xii)[6]

The middle tier of Saint Domingue society was made up primarily of free people of color,[7] two-thirds of whom "were of mixed racial descent; some had both whites and slaves for relatives" and "were more numerous than in most Caribbean colonies and notably more wealthy" (xiii). Specifically, Carolyn E. Fick notes that "by 1789, the *affranchis* [free people of color] owned one-third of the plantation property, one-quarter of the slaves, and one-quarter of the real estate property in Saint Domingue" (1990, 19). At the same time, however, by way of "repressive social legislation, . . . the affranchise were legally defined . . . as a distinct and subordinate social 'caste'" (20).[8]

According to Geggus, despite its being a French colony,

> historians disagree whether Saint Domingue would have undergone revolution without being destabilized by the French Revolution of 1789. . . . [Notably,] the American Revolutionary War also boosted the ambitions of the fast-growing free colored population; having contributed two battalions of soldiers to overseas expeditions, its leaders began to lobby the government for more equal treatment, albeit very discreetly. (2014, xiii)[9]

In the simplest of terms, we know that a colonial and racist state (in this instance, France) sought to maintain its power and the status quo through the disenfranchisement of the enslaved population of Saint Domingue. Furthermore, we know that the Haitian Revolution sought to upend this power of the colonial state and that it simultaneously sought the emancipation of the enslaved population. On Badiou's terms, this would mean that the inexistent of the state aimed to become existent.

However, my concerns in this book are the motivations or terms through which the Haitian Revolution came about. Nesbitt's Badiouian framework focuses his analysis on the Haitian Revolution, and he describes the revolution's aims in the following manner: (a) "Acting decades in advance of the North Atlantic powers, they turned the abstract assertion of a human right to freedom for all citizens into historical fact and created a slavery-free society, without discrimination other than that one be human and present within the borders of the new state" (2008, 1); (b) the unique contribution of the Haitian Revolution to humanity was "the construction of a society without slavery, one of a *universal* and *unqualified* human right to freedom" (2); and (c) "the agent of this process [is] one whose 'sufferings are universal' [and] one that has experienced no particular wrongs *(against a class, gender, or race)* but the denial of humanity itself, a class whose emancipation necessarily implies the emancipation of humanity as a whole" (2013, 7, emphasis added). Each of these three statements offers some clarity regarding Nesbitt's framing of the Haitian Revolution.

In other words, for Nesbitt the Haitian Revolution sought to destroy the racist colonial state and bring about a politics that was anticolonial and antiracist, thus unconditionally ending slavery. It sought to create a state that would not be exclusionary but instead would be open to all persons. Second, the Haitian Revolution was founded upon principles that were universal and unqualified, such as the political truths of equality and justice. Third, the motivations for the Haitian Revolution were not based on any particular identity (such as race) but instead were motivated by sufferings that could be universalized—the denial of humanity itself. For this reason, the revolution sought the emancipation of all humanity. Furthermore, Nesbitt claims that the Haitian Revolution "fundamentally transformed this transnational, world-systemic historical process" (2008, 2). As a result, the Haitian Revolution exceeded mere national and civil rights—those rights bound up within a state—and made universal claims of the Rights of Man (11).[10]

Nesbitt locates these principles of the Haitian Revolution in the following way: "The universal prescription announced by the signatories of June 1792 [discussed at greater length below] is not the negation of specificity in some abstract universal sense, but rather the recognition that there is no possible politics of identity . . . [and furthermore that] the realm of identity—specifically, racial identity—is purely negative" (2013, 2). Nesbitt cites a letter written to the General Assembly of Saint Domingue by Toussaint L'Ouverture, among others, in July 1792 as the most explicit exemplification of the universal principles motivating the Haitian Revolution.[11] The universality to which Nesbitt refers in this history of the Haitian Revolution is reflective of the Declaration of the Rights of Man and of the Citizen in France following the French Revolution (1789–94). In Nesbitt's 2008 book, titled *Universal Emancipation: The Haitian Revolution and Radical Enlightenment,* he outlines the manner in which the Haitian Revolution was "inspired by Radical Enlightenment ideas" including the French Revolution (2).

Indeed, when one reads the 1801 Constitution of the colony of Saint Domingue written by Toussaint L'Ouverture and members of his army, it is apparent that this constitution draws heavily upon the language of both the French Revolution and the American Revolution. In addition, consistent with Badiou's critique of identity politics, Nesbitt claims that identities, and specifically racial identities in this context, operate in a merely negative fashion that cannot be progressive in character. For example, as Nesbitt states, "a *politics* ... can take place only under the proposition of undivided universality" (2013, 2–3). The Haitian Revolution can only be considered "political" if it adheres to the principles of universality and seeks justice and equality for all. Of course we must also keep in mind that for Badiou the political is "something that, in the categories, the slogans, the statements it puts forward, is less the demand of a social fraction or community to be integrated into the existing order, than something which touches on a transformation of that order as a whole" (Badiou and Hallward 1998, 119). Unlike cultural movements that seek integration into the existing logic of the state, to be progressive (and political) implies some kind of transformation of the logic of the state for Badiou.

RACE AND THE HAITIAN REVOLUTION

Nesbitt's ultimate concern is to demonstrate the correlations between Badiou's political theory and the Haitian Revolution. However, there remain some historical events pertinent to the revolution that Nesbitt fails to address and that fail to fit within a Badiouan framework. Drawing from Geggus's account of the Haitian Revolution, I raise several concerns about Nesbitt's use of a Badiouian framework for understanding this revolution, as well as concerns about Badiou's politics of indifference. George Ciccariello-Maher's "'So Much the Worse for the Whites': Dialectics of the Haitian Revolution" (2014) provides a useful framework for understanding these concerns.

In his essay, Ciccariello-Maher speaks to the fraught relationship between dialectics and decolonization most evident at the intersection of dialectical thought and the Haitian Revolution (2014, 19). Generally, he is concerned with whether it is possible to conceive of a dialectics that is decolonial, and he turns to the Haitian Revolution in order to do so. He discusses Susan Buck-Morss's essay "Hegel and Haiti" (2000) as well as her book titled *Hegel, Haiti, and Universal History* (2009) in an attempt to "draw upon both the contours of the revolutionary process, but more importantly the meaning and interpretations of those contours, in an attempt to rethink the relationship between identity, dialectics, and the universal" (Ciccariello-Maher 2014, 38). Ciccariello-Maher is concerned with the interplay and representation of universality and particularity within the framework of the Haitian Revolution, as well as Buck-Morss's use of such categories.

A number of Cicariello-Maher's critiques of Buck-Morss's articulation of the Haitian Revolution apply to Nesbitt's articulation of the Haitian Revolution as well. Most notably, Ciccariello-Maher analyzes the justifications Buck-Morss offers to support her claim that the Haitian Revolution was universal by addressing (a) her use of the 1801 Constitution, (b) her representation of the figure Toussaint L'Ouverture, and (c) her recentering of whites in the Haitian Revolution. First, the 1801 Constitution was written by Toussaint L'Ouverture and was the first constitution composed following the start of the revolution (1791) and not long after the French Revolution and the Declaration of the Rights of Man and Citizen, hereafter referred to as the "Rights of Man." The 1801 Constitution followed the declaration of the end of slavery by Sonthonax, a French official, but also the threat of the reinstatement of slavery following Napoleon's rise to power in France. That said, Ciccariello-Maher notes that "Buck-Morss seems strangely unconcerned with the precise wording of this ostensibly universal statement [the 1801 Constitution]—which declares all Haitian men 'free *and French*'— . . . in which the very notion of freedom is bound as if by synonymy to the mother country. How universal could colonial rule possibly be, especially given the constant threat of re-enslavement?" (2014, 23).

The dilemma, as correctly noted by Ciccariello-Maher, is twofold. First, it locates strong ties between the 1801 Constitution and the French Revolution (including the Rights of Man, of which the 1801 Constitution draws heavily). Second, this document further cements the relation of colonial rule of Haiti by France, and a Napoleonic France at that. Given these concerns, a question that ought to arise is the following: If the goal of the Haitian Revolution was the emancipation of those who were enslaved, then to what extent can the 1801 Constitution be considered exemplary of this goal? This question seems especially pertinent given that in 1801, Haiti continued to be under colonial rule, and the threat of re-enslavement remained.

Nesbitt's articulation of the Haitian Revolution follows a similar problematic line of argument in three ways. First, Nesbitt utilizes Toussaint's 1792 document in which he invokes the Rights of Man for framing the

Haitian Revolution. However, the rendition of the Haitian Revolution offered by Nesbitt seems to overlook various important historical moments. For instance, Haiti declared independence in 1804, and thus until this point in time Saint Domingue was still a French colony and subject to French rule. This relation between Saint Domingue and France is of particular importance, given that in 1801 Napoléon Bonaparte[12] attempted to reinstate slavery in Saint Domingue.[13] Why, then, are the documents of 1792 and 1801 exemplary of the Haitian Revolution and demonstrative of the emancipation of those who were enslaved? In actual practice it would seem as though we should, as Ciccariello-Maher does, maintain "skepticism toward the formalism with which Toussaint embraced the Rights of Man and a suspicion that, beneath the formal equality of emancipation, white supremacy continued to operate in a manner that threatened even formal freedom" (34).

Second, regarding the figure of Toussaint, Buck-Morss is described by Ciccariello-Maher as celebrating Toussaint's uncritical embrace "that led [him] to oppose not only discrimination, but any form of racial identity that interfered with the establishment of formal equality in the here and now" (25). In other words, the political emancipation of people who were enslaved in Saint Domingue was not made on the basis of any particular race; rather, any form of racial identity had to be subtracted from the Haitian Revolution. However, Ciccariello-Maher critiques this position by stating that "it was *this* [his uncritical embrace of the universal] that led to Toussaint's favoring of the whites, [and] his concomitant distancing from the Black masses" (25). Unlike various other figures of the Haitian Revolution (such as Jean-Jacques Dessalines and Hyacinthe Moïse) Ciccariello-Maher argues that Toussaint's push toward the subtraction of racial identity from the Haitian Revolution in favor of a "universal" was for the purpose of reassuring whites who still lived in Saint Domingue (27). As noted by Laurent Dubois, "To preserve emancipation, Louverture decided that he must preserve the plantation economy and encourage the return of white planters who had fled. Locked in conflict with ex-slaves who had a very different vision of what freedom should mean, he maintained and perfected a coercive system that sought to keep them working on plantations" (2004, 4)

As such, one ought to be careful not to attribute too much to Toussaint. It is important to remember that Toussaint, Jean-François, and

Biassou—three figures to whom the Haitian Revolution and the Constitution of 1801 are often attributed—were fighting for the Spanish against the French in an attempt to maintain the rights of "free colored people" while also maintaining slavery in 1792 (the year of the document Nesbitt upholds as exemplary of the universal principles of the Haitian Revolution).[14] Furthermore, during Toussaint's tenure as governor of Saint Domingue, he upheld a system of forced labor until the time he surrendered to the French to ensure that the plantations on the island were productive. It is thus surprising that Nesbitt would turn to the 1792 document written by Toussaint, Jean-François, and Biassou as exemplary of the ideals of the Haitian Revolution. Similarly, in *Logics of Worlds*, Badiou chooses to emphasize 1796 as a pivotal moment of the Haitian Revolution. He describes this moment of the revolution as the "peaceful organization . . . under Toussaint's dictatorship, of the first interracial egalitarian society that humanity has ever known" (Badiou 2009, 524). However, as a number of historians have pointed out, Saint Domingue at this time was a society that was still entrenched in the alienation of former slaves due to the implementation of forced labor.

Third, "Whereas Buck-Morss, however inadvertently, centers the biologically-white colonists in her determination of what period of the Haitian Revolution matters, [C. L. R.] James [in *The Black Jacobins*] instead explicitly decenters the politically-white colonists as a measure of progress and instead insists that they stood as little more than a barrier to the universal" (Ciccariello-Maher 2014, 27–28).[15] Progress, according to Nesbitt, is determined by the ability of Toussaint to employ the language of the French Revolution in the 1801 Constitution for Buck-Morss, and the 1792 letter written by Toussaint. The implication is that the importance of this revolution did not lie in Haiti but elsewhere, and as a result "notions of formal freedom and universal equality are worse than empty words, [and] even constitute an active barrier to the universal by foreclosing . . . struggles that might be deemed too particular" (32). As I demonstrate below, the analyses of the Haitian Revolution offered by Buck-Morss and Nesbitt fail to adequately represent the motivations of the Haitian Revolution due to the conception of universality that they employ.

There are two implications that follow from the dilemma of framing the Haitian Revolution through the universal principles of equality and liberty enacted through the Rights of Man. First, the emancipation of those who were enslaved, given that this is the goal of the Haitian Revolution, *requires* the independence of Saint Domingue from colonial rule (Geggus 2014, xv). Second, it is pertinent to analyze documents other than those discussed by Buck-Morss and Nesbitt, which in practice did not actually aim toward the emancipation of those who were enslaved. It is for these reasons that I suggest that instead of turning to the 1801 Constitution, or to the 1792 document written by Toussaint et al., we should turn instead to the 1804 Declaration of Independence of Hayti. Regarding this document, Ciccariello-Maher states the following:

> The 1804 Declaration constitutes a riposte to Toussaint's errors and the abstract universalism of the 1801 Constitution. The document openly critiques the formalism of the Rights of Man, going a step further to argue that not only were words like "liberty," "equality," and "fraternity" insufficient, but such abstract principles had proven positively danger-ous. (2014, 28)[16]

For similar reasons one should also turn to the 1805 Constitution that was drafted by the free nation of Hayti and by Dessalines, who declared Hayti free from colonial rule and also from slavery. Such a document is impor-tantly distinct from the 1792 and 1796 documents that Nesbitt and Badiou use respectively.

There are a number of reasons why the 1805 Constitution is excluded from, in particular, Nesbitt's analysis of the Haitian Revolution. Namely, "The 1805 Constitution . . . fills that identitarian opposition with a new racial content by declaring all Haitians to be Black" (29). Thus, unlike the 1801 Constitution and the 1792 letter written by Toussaint, the 1805 Con-stitution does not purport to end slavery through the elimination of racial categories altogether, rather it upends slavery and seeks the emancipation of those who were formerly enslaved by centering Black people and by constituting the racial category of Blackness *as political*. Of particular im-portance are Articles 12–14, which state the following:

> Article 12: No whiteman [*sic*] of whatever nation he may be, shall put his foot on this territory with the title of master or proprietor, neither shall he in future acquire any property therein.

> Article 13: The preceding article cannot in the smallest degree affect white women who have been naturalized Haytians by Government,

nor does it extend to children already born, or that may be born of said women. The German and Polanders naturalized by government are also comprised in the dispositions of the present article.[17]

Article 14: All acception [*sic*] of colour among the children of one and the same family, of whom the chief magistrate is the father, being necessarily to cease, the Haytians shall hence forward be known only by the generic appellation of Blacks.

As we can see here, within the 1805 Constitution, Blackness is a condition for citizenship. That said, while one might argue that the use of the "generic" in Article 14 denotes that Blackness is a category that is open to all persons, Articles 12 and 13 make evident that this is not the case. Article 12 denotes the importance of ensuring that there are no longer slaves and white slave holders in Saint Domingue (in reference to the use of "masters" therein), and that the goal of the constitution is, in this sense, to upend slavery. In addition, white men, with a few exceptions clearly noted in Article 13, are explicitly refused citizenship. As stated by Anne W. Gulick regarding Articles 12–14, the "three-part negotiation of Haitian citizenship first transforms whiteness from the only legible political identity to the only identity that will henceforth be *illegible* to the new nation-state" (2006, 808). Thus, with the invocation of the new nation-state, not only does whiteness become illegible and thus exist outside the possibility of citizenship, but arguably within Badiou's framework, whiteness could be said to be *illegal* insofar as white men are expressly excluded from citizenship. Furthermore, as noted by Gulick, "Articles 12 through 14 announce that Haiti, perceived already by the rest of the world as black, has the same claim to political legibility as the French Republic or the United States of America—not in spite of, or even without reference to, but *because* of its blackness" (808). Thus, racial particularity is central to the Haitian Revolution.

Similarly, Gulick writes, "This text contains what in today's lexicon would be called a set of radical postcolonial aspirations, a community imagined, through a legal narrative, as capable of doing something none of its models had done before: identifying both blackness and humanity as the basic signifiers of citizenship" (802). Importantly, Fanon's identification of the "zone of nonbeing" employed by Ciccariello-Maher confirms this reading of the 1805 Constitution: "Rather than enforced uniformity . . . the declaration that all Haitians would henceforth be Black constituted a promotion to Being of those who had previously been condemned [dam-nés] to nonbeing" (2014, 34).

Likewise, "In his [James's] 1963 appendix to the revised edition of *The Black Jacobins*, . . . Haiti became the birthplace of negritude long before Haitians themselves (along with The 1805 Haitian Constitution African diasporics on multiple shores of the Atlantic) identified and defined a transcontinental resistant political identity predicated upon blackness" (Gulick 2006, 812–13). In other words, there is a consistency between the Négritude movement and the Haitian Revolution, and additionally, the consistency between these two movements depends on a political identity predicated upon Blackness. Thus what distinguishes the 1805 Constitution from French or U.S. Constitutions is that it brings the particularity of race to the forefront of its very inception. In this vein, Gulick writes, "In the Haitian Constitution, these experiences are brought to the fore, integrated into the text's narrative structure in direct contrast to the kinds of *silences* the North American model was legitimizing in its own textual-legal foundations of nationhood" (808, emphasis added). Within this vein of argument, the goal of the Haitian Revolution was not to erase the language of race altogether from the legal structure of the nation-state—that is, a state that was supplanted by a language of equality for all. Nor was the undergirding of the 1805 Constitution an aim to subtract the particularity of race from the nation-state. Rather, the revolution aimed at turning a racial ideology on its head; that is, instead of whiteness being the defining feature of citizenship, Blackness became the new measure of citizenship.

Of course, I am not proposing that the 1805 Constitution was written ex nihilo. Rather, the principles of the 1804 Declaration and the 1805 Constitution are the culmination of the slave revolution that began in 1791. In order to demonstrate this correlation, we need only to turn to the writing of Moïse, who condemned Toussaint's 1801 Constitution (James 1989, 267) and also eventually fought against Toussaint's implementation of forced labor and for the emancipation of Blacks. As noted by James, "What these old revolutionary blacks objected to was working for their white masters. Moïse was the Commandant of the North Province, and Moïse sympathized with the blacks. Work, yes, but not for white. [Moïse states,] 'Whatever my old uncle [Toussaint] may do, I cannot bring myself to be the executioner of my color'" (275). Moïse was ultimately executed in 1801 for leading a revolt against Toussaint that same year. As noted by Ciccariello-Maher, "It is clear that the rebellion [against Toussaint] sought Black unity and slaughter of the whites as at least a partial means toward 'complete emancipation'" (2014, 24). There is thus significant documentation that demonstrates that universal categories, such as the Rights of Man, were used by Toussaint in the Haitian Revolution in order to appease the whites. Furthermore, the masses, who comprised the revolution and whose freedom the Haitian Revolution is meant to address, were motivated by a conception of Blackness as a political category.

Unlike Badiou's politics of indifference described in chapter 1, the 1805 Constitution does not propose truth that is indifferent to difference or particularity. Rather, it assumes difference as a political *necessity* for emancipation. Given the tension between Nesbitt's Badiouian framing of the Haitian Revolution and the 1805 Constitution of Hayti, I propose that this leaves us with a series of questions. Most importantly, one should ask: Is the Haitian Revolution an example of a political event or should it be considered an example of a cultural movement? There are two plausible responses to this question. First, if one were to say that the Haitian Revolution *is* political,[18] then it would have to follow that race is no longer a difference to which the truth of an event must be indifferent. Second, if one were to say that the Haitian Revolution is *not* political and therefore cultural because of the language of the 1805 Constitution, then it would seem unlikely that Badiou's theory of emancipation could be properly inclusive of nonwhite persons.

This brings us to a third option that one might propose as a response to the tensions that exist between the 1805 Constitution and the Badiouian framework—namely, to disregard the 1805 Constitution as a defining moment of the Haitian Revolution. Indeed, it is true that a new Constitution was written in 1806 following the assassination of Dessalines and the founding of the Republic of Haiti (Gulick 2006, 804). However, to reject the 1805 Constitution because it does not fit into Badiou's theory of emancipation would seem to propose that this constitution was a step toward universality (which reduces it to a moment in a dialectic of liberation). Furthermore, one might argue that the 1805 Constitution was a first attempt at emancipation and that its authors improved the 1805 Constitution on their second attempt. The first assertion is problematic given that it reduces race-based liberation to a moment that is subordinate to something else. The latter assertion is also problematic insofar as it assumes that one can only get emancipation right, or think through emancipation, if it is inclusive of white people.

In summation, it is my contention that the Haitian Revolution ought to be understood as a political movement.[19] However, given the 1805 Constitution and its emphasis on race as a political category, Badiou's theory of emancipation fails to count the Haitian Revolution as political. This is not a failure on the part of the Haitian Revolution itself; rather this tension is an example of a limitation of Badiou's emancipatory politics.

My analysis of Badiou's discussion of Négritude above, as well as Nesbitt's Badiouian framework of analysis of the Haitian Revolution, aims to support my argument that Badiou's political project juxtaposes identity and emancipation. Briefly, Badiou claims that the Négritude movement is cultural because of its emphasis on identity. It is inconsistent with political emancipation except that it serves as a moment that needs to be sublated before universal emancipation is possible—thereby demonstrating the tension he maintains between identity and universality. Similarly, for Nesbitt, the Haitian Revolution should be understood as aiming toward politics and truths, such as universal conceptions of equality and justice. To this end, he emphasizes a correlation between the French Revolution over and against what I have argued is a conception of emancipation that centralizes race.

To what extent is it necessary to emphasize a tension between particularity and universality? And to what extent are they necessarily incommensurable? My concern with Badiou's political theory is that the tension he locates between universality and particularity, and his inability to recognize the importance of meaningful differences as the basis for solidarity and emancipatory politics, means that his political theory cannot safeguard itself against assimilationist or Eurocentric frameworks. And while Badiou's conception of political emancipation presupposes such transformative relation between the inexistent and the construction of a world, the framework for his own political theory itself does not perform or enact such safeguards. Instead, most of his references to minority perspectives and frameworks that are alternative to a Western or European framework become assimilated into his own already-constructed politics, like the Négritude movement that becomes a moment within his dialectic of universal emancipation. Such assimilationist, or even perhaps colonial, practices, thus lie at the heart of Badiou's presumably universal politics of emancipation.

WHY DO POLITICS NEED TO BE EMANCIPATORY?

A question that motivates this final section is: Why do politics need to be emancipatory? In a certain sense, one should ask whether there are important movements that Badiou would describe as cultural, but which ought to be thought of as political (albeit not in the sense employed by Badiou). Generally speaking, my goal is to demonstrate that his theory of political emancipation is limited because of what it excludes from the political realm.

In "The Political Critique of Identity," Alcoff states, "Identity is not merely that which is given to an individual or group, but is also a way of inhabiting, interpreting, and working through, both collectively and individually, an objective social location and group history" (2016, n.p.). With this in mind, to what extent can group histories be preserved in Badiou's politics of indifference? Or, to what extent does a group history matter for his theory of emancipation? There are two points that I raise in order to address these questions. The first concerns his conception of history, and the second point concerns the relation between history and a political event.

In *Badiou in Jamaica,* Wright provides an account of Badiou's theory of history as anti-historicism. He describes it as follows:

> [Badiou's] anti-historicism by no means implies ahistoricism. To leap to such a conclusion would simply be to repeat the dominance of the historicist account of History (rather as pessimistic accounts of the omnipresence of domination collude with and extend that domination). The term "ahistoricism" implies a complete indifference to historical factors, a pure and uncompromising rejection of their relevance, or—given that it is most frequently used as an insult—an outright ignorance of supposed historical facts. Badiou cannot be justly accused of any of these things. What is required, then, is an investigation into the possibility of anti-historicist conceptualizations of history. Such an investigation paves the way . . . for the affirmation of a mode of historiography that is integral

to the transformative labor of the subject. Such an affirmation prevents us from adopting the essentially idealist position of viewing history tout court as something to be definitively broken away from. As we shall see, recently Badiou has allowed for a relation to History that sustains a radical, because historically informed, political imaginary, something surely relevant to the possibility of preevental resistance. (2013, 188)

Wright is careful to distinguish between categorizing Badiou's political theory as anti-historical rather than ahistorical, arguing that the term "ahistorical" implies that a theory is completely taken out of a historical context. As noted in chapter 1, the truth of the event is always located in a particular world. At the same time, however, this truth also transcends that particular world and all particularity is subtracted from it. Yet, as noted by Wright, "peasant revolts are put down to grain shortages, workers movements are ascribed to foreign interference, slave uprisings are explained away as expressions of racial difference, and so on. It is this façade of misleading contingency that prevents the dialectical momentum of class struggle from appearing as an historical necessity" (188–89). How then are we to conceive of the anti-historicism Badiou proposes in regards to what I have offered above about emancipation?

Badiou's theory of history is not ahistorical, according to Wright, because political events still occur within a given historical situation. Yet we also know that a political event ruptures with the situation and provides the conditions for thinking politics anew. At the same time, however, even though his politics is anti-historical rather than ahistorical, group history (as described by Alcoff above) as well as collective memory (as described by Belle, discussed in chapter 3) does not seem pertinent for his emancipatory politics. Badiou's exclusion of group history and collective memory is most evident in his emancipatory politics because of the negative conceptions of identity (to the exclusion of positive conceptions of identity) that he utilizes in his politics of indifference. Recalling Belle, a positive conception of race "encompasses a sense of membership or belonging, remembrance of struggle and overcoming, and the motivation to press forward and endeavor towards new ideals and achievements" (Gines 2003, 56), and furthermore "challenges the history of oppression and rejection that is associated with being black" (64). Or, in Fanon's words: "Without a black past, without a black future, it was impossible for me to live my blackness.... Jean-Paul Sartre forgets that the black man suffers in his body quite differently from the white man" (2008, 117). It thus becomes important to understand the history of oppression "so that we are not condemned to repeat those sufferings in the future" (Gines 2003, 65). It is also important to maintain collective memory in order to avoid future harms, and for theorists such as Belle this is possible through a conception of race that exceeds the logic of an oppressive structure. At the end of her essay on Fanon and Sartre, Belle provides her readers with a cautionary tale:

> When we realize the complex and arduous task of developing an authentic race consciousness, rather than hastily moving to rejecting race altogether; the importance of conserving and preserving race should become more evident. We cannot simply jump from aiming at an authentic race consciousness to the goal of attaining a raceless society. We must first acknowledge the difficulty involved in achieving an authentic race consciousness before we can even imagine a society without racial oppression or without race. And even if such a society is possible, I refuse to struggle to discover and take up my racial identity in a positive way only to later deny it for the sake of the class struggle or in an attempt to escape the past. (66)

Given Badiou's conception of race, it is unclear how racial collective memories could conceptually continue to operate in his emancipatory politics. Or, perhaps more accurately, it seems that racial collective memories cannot continue to exist in his emancipatory politics. His articulation of Négritude is one such example of how a conception of authentic race consciousness and/or liberation ought to be denied for the purpose of universal emancipation, especially in a manner that is consistent with Belle's critique of Sartre. Even if a raceless society were possible (a contentious claim that Belle does address in her essay), the issue that still remains is the means or method through which it could become possible. For Belle and Fanon, a raceless society cannot evolve out of the erasure of race.

In addition to the role of collective memory, the framework of Badiou's political theory raises a few conceptual problems for the figure of the faithful subject for several reasons. First, his politics of indifference presupposes that the subject of the event—that is, the faithful subject—is a generic subject, which means that it is constituted independent of any particular identity (whether this be an individual or a group). Second, this articulation of the faithful subject forecloses the possibility of a gender or racial analysis (for instance) of that particular location of the subject faithful to the event. This faithful subject is constituted insofar as it seeks a universal political truth (such as justice and equality) nominated through the appearance of the inexistent in a world and the creation of a new world or state through which the inexistent can be apparent or counted. The subtraction of particularity from the faithful subject, however, also erases differences as relevant political categories, and thus such a form of subtraction fails to remain aware of meaningful differences. Similarly, it is important to note that this conception of the generic subject forecloses the possibility to pay attention to how the concept of the knowing subject is defined and oriented.

Recalling chapter 1, Badiou proposes that identitarian logic, whereby a "culture's constitutive elements are only fully comprehensible on the condition that one belongs to the subset in question," to be "genuinely *barbaric*" (2003, 12). If one does not need to remain aware of the most salient meaningful differences in the construction of the subject of the event, and thus of political emancipation, then what implications might arise?

It is important to note that Badiou states that the production of truth emerges by way of the event and through the work of the newly formed subject of the event. The implication is that knowledge pertaining to the new principles on which the revolution is predicated, or the new principles for political universal emancipation, cannot be known in advance of the political event. Instead, they emanate from it. This means that the ideas of the revolution are transcendent and not dependent upon the knowledge that was immanent to the logic or ordering of the world prior to the event. More specifically, this means that an event does not rely on prior knowledge. This is also the reason why a new language is required as that through which new principles or ideas can be upheld and maintained. In addition, in order for the truth to be universal, it must have "a meaning that is intelligible to all" (Badiou and Hallward 1998, 119). If the desire is to change the structure or logic of a given world such that it is founded on different (and emancipatory) principles, then the people who occupy it would need to understand the new principles in order to properly effectuate this change.

That said, if one were to employ a positive conception of identity (such as the positive conception of race described in chapter 3), then it remains unclear to me why this (positive) identity would need to be excluded in order to achieve universal emancipation. Furthermore, is not the knowledge that one might attain in virtue of being inexistent in a world valuable knowledge that would be beneficial to (universal) emancipation?

My articulation of Négritude and the Haitian Revolution in this project is helpful for understanding Badiou's conception of universality. Badiou states the following: "In each case we have to work to make a category pass from what I called its identitarian or syndical status, to a political status" (119). This description of the identitarian to the political is dialectical, whereby the one (identitarian status) must be subtracted in order to attain the other (political status) in a move toward universality. As previously noted, he allocates the Négritude movement to the identitarian status because it is a conception of liberation that fails to become universal and therefore emancipatory. The Haitian Revolution, according to Nesbitt, achieves this political status and thus is universal. Or similarly, in *Black* Badiou describes how the dissolution of the black–white binary was necessary for political universalism (2017, 100). Therein, Badiou emphasizes a relation between difference and universality whereby difference is a moment prior to universality, and a moment that ultimately needs to be surpassed (one step further) in order to achieve universal emancipation.

Consistent with my critique of Eurocentrism in chapter 3, one ought to be cautious of the kind of move that Badiou is proposing. Namely, one should ask whether there is already at play a kind of identity informing when something is constituted as a political event. Regarding Nancy Fraser and Todd Gitlin, Alcoff states, "I would suggest that the identity politics at play in this case is white identity, in which whiteness is associated with the privilege to name others, to choose one's own form of discursive banter with total autonomy, as well as with the vanguard narratives of Anglo-European cultures which portray the rest of the world as existing in various stages of 'backwardness'" (2016, n.p.). Badiou's juxtaposition of culture and politics seems in part to perform the distinction between the progressive (political) and the "barbaric" or backward (cultural and identitarian). For example, Nesbitt's articulation of the Haitian Revolution is progressive only because, in his view, it rejects identity politics and implements the ideals of the French Revolution (equality, for instance). Even though a political truth appears through the enactment of the subject of an event, and an event is always locatable within a particular site, it is only through the subtraction of identity that politics can take place. Badiou's theory of political emancipation lends itself to Western frameworks (e.g., the French Revolution) that impose upon a non-Western context (e.g., the Haitian Revolution). As a result his theory runs the risk of enacting "an extension of the privilege associated with whiteness to name and signify difference and to determine its place in a progressive narrative of united struggle" (Alcoff 2016, n.p.).

Once again, I ask: Why must politics be emancipatory? In *Badiou in Jamaica*, Wright analyses the Rasta movement through Badiou's theory of the event in an attempt to demonstrate that it *too* is political. Similarly, Michael Neocosmos and Grant Farred each respectively analyze the South African anti-apartheid movement in an attempt to demonstrate that it *too* is an example of a Badiouian political event (see Neocosmos 2018; Farred 2018). However, given the structure of Badiou's political theory, his conception of what counts as political becomes quite limited and, as a result, much labor and activism get lost.

There are many texts that speak to the role and the relevance of acts of resistance that did not follow from an evental sequence, and yet there is cause to consider them as political acts of resistance in the face of oppression. In "Reflections on the Black Woman's Role in the Community of Slaves" (1972), Angela Davis discusses various acts of resistance by Black women within the history of antislavery struggles, an area of analysis that continues to be underserved by academic writings. As noted by Davis, "Black women often poisoned the food and set fire to the houses of their masters. For those who were also employed as domestics these particular overt forms of resistance were especially available" (1972, 91). In her essay she provides numerous accounts of acts of resistance against white slave owners by Black female slaves. One might ask, should these acts be considered political?

Furthermore, why should we assume that identity is problematic for universal emancipation? (Alcoff 2016). In fact, there are various moments in history of resistance movements in which solidarity of identity was central to working toward emancipation. As noted by Alcoff, "The Communist Party USA of the 1930s demanded 'Self-determination for the Afro-American Nation' in its basic party platform, and supported black nationalist demands even unto the right of separation" (n.p.). Additionally, regarding the division between class and race, Alcoff states the following: "Picturing class formations as ideal types without race or gender disenables our ability to use the concept of class as an explanatory concept in social theory" (n.p.).

As such, perhaps Badiou's political theory ought not be the standard for what counts as political. It has been my intention to make evident that Badiou's political project is actually susceptible to the same problems that he seeks to upend. Whereby Badiou seeks to create a structure for thinking political revolution that transcends any particular political order, he has actually failed to relinquish the norms, structures, and harms of Eurocentrism. Furthermore, whereby Badiou sought to propose a political project that was universal, he has actually proposed a political project that reinforces structures of exclusion when applied globally to the extent that it is only by a proximity to whiteness or Europe that emancipation is possible.

In summation, as we go forward it is important to keep in mind the question with which this conclusion began. The aim of this section has been both to describe the ways in which politics ought to be more than what gets counted as emancipation and to demonstrate that the conception of politics offered by Badiou (as only that which is emancipatory) is insufficient. That said, in the following chapter, I aim to provide an alternative (and what I believe to be a superior) conception of political emancipation, one that is not premised on the politics of indifference offered by Badiou. Instead, I propose that Sylvia Wynter offers a conception of universal humanism that maintains the importance of identity for the purpose of universal emancipation.

5. Sylvia Wynter's Theory of Emancipation

Given the tensions outlined in the previous chapters regarding Alain Badiou's conception of emancipation and his politics of truth as indifferent to differences, one might ask: What responses might Badiou or other scholars interested in emancipatory politics and universalism provide? I propose that one helpful answer to this question is located in the work of Sylvia Wynter.

While the projects of Badiou and Wynter are distinct in ways that I develop throughout this chapter, there are a number of reasons why it is appropriate to bring Wynter and Badiou into conversation. First, like Badiou, Wynter describes how worlds are organized by a particular logic (or what she calls a worldview) that determines who appears (exists) in a world and who does not appear (inexists). Wynter's project is a response to a specific problem: the inexistence and oppression of particular groups of people due to the logics of a state. Or more specifically, she analyses particular logics of worlds by drawing correlations between colonialism and conceptions of the subject (or Man) that are operating in contemporary Western societies. "Unsettling the Coloniality of Being" (2003) is a demonstration of how "Man" is constructed through a binary that presupposes the existence of, and simultaneously the creation of, its negation (or what inexists in a state). In other words, we can think of the concept Man as constituted through a articulation of non-Man (see McKittrick 2015, chapter 4; Wynter 1995). As a result, what it means to be human is founded upon the presupposition of a group of persons who are *excluded* from the category human. For instance, below I develop Wynter's analysis of a particular kind of subjectivity (or Man)— namely, the "rational subject." The rational subject is important for her project because this conception of subjectivity is bound up with European expansionism and the colonization of Africa, Asia, and the Americas (Wynter 1995). The implication is, therefore, that "rationality" is in fact not universal, as it purports to be; rather, it is dependent upon an other that is effaced from humanity. Thus, like Badiou, Wynter's political theory and theory of emancipation offer a critique of systems of oppression and domination, and she does so by focusing on the description of the "subject" around which a worldview is organized. The first section of this chapter develops constructions of "subject–other" relations for Wynter in conversation with Badiou.

Second, like Badiou, Wynter's theory of emancipation seeks to change oppressive structures and turns to what is outside the dominant logic that orders a particular world. Recall how Badiou develops his conception of truth, as indifferent to the differences and identities that are formed within a particular logic of a world. For him, truth provides the conditions for rupturing the logic of a world insofar as it transcends that world. Wynter, on the other hand, does not turn to the same kind of universal truths that are indifferent to differences; instead, she develops a conception of liminality. For Wynter the "liminal" is a position through which conscious awareness of the logic of a particular world can be made evident. Contra Badiou, the operation of the liminal or marginal subject is not to *subtract* particularity and identities from truth, emphasizing the importance of universal truths. Rather, Wynter emphasizes the importance of identities *for* emancipation through her analysis of the Négritude movement. For her, Négritude is exemplary of emancipation because it operates outside the subject–other binary that determines who exists according to a particular logic. Wynter's analysis of Négritude is juxtaposed with Badiou's, for whom Négritude cannot be thought of as either political or emancipatory because it is based in particularity and, as such, fails to rise to the level of universality. Contra Badiou, for Wynter, Négritude is demonstrative of her formulation of emancipation and the political. The second section of this chapter outlines the importance of the liminal for Wynter's project juxtaposed with Badiou's conception of subtraction and his politics of indifference.

Third, Wynter expands her analysis of Négritude in "Beyond the Categories of the Master Conception: The Counterdoctrine of the Jamesian Poiesis" (1992) in order to demonstrate how it is possible to conceive of a politics of emancipation that is universal while also maintaining the importance of particularity for the purpose of political emancipation. In this essay, she provides what she calls a "pluri-conceptual" model for emancipation that emphasizes multiplicity over singularity. The third section of this chapter develops Wynter's "pluri-conceptual" model for political emancipation in conversation with Badiou's politics of indifference.

This chapter is thus broken down in the following way: (1) I draw a comparison between Wynter's construction of subject–other relations and Badiou's description of existence–inexistence, (2) I develop Wynter's conception of the liminal in order to distinguish it from Badiou's method of subtraction, and (3) I develop Wynter's pluri-conceptual model for politics and emancipation compared with Badiou's politics of indifference.

ON CONSTRUCTIONS OF SUBJECT–OTHER

The first section of this chapter addresses problematic, dominant conceptions of historical subjects and the production of knowledge as a kind of perpetuation of colonialism or, more specifically in this case, "coloniality." Coloniality is a term introduced by Aníbal Quijano in "Coloniality and Modernity/Rationality" (2007). Quijano proposes that coloniality is a correlate to, and an extension of, colonialism and modernity. In short, if one were to conclude that European colonialism no longer exists in a particular place, the effects of colonialism, through the dependency relation between colonialism and modernity, would continue to exist. For example, such continuations of coloniality/modernity exist in contemporary societies through racialized oppression and Eurocentric structures of knowledge. This continuation of colonialism and its support for European modernity is what Quijano names "coloniality." Coloniality refers to a framework of power created by European groups over "racially" and "ethnically" marginalized communities. Specifically, coloniality refers to the exploitation and domination of cultures and the imagination of marginalized groups (Quijano 2007, 168–69). In naming coloniality, and through his critical interrogation of it, Quijano proposes a decolonial project.

Similar to Quijano, Wynter offers a decolonial project that critiques coloniality; however, she uses the term "enchantment" in several essays to describe her approach to coloniality. She portrays enchantment as a state of existence that is undergirded with colonial histories and yet wholly unreflective of the various implications of coloniality. Enchantment is also meant to express a social condition and a collective state of mind (or social imaginary) that might accompany the lack of reflexivity within a given worldview. As a result, enchantment is a term she uses that has political and colonial implications, as well as psychological and cognitive ones. The manner in which she is able to interweave such seemingly disparate systems of thought is developed throughout this chapter. For the time being, we can think of enchantment as a kind of lack of reflexivity about (colonial) realities.

The aim of her decolonial project is a process of "disenchantment"—that is, to throw off the blinders of enchantment and engage in critical projects. Additionally, one must also guard against what she calls the "re-enchantment," whereby the social imagination falls back into an unreflexive and uncritical position supported by coloniality. What follows is a development of various historical moments that exemplify modes of enchantment.

The geopolitical context that Wynter is concerned with begins with Europe. Specifically, she is concerned with what led to European expansion in the "New World."[1] The manner in which I provide an account for this European expansionism (or more specifically, European colonialism) is via differing conceptions of dominant European subjects (i.e., of the human, or of Man). In other words, we can better understand how European colonialism was possible and conditioned through dominant conceptions of what was meant by "human" at various points in history. According to Wynter:

> Whether religious or secular, all such schemas/programs and their formulations of a "general order of existence" also function to inscribe the specific "descriptive statement" of the human that is enacting of the ontogeny/sociogeny, nature-culture mode of being human, for whom the specific ensemble of motivated behaviors will be adaptively advantageous. (2003, 280)

In other words, the conception of what it means to be human that dominates any particular world reflects, or more specifically, *is* the inscription of a kind of ordering that dominates that world. Three distinct conceptions of the subject are discussed below: (1) the Judeo-Christian conception of the subject (i.e., the Human, or the True Christian Self), (2) the rational self as a political subject of the state (i.e., Man 1), and (3) the economic and biological man (i.e., Man 2).[2] It is important to understand these conceptions of subjecthood because we can draw various correlations between them and because the economic and biological man (Man 2) continues to influence present-day Western social and political relations. In addition, in each case we can locate the correlation between the descriptive statement of what it means to be human and the general order of existence that it perpetuates. This conception of the human thus serves as an analogue to Badiou's conception of the transcendental operator that will be discussed in further detail below.

The Judeo-Christian Subject: The "Human," or the "True Christian Self"

The Christian conception of the subject is theocentric and loosely corresponds to conceptions of the subject in Medieval Latin Christian Europe (Wynter 2003, 268).[3] Generally speaking, the Christian subject presupposes a notion of the existence of the True Christian Self (281). The True Christian Self can be understood as being "gifted with spirit" and thus blessed by the grace of God. At the same time, not all persons were attributed this position of the True Christian Self. Instead, outside of this order of existence, there is a space of Otherness for those who have succumbed to the "ills of fallen flesh," those who exist outside of the grace of God, and those who are sinful by nature. Specifically, this refers to heretics and "enemies of Christ," or pagan-idolaters (266). Of course, within this general order of existence, there is a plan of salvation to cure the ills of those who were enslaved by original sin, insofar as original sin threatened all the subjects of the order (278–79). Interestingly, in this sense, there were degrees of spiritual perfection and imperfection, resulting in a hierarchy of humanness (287).

The general order of existence in Medieval Christian Europe is mapped onto the dichotomy between "Spirit" and "Flesh."[4] In addition to its production of a dominant conception of the subject operating at the time, the Christian order of existence was also projected onto the cosmos.

As Wynter states, "This Spirit/Flesh code had then been projected onto the physical cosmos, precisely onto the represented nonhomogeneity of substance between the spiritual perfection of the heavens ... as opposed to the sublunary realm of earth, which ... had to be at the center of the universe as its dregs" (278). In other words, there was a difference in substance between the heavens (spirit) and the earth (flesh). In addition, the earth was the center of the universe insofar as it lacked the capacity for motion (motion being a divine attribute). This general order of existence has implications for the subject that it constituted (or that was attempted to be created, in its most perfect form) and also has structured the conception of the universe. This order was all-encompassing.

In addition, the mapping of the geography of the earth can also be understood in terms of the existing order of Spirit/Flesh. During this period, the Christian conception of the world was divided up between realms that were habitable and were in the grace of God (centering on Jerusalem) and regions that were considered uninhabitable because they existed outside the grace of God. Thus, "Before the fifteenth-century voyages of the Portuguese and Columbus ... the Torrid Zone beyond the bulge of Cape Bojador on the upper coast of Africa ... had to be known as too hot for habitation, while the Western hemisphere had had to be known as being devoid of land" (279). The Torrid Zone comprised those areas of the world that existed outside of the grace of God and that were therefore uninhabitable.

The theocentric conception of what it meant to be human was produced through the master code of Spirit/Flesh and further reified through the nonhomogeneity of the heavens and the earth as well as the geography of the earth. However, this descriptive statement of what it meant to be human was unsustainable for a few reasons. First, the fifteenth-century voyages "proved that the earth was homogenously habitable by humans, seeing that the Torrid Zone was indeed inhabited, [and that] ... the land of the Western hemisphere ... turned out to be above water" (280). In other words, the geography of the theocentric framework described above was proven to be false. Together with Copernicus's new astronomy, that proposed that the earth moves around the sun, the nonhomogeneity of the heavens and the earth, as well as the previous conception of how the earth was mapped, could no longer be sustained.

As a result, "an epochal rupture" was set in motion (281). The theocentric conception of the subject as the True Christian Self was no longer feasible because the master code upon which it was structured (Spirit/Flesh as evident through the geography of the earth and manifest in the study of the cosmos) had been swept away in favor of a new science and new mapping of the earth.

It is important to note here that there continues to be some similarities between Badiou and Wynter, given the description of Wynter's project provided above. First, for both figures a state or world is organized according to particular principles—that is, what Badiou calls the "transcendental index" and what Wynter has described as the theocentric framework ordered by the master code of Spirit/Flesh. Second, both figures regard the Copernican Revolution as an event, albeit in different ways. Recall from chapter 1 that for Badiou an event is a rupture with the current transcendental order through which a new transcendental order takes place. Within this framework, the Copernican Revolution attests to an evental rupture that radically changed the manner in which the universe was ordered. Again, this has serious implications for the sciences, and as a result a new (physical) science emerges. In addition, for both Badiou and Wynter, it follows that the principles that order any particular world are contingent.

There are also notable differences between Wynter and Badiou at this juncture. While for Wynter the Copernican Revolution, and the discovery of inhabited land in the Torrid Zone, result in an epochal rupture and the creation of a new set of ordering principles, the epochal rupture is not a totalizing break between the two. While these two ordering principles are different in kind, and the former did not cause the latter, there remains some continuity between them. Recalling the discussion of Badiou's conception of an event in chapter 1, we know that for him there can be no continuity between the transcendental order prior to the event and the transcendental order that follows from the event. For Badiou a total break is imperative in order to constitute a new political structure. In other words, in order to avoid an adaptation or adjustment of a previous transcendental order, a total break is required. For Wynter, as I demonstrate below, elements of the Spirit/Flesh master code will reappear in different worldviews, despite the logic of the worldview (including sciences, geography, and subject-formation) being distinct. Finally, for Wynter a new subject emanates from the rupture of the dominant ordering principles of Spirit/Flesh; it is the rational political subject of the state.

The Rational Political Subject of the State: Man 1

The rational political subject of the state roughly corresponds historically to the Renaissance period. The emanation of the rational political subject of the state from the Christian conception of the true self can be located in part by drawing out the differences between a religious concept of man/ humanity that preceded the Copernican Revolution and a rational concept of man/humanity that followed. The narrative Wynter develops in "Unsettling the Coloniality of Being" draws upon the fluctuating influence of science and religion in knowledge production. In summation, she states:

> It was therefore to be on the basis of this new conception, and of its related civic-humanist reformulation, that Man was to be invented in its first forms as the rational political subject of the state, as one who displayed his reason by primarily adhering to the laws of the state—rather than, as before, in seeking to redeem himself from the enslavement to Original Sin by primarily adhering to the prohibitions of the Church. (277)

Put simply, following the Copernican Revolution, we find in the Enlightenment era a concept of man/humanity that presupposes reason—via the new role of science—as a founding idea for the new universal "man." Within this new framework, God became knowable to human beings insofar as human beings were conceived as being created in God's image, contra the theocentric conception of the human for whom knowledge of God was foreclosed (278). Similarly, there was a shift from understanding the cosmos via supernatural causation to understanding the universe through natural causation, a shift that was required for the rise of the natural sciences (305).

Regarding the formation of the subject in particular, with the epochal shift described above, Wynter is pointing to the "systemic representational shift being made out of the order of discourse that had been elaborated on the basis of the Judeo-Christian Spirit/Flesh organizing principle . . . to the new rational/irrational organizing principle and master code" (300). In other words, what it meant to be human in this era became equated with the capacity for rationality, which additionally came to adhere in the degree to which one could obey the laws of the state. As a result, the state itself is what determined what it meant to be rational.

According to Wynter, Man 1 was still dependent upon a certain conception of God; however, the manner in which God was conceived is strikingly different from the previous era. She writes:

> It was this new premise that God had created the world/universe for mankind's sake, as a premise that ensured that He would have had to make it according to rational, nonarbitrary rules that could be knowable by the beings that He had made it for, that would lead to Copernicus's astronomy, . . . that since the universe had been made for our sake by the best and wisest of craftsmen, it had to be knowable. (278)

Within this framework, God became more beneficent and mankind was now considered capable of understanding God's plan.

The historical narrative used by Wynter demonstrates that dominant conceptions of man or of human are not accidentally constituted. Rather, there is some impetus or force that is responsible for creating such dominant conceptions. As previously noted, prior to the Copernican Revolution, the dominant concept of humanity was founded upon natural law, and was implemented by the laws of Christianity. Part of her project is to ascertain what led to the shift from natural law to reason. There are a few ways in which we can understand the shift from the Christian to the Enlightenment concept of man/human that the Copernican Revolution marks. For instance, she notes it could be attributed to the rise of science as changing the structure of knowledge production at that time. Along the same lines, it could be attributed to a notion of equality that was becoming more prevalent. In other words, in lieu of one's position being dependent upon natural law, the Enlightenment era assumed the rational subject to be capable of presupposing a kind of universality that had previously been foreclosed—that is, that all persons could be rational but not all persons could be touched by the grace of God. However, she stipulates that these are, in fact, *not* the overarching reasons for the shift to the Enlightenment concept of humanism. First, she states, "it was a constitutive part of the new order of *adaptive truth-for* that had begun to be put in place with the rise to hegemony of the modern state, based on the new descriptive statement of the human, Man, as primarily a political subject—of, therefore, the West's own self-conception" (300). In other words, the new world order was founded upon, and indeed perpetuated, a specific conception of man that was of its own making. But it is the manner in which this self-conception was constructed that renders it a worthy object of critique regarding the racial hierarchies and conceptions of universality that issued from it. Wynter emphasizes the role of the subject over the role of sciences as shaping the order of the modern state. Whether or not it is an accurate portrayal of the shift from the Christian worldview to the Enlightenment worldview, her primary concern is the experience of what it means to be human in each worldview in order to make evident those who are excluded from what it means to be human. In addition, and by implication, her intention is to demonstrate how the logics of particular worlds are built on the creation of those who are excluded from the experience of being human. Furthermore, to assume that the shift to the Enlightenment was based upon a notion of equality would be to overlook the context in which this transition takes place. Specifically, the context through which she develops this analysis of the shift from the Christian conception of the human to Man 1 is European expansionism and colonialism. She reminds us that "it is important to realize that this reinvention of the Western self was determined by a concrete relation" (Wynter 1976, 84). This new order was also made possible through the reinvention of the dominant conception of the subject as rational.

Before we move to the conception of the human that Wynter claims continues to exist in the contemporary Western world (Man 2), it is important to note the similarities between the two conceptions of the subject just discussed—that is, the theocentric True Christian Self (the Human) and the rational conception of the political subject (Man 1). On this topic, she states:

> In the wake of the West's reinvention of its True Christian Self in the transumed terms of the Rational Self of Man, however, it was to be the peoples of the militarily expropriated New World territories (i.e., Indians), as well as the enslaved peoples of Black Africa (i.e., Negroes), that were made to reoccupy the matrix slot of Otherness—to be made into the physical referent of the idea of the irrational/subrational Human Other. (Wynter 2003, 266)

The construction of the dominant conception of the mode of being human is dependent upon the simultaneous construction of its own negation. We see this in what it means to be a True Christian Self, a position that maintains a fear of the enemies of Christ and the explicit desire to save those enemies of Christ for the purpose of preserving a specific world order. Similarly, the construction of the rational subject can be understood as being for the purpose of delineating a group who is considered irrational or subrational. The categories of irrational and subrational human other, for example, are not unintended consequences of the idea of the rational subject; rather, they are intentionally created alongside and for the purpose of the creation of the dominant subject category. In addition, while the rational subject might be categorized as an idea, the subrational and irrational positions are inherently physically and materially experienced (for example, the military expropriation and genocide of Indigenous populations and the enslavement of people from Black Africa). All this is to say that "Cultural racism is therefore organic to—and not anomalous to—Western capitalism, and *ipso facto* to Western civilization" (Wynter 1976, 86). As a result, it is important to understand the dominant conception of the subject and the role it plays in perpetuating the logics of worlds.

For example, the Valladolid controversy of 1550–51 was the first European debate about the rights of colonized people. Of course it should be noted here that the rights of the colonized people need to be thought in relation to arguments for the justification or legitimation of the rights of European settlers over the New World and the peoples who inhabited these new worlds. The two figures who were engaged in this debate were Bartolomé de las Casas and Juan Ginés de Sepúlveda. Las Casas was a sixteenth-century Dominican friar (and one of the first European settlers in America),[5] while Juan Ginés de Sepúlveda was a sixteenth-century philosopher and theologian. The Valladolid controversy is of particular importance for the purpose of this project because it makes evident the two distinct conceptions of the subject just described—that is, the Human and Man 1.

Generally speaking, Las Casas's position in the Valladolid debate can be thought of as operating within the theocentric model of the subject—that is, within the Spirit/Flesh master code of the Judeo-Christian conception of what it means to be human. As noted by Wynter, for Las Casas,

the indigenous peoples of the New World could not be classified as Enemies-of-Christ, since Christ's apostles had never reached the New

> World, never preached the Word of the Gospel to them. Which means that because they could not have ever refused the Word they could not ... be classified as Christ-Refusers, their lands justly taken, and they themselves enslaved and/or enserfed with a "just title." (Wynter 2003, 293)

The Indigenous peoples of the New World (who obviously were not Christian prior to European settlers' arrival in the New World) could not be thought of as enemies of Christ because they had never heard the word of God and therefore could not have denied it. As a result, within this world order there was no justification through which Indigenous peoples could be disenfranchised of their rights and their lands. At the same time, however, "African slaves, whom he then believed to have been acquired with a just title, should be brought in limited numbers as a labor force to replace the Indians" (293). According to Las Casas, the colonization of Africa was justified because the peoples of Africa were enemies of Christ—enemies because, he believed, they had heard the word of God and denied it. As a result, he contended that the African continent belonged to no one prior to European colonization (terra nullius), and thus European conquest of the continent was justified. This was, then, the start of the trans-Atlantic slave trade (293–94). It should be noted that once Las Casas learned about the unjust methods used by the Portuguese to obtain African slaves, he regretted his decision (Las Casas 1971).[6]

As is made evident in the Valladolid controversy, Las Casas's position was neither the only position regarding the Indigenous populations in the New World nor the dominant one. As Wynter states, "Las Casas had thought and acted in the terms of his Christian evangelizing imperative. The Spanish state's primary imperative, however, was that of its territorial expansion, of realizing its imperial goals of sovereignty over the new lands" (2003, 294). Las Casas's position reflects the theocentric master code described above. For him, the aim was to provide the conditions through which the True Christian Self could be achieved by all persons, including Indigenous populations of the New World. Presumably, the kind of European expansionism that he was concerned with was in reference to this theocentric model and genre of human being. However, with the epochal rupture on the geographical and cosmological level, and the corresponding effects in the sciences, a new set of goals was constructed. And with this new set of goals came about the new rational conception of the subject. What Wynter draws our attention to, in conversation with various theorists such as Aníbal Quijano and Walter Mignolo, is the motivation for this new conception of the subject for the purpose of European expansionism. This correlation is most evident in Sepúlveda's justification for the colonization of Indigenous populations of the New World.

In *Aristotle and the American Indians*, Lewis Hanke outlines the four reasons Sepúlveda offers as justification for war against Indigenous peoples:

> "For the gravity of the sins which the Indians had committed, especially their idolatries and their sins against nature.
>
> On account of the rudeness of their natures, which obliged them to serve persons having a more refined nature, such as the Spaniards.
>
> In order to spread the faith, which would be more easily accomplished by the prior subjugation of the native.
>
> To protect the weak among the natives themselves." (1959, 41)

As noted by Hanke, the second point noted above laid the foundation for the argument that "some men are born to be natural slaves" (44), an argument that stems from his reliance on Aristotle, as well as the presumptive superiority of Spaniards (45). Despite the use of sin and idolatry in the four points listed above, there is something that is fundamentally distinct about Sepúlveda's discussion of Indigenous peoples, located squarely in his invocation of natural slaves. For Las Casas, conversion was possible for all persons, and therefore (presumably) there were no natural distinctions between groups of peoples. For instance, according to Hanke, Las Casas "concludes, from a vast array of evidence, that the Indians are no whit less rational than the Egyptians, Romans, or Greeks, and are not much inferior to Spaniards. Indeed, in some respects, he declares them even superior to Spaniards" (55).[7] But, for Sepúlveda, to be born a "natural slave" meant that there was no changing one's social and political location. Put most simply, for Sepúlveda, Indigenous populations, as well as African populations, could justifiably be enslaved based on a new conception of order: rationality.

For Sepúlveda, Indigenous populations were considered irrational, and the mass of enslaved peoples of Africa were considered subrational. The explicit culmination of this point for Sepúlveda in particular (and in the context of the Valladolid controversy) was that Indigenous and African populations were *natural* slaves and therefore their enslavement was justified. As a result, "it was here that the modern phenomenon of race, as a new, extrahumanly determined classificatory principle and mechanism of domination, was first invented" (Wynter 2003, 296). Rationality, or the degree to which one is in the mode of being human, becomes constructed through phenotypical and religio-cultural differences.

The existence of a self–other distinction in Wynter's project— whereby the dominant conception of what it means to be human (i.e., the True Christian Self or Man 1) simultaneously creates its own negation (i.e., the fallen or the irrational)—is similarly part of Badiou's critique. As noted in chapter 1, Badiou aims to develop a theory of politics that is *not* based upon exclusion and thus his view seeks to address this dichotomy of the self–other. Wynter also conceives of this dichotomy as appearing problematically in European colonial history, as noted above. However, as previously discussed, the manner in which Badiou attempts to dismantle this exclusionary construction of the state (a requirement for his theory of emancipation) is by way of his politics of indifference. As I move forward with this project, my attention is focused on the manner in which Badiou and Wynter each respectively attend to the inexistent or the position of negation, as well as the role they each respectively assign to this position. Briefly, Badiou and Wynter seek the emancipation of the inexistent, to use Badiou's language. However, Badiou's theory of emancipation requires an indifference to differences (such as race) in order to achieve universal emancipation, whereas Wynter's theory of emancipation works through differences (such as race) in order to achieve universal emancipation.

The Economic and Biological Man: Man 2

The third example of the self–other master code is the economic and biological man, or Man 2. The economic and biological genre of being human that continues to pervade Western social and political contexts begins roughly in the nineteenth-century by way of liberal humanist intellectuals (314). As we will see below, while Man 2 is both continuous and discontinuous with Man 1 and the theocentric conception of being human, the principles that Man 2 presupposes are quite distinct (318). Man 2 is a secular conception of what it means to be human. The distancing of Man 2 from a religio-centered construction is due to its focus on biocentric and economic modes of being human.

Generally speaking, this conception of the human is dependent upon Charles Darwin's theory of evolution. In particular, two premises of Darwin's theory are particularly important for Wynter's construction of Man 2: (1) the human exists "in a line of pure continuity with all other organic forms of life" (314), and (2) natural selection impacts the fitness of species, resulting in certain traits being passed down to future generations through reproduction. The implications of these two premises are developed below. Alongside the biocentric conception of the human is the economic conception of the human—that is, *"homo economicus."* Like the theocentric and rational conceptions of what it means to be human, the biocentric and economic co-constitution of the genre of being human is defined through its negation.

What then is the negation upon which Man 2 is dependent? The new category of human Otherness is "now comprised of the jobless, the homeless, the Poor, the systemically made jobless and criminalized—of the 'underdeveloped'—all as the category of the economically *damnés,* rather than, as before, of the politically condemned" (321).[8] Man 2 is, on the one hand, constructed on the basis of what it means to be an economically productive member of society. The ills of the society, as a result, concern the population who are perceived as not contributing economically. For example:

> Enslavement here is no longer tied to Original Sin, or to one's irrational nature. . . . Rather, enslavement is now to the threat of Malthusian over-population, to its concomitant "ill" of Natural Scarcity whose imperative "plan of salvation" would now be postulated in economic terms as that of keeping this at bay—of material, in the place of the matrix spiritual, Redemption. (320)

At the same time, however, Wynter claims that the economic genre of being human is mapped onto a Darwinian chain of being that is manifest in two manners (309). First, "This principle, that of bio-evolutionary Natural Selection, was now to function at the level of the new bourgeois social order as a de facto new Argument-from-Design—one in which while one's selected or dysselected status could not be known in advance, it would come to be verified by one's (or one's group's) success or failure in life" (310).

An economic hierarchy is mapped onto a biocentric hierarchy. Or, in other words, economic success (and thus economic failure) is mapped onto a conception of who is most fit (or least fit) in society. As a result, the economically damned in society, or the dependents of society, can thus justifiably (according to this system) be dysselected from society and found undeserving of social aid. Second, drawing from a Darwinian conception of the continuity between all living creatures, the economic and biocentric conception of man also operates upon a continuity of those who are most fit and those who are least fit.

An important implication of this new space of Otherness is confirmed by Frederick Douglass's "The Color Line" (1881), echoed in W. E. B. Du Bois's *The Souls of Black Folk* (1903). Wynter describes the color line as "a line drawn between the lighter and the darker peoples of the earth, and enforced at the level of social reality by the [law, likely] instituted relation[s] of socioeconomic dominance/subordination between them" (310). As a result, the color line comes to demarcate what in previous systems were the Spirit/Flesh dichotomy and the rational/irrational dichotomy, culminating in the demarcation of those who are deserving of reward (and the most fit) from those who are not (322). More specifically, those who were economically disenfranchised because of their race, through racial segregation and red lining, for instance, are deemed less fit within a given social reality—that is, economic failure is a failure of one's ability to adapt and survive in a social context.

For Du Bois, the color line refers to the racial segregation of African American peoples in the United States, segregation that occurred through legal structures as well as discursive means. In addition, his discussion of the color line also establishes what he calls "double consciousness." In *The Souls of Black Folk*, he states the following:

> It is a peculiar sensation, this double consciousness, this sense of always looking at one's self through the eyes of others, of measuring one's soul by the tape of a world that looks on in amused contempt and pity. One ever feels his two-ness—an American, a Negro; two souls, two thoughts, two unreconciled strivings; two warring ideals in one dark body, whose dogged strength alone keeps it from being torn asunder. (1994, 2)

In other words, double consciousness is when a marginalized person recognizes not only their own self-perception but also how they are perceived as a member of a marginalized group by a dominant group. A further implication here is that someone who has the sensation or experience of double consciousness has a particular kind of epistemic position in the world, whereby they have access to different kinds of knowledge based on their position in relation to the color line. As a result, for Du Bois and for Wynter, marginalized people have access to knowledge that is not immediately accessible (if accessible at all) to those who occupy dominant positions within the same social reality.

There are various examples that we can draw from in order to understand the ramifications of this genre of being human. We could look to the recent (and historical) anti-economic migrant sentiment in Europe and North America. For instance, in the UK the anti-immigrant sentiment that was central to the 2016 Brexit vote was based on the idea of job scarcity for UK citizens, a distinction that is likely based upon the color line just described, albeit an extension of the color line based upon a racialized other that is "not British." One might also consider "the criminalized majority Black and dark-skinned Latino inner-city males now made to man the rapidly expanding prison-industrial complex" (Wynter 2003, 261) or the criminalization of Indigenous communities in Canada and the United States (Ross 2016; Teran 2016; Lumsden 2016). In all these cases, racial profiling presupposes the evolutionary natural selection of those who will "make it" and those who will not.

At this point it should be apparent that there are some similarities between the conceptions of a worldview and the notion of worlds developed by Wynter and Badiou respectively. For instance, for Badiou, "world" implies a series of relations, a network through which objects appear (Badiou 2009, 99). Additionally, "a world articulates the cohesion of multiples around a structured operator (the transcendental)" (102). In other words, worlds provide the conditions through which objects appear, but are ordered by what he calls the transcendental index. Furthermore, the ordering of any world is wholly contingent. For Wynter, a worldview refers to a dominant narrative that organizes worlds according to a particular conception of what it means to be human (i.e., the True Christian Self, the rational political Man 1, or the economic and biological Man 2). Similarly, for Wynter the organization of worlds according to some master code is contingent and thus could be organized differently. Generally speaking, both Wynter and Badiou offer a critique of these dominant and oppressive conceptions of worlds and also seek solutions to oppressive world orders. The continuities between Badiou's and Wynter's political theories of emancipation provide the conditions for my analysis of why and how Wynter's political theory offers a substantial alternative to Badiou's project without radically changing the kinds of goals he has for his project. Alternatively, the continuities between their projects also allow me to demonstrate that there is an alternative solution to Badiou's project in Wynter's work. To these ends it is the distinctions between their projects with which I am concerned. Whereas Badiou focuses on a politics of indifference based upon a theory of political truths, Wynter focuses on liminal positions and a theory that emphasizes differences in addition to universal emancipation through her pluri-conceptual framework. These points of comparison are the focus of the next two sections.

ON LIMINALITY AND NÉGRITUDE

In "The Ceremony Must Be Found," Wynter defines liminality as follows:

> [It is the] experience [of] a structural contradiction between [one's] lived experience and the grammar of representation which generate the mode of reality by prescribing the parameters of collective behaviors that dynamically bring that "reality" into being. The liminal frame of reference therefore, unlike the normative, can provide . . . the outer view from which perspective the grammars of regularities of boundary and structure-maintaining discourses are perceivable. (1984, 39)

Unlike the normative/dominant position, the liminal position is thus situated such that it marks the lives of those whose experiences are in contradiction with that dominant position. Recall, for instance, the discussion above of Du Bois's conception of double consciousness, whereby an African American experiences the contradiction between being American and being Black. Such a contradiction is experienced because their lived reality is imposed upon by dominant positions that exclude them. At the same time, however, because of the experiences of the liminal position, marginalized persons are well situated to see the contradictions inherent to the normative view. There are a number of ways in which one can be marginalized and, as a result, a plethora of liminal positions that one could occupy. For this reason, I will not attempt to name them here. However, a significant amount of work on the experiences of marginalization and the kind of knowledge that is produced out of this marginalization has been done. Most notably, Du Bois wrote on the topic most explicitly in *The Souls of Black Folks*. One could also consider Simone de Beauvoir's *The Second Sex* (1949) as providing an account of the epistemic situatedness of (white) women in a male-centered society.[9] Similarly, Monique Wittig's *The Straight Mind* (1980) offers a conception of "the lesbian" as epistemically situated differently within a heterosexual social reality. It is important to note, however, that one's identity as Black, gendered, and gay, for instance, does not mean that one inherently has conscious awareness of the epistemic situatedness of their liminal positions. Rather, as stated above, they are *better situated* to gain this epistemic position.

Similarly, in "Beyond Liberal and Marxist Feminisms," Wynter draws on the work of Asmaran Legesse, stating that "it is the liminal category who 'generates conscious change by exposing all the injustices inherent in structure'" (Wynter 1982, 36). Thus, for Wynter, liminality can provide a view from which to understand a dominant/normative structure and ordering of the dominant referent through which the subordinate being and the dominant referent are both constituted. In this sense it is very important to provide space for a discursive intervention from the liminal frame of reference.

According the Wynter, "The category minority is always already a subordinated category within the organizing principle of difference/deference of our present 'symbolic contract' and of the mode of particular 'nature' to which its specific secular ontology 'tied us down' metaphysically" (1987, 233). However, "in order to call in question this ontologically subordinated function, 'minority discourse' can *not* be merely another voice in the present ongoing conversation or order of discourse" (233). In other words, the significance of the liminal over the dominant referent is that the liminal provides a point of view that can shift/disenchant the dominant referent; it is to disenchant, to make unstable, the structure that seeks its own stability. The liminal can provide the conditions for a critique of the dominant worldview, according to Wynter. However, the manner in which the liminal becomes manifest for Wynter is such that it is firmly entrenched in particularity and difference.

In many of Wynter's essays, she notes the prevalence of a conception of Being formed on the basis of a lack-of-Being (Wynter 1976, 1987, 2003)—for example, the rational–irrational or subrational binary and the True Christian Self–pagan idolater binary, both of which emulate the Being–lack-of-Being binary. Noting the problems of this binary above, the central aim of this section is to determine how it is possible to move beyond this binary logic. Or, alternatively, I am going to consider the ways it is possible to conceive of the emancipation of those who are allocated to the position of lack-of-Being. For Wynter the creation of the liminal, or "minority," category alone is insufficient to transcend the binary, as noted in the previous paragraph. As such, she provides an alternative to a conception of lack-of-Being that is juxtaposed to Being, or a "we" juxtaposed against a "they." According to Wynter, the juxtaposition of these two locations is one of codependence, or, more specifically, each position is constructed for the benefit of the dominant location. An attempt to rethink and unravel this system requires a different positionality, one that exists outside the binary logic. This third position that exists outside of the binary is akin to Du Bois's description of double consciousness. Namely, it is a marginalized position, but one that is also epistemically situated and conscious of the manner in which the binary operates. It is thus important to note a difference between those who are relegated to the position of other within the self–other binary and those who are marginalized in society and have gained double consciousness. While the former can be construed as a product of the binary, the latter should be thought of as existing outside the determination of the binary, or at least not wholly determined by it. For Wynter, Négritude is an example of a position that exists outside an oppressive binary logic and is helpful in shedding light on the importance of the liminal position and its role for a theory of emancipation.

In "Ethno or Socio Poetics," Wynter makes reference to Césaire's famous poem "Notebook of a Return to the Native Land." She states the following:

> [This poem] comes from the fact that in creating the concept of Negritude, he was contesting an implicit Western assumption of Blanchitude (the term is Jacques Leenhardt's) that created characteristics of its own negation in the Negro; so that Negritude took as much issue with this

implicit concept of the negro as it did with the assumptions of blanchitude. (1976, 92)

One of the central features of the Négritude movement for Wynter is evident in the delineation between blanchitude/Negro and Négritude. Similar to previous discussions of the problem of enchantment, the correlation between blanchitude and "Negro" is one of negation. In this example, blanchitude presupposes the position of the dominant or normative position (or Being) and Negro is the negation of this position (or lack-of-Being). This is akin to Badiou's conception of (negative) identity discussed in chapter 3. However, what distinguishes Wynter from Badiou is evident in her articulation of the different roles of Negro and Négritude. As previously noted, the category of Negro is produced for the purpose of the creation of the dominant position—blanchitude in this instance. Negro is dependent upon blanchitude. Recalling chapter 3 and my discussion of negative identity, Negro can be thought of as constituted through the white gaze. Négritude, however, is not constituted through the white gaze, nor was it created for the purpose of maintaining the dominant position. Rather, as noted above, for Wynter, it serves to demarcate a position that is critical of both blanchitude (Being) and Negro (lack-of-Being). In this sense it would be problematic for Wynter to equate Negro and Négritude because doing so would erase the source from which Négritude gains its meaning, and it would erase the existence of those who named it. Given that Négritude offers a critique of both the conception of Negro and blanchitude from a marginalized position, Négritude exists outside of the self–other binary. Thus she maintains a conception of identity that is not merely negative, but alongside Belle, she affirms that such conceptions can also be construed as positive.

Wynter provides us with a second example that utilizes her analysis of the Négritude movement in an alternative way. She states:

> The black experience in the New World . . . constituted an existence which daily criticized the abstract consciousness of humanism; that the popular oral culture which the black created in response to an initial negation of this humanness, constitutes as culture, the heresy of humanism; and that is why black popular culture—spirituals, blues, jazz, Reggae, Afro-Cuban music—and its manifold variants have constituted an

underground cultural experience as subversive of the status quo Western culture as was Christianity in the catacombs of the Roman Empire. For it was in this culture that the blacks reinvented themselves as a WE that needed no OTHER to constitute their Being; that laid down the cultural parameters of a concretely universal *ethnos*. (92)

Similar to her description of Négritude above, she provides an example of identity that is not premised upon a binary system. For instance, when she states that the reinvention of Blackness is a *we* that needed *no other,* she is proposing that it is possible to create an identity that is produced outside a dominant binary and not merely a negation. Importantly, she also describes this movement as both cultural and universal, the implications of which are developed below. The concept of Négritude simultaneously creates a new concept (sign) and exists outside the negative dialectic of blanchitude and Negro.

In a similar manner, Wynter describes Black aesthetics more generally as "the transformation of consciousness from being 'Negro,' in the negative sense defined by the dominant society, to being self-defined positively as 'Black,' with the suffering of a Negro-Black conversion experience" (1998, 273). A reordering of Western aesthetics, like Western politics (as one that "saw the exclusion and denigration of the black historical experience and the 'white orientedness' of the universality as a whole" [273]), requires that Black people and Black artists "define the 'world in their own terms'" (274). The importance of the Négritude movement is in part because it provides the conditions to get outside the normative binary (of positive and negative identities, in this case blanchitude and Negro). At the same time, the liminal position is important because it provides the conditions for the creation of new objects of knowledge as evidenced by the Négritude movement. Wynter's articulation of the role of the creation of new objects of knowledge from the liminal position is evidenced in her conception of epistemic disobedience, the focus of the next section.

Before I delve into epistemic disobedience, it is important to note the differences between Wynter's and Badiou's respective conceptions of Négritude. Recall that, for Badiou, Négritude is neither political nor progressive. Instead, Négritude is categorized as cultural; it is cultural because it is mired in identity—that is, identity that is also subsequently determined by the oppressive structure that it seeks to upend. Contra Badiou, for Wynter, Négritude is not determined by the oppressive structure that it seeks to upend. Rather, Négritude exists outside of the self–other binary that orders a particular world. Thus, contra Badiou, Wynter claims that Négritude produces itself outside the self–other, or subject–other, binary and therefore can be progressive and political.

EPISTEMIC DISOBEDIENCE

What, then, is the correlation between the liminal position, Négritude, and the ability to constitute new worlds? The answer is located in a conception of epistemic disobedience. There are various ways in which Wynter performs epistemic disobedience. In "Unsettling the Coloniality of Being" and "1492: A New World View" (1995), two of her most foundational essays, she investigates specific representations of what it means to be human and the structure that gives rise to, or produces, such representations. For instance, the production of Man 1 (the rational subject) discussed above already presupposes what counts as knowledge. In a circular fashion, Man 1 presupposes that knowledge can only be produced by rational subjects, yet rationality is attributed only to select groups of persons. Accordingly, groups of people who are not considered rational are thereby excluded from humanity, and are thus considered incapable of producing knowledge. As a result, knowledge has a very specific function that Wynter claims is bound up with colonial conquest (see Wynter 2003, 1995). Walter Mignolo describes epistemic disobedience in the following manner:

> Under the rules of the epistemic canon, and according to its racial mandates, if you have been classified in/as difference, then you are required to submit and to assimilate to the canon or remain outside. Wynter does not follow either of these pathways. She instead engages what I call the decolonial option, a practice of rethinking and unraveling dominant worldviews that have been opened up by Indigenous and black and Caribbean thinkers since the sixteenth century in América (with accent) and the Caribbean. The decolonial option does not simply protest the contents of imperial Coloniality; it demands a delinking of oneself from the knowledge systems we take for granted (and can profit from) and practicing epistemic disobedience. (2015, 106–7)

The practices of epistemic disobedience that Mignolo attributes to Wynter are not reactionary positions *against* dominant systems of knowledge. Rather, epistemic disobedience is an interrogation of the manner in which knowledge production transpires. The act of "delinking" that he makes reference to as an important aspect of epistemic disobedience denotes a specific location from which practices of epistemic disobedience can be enacted. From such a location, an interrogation of dominant knowledge systems can take place *outside* the dominant system of knowledge itself. For her, however, this "outside" does not reify the binary logic discussed above, whereby the dominant system of knowledge exemplifies the "One" and practices of epistemic disobedience represent what is "Other." Rather, dominant systems of knowledge are founded on a binary logic, whereby what is (e.g., the rational subject, the counted) always already presupposes what is not (i.e., its negation). The act of delinking and practices of epistemic disobedience necessitate a location outside this binary logic, a kind of third position. It is this position of radical differentiation from the structure of knowledge production itself that makes possible a "rethinking and unraveling of [a] dominant worldview."

As noted by Mignolo above, "Indigenous and black and Caribbean thinkers since the sixteenth century" have been engaging in decolonial practices of epistemic disobedience. Jane Gordon's practice of creolization enacts similar decolonial practices, whereby it is imperative to engage with theorists outside of the dominant system of knowledge production (Frantz Fanon in her case) in order to reconceive of figures in the philosophical canon (Jean-Jacques Rousseau, for instance) (Gordon 2014; Gordon and Roberts 2015). The manner in which this engagement is enacted, however, is equally important. For instance, Gordon is careful not to appropriate Fanon for the purpose of developing a theory based on Rousseau. Rather, as she states explicitly, Fanon and Rousseau must equally be imposing on the other. Through this method of creolization, she is not enacting the rejection of the Western European philosophical canon; instead, she is providing the conditions for a new structure of knowledge by meaningfully introducing thinkers that have been delegitimated and marginalized within philosophy. One might also consider Sean Glen Coulthard's (Yellowknives Dene) *Red Skin, White Masks* (2014). In this book he discusses the importance of the reintroduction of Indigenous values, politics, and practices for decolonization.

Within practices of epistemic disobedience, Wynter's goal is "to introduce and integrate . . . several 'new objects of knowledge' which cannot meaningfully exist within the discursive *vrai* (truth) of our present 'fundamental arrangements of knowledge' nor within the analogic of its '(ethic-) theoretical foundations'" (Wynter 1987, 207). In addition, what becomes possible is the establishment of new ground, upon which "new objects of knowledge can find their efficient criterion/condition of truth" (207–8). According to Mignolo, Wynter is not attempting to overturn existing systems of knowledge. Rather, through her critique, she is attempting to change the way in which knowledge is produced and through which *knowing itself* is constituted. At the same time, however, he claims that "Wynter is not proposing to contribute to and comfortably participate in a system of knowledge that left her out of humanity (as a black/Caribbean woman), but rather delink herself from this very system of knowledge in order to engage in epistemic disobedience" (Mignolo 2015, 106). Thus it would seem that, for Wynter, in addition to offering a critique of how knowledge is produced, she is attentive to her own positionality (as an academic) in relation to systems of knowledge production. While epistemic disobedience is not a concept Wynter herself employs, it nonetheless provides a manner through which one can understand her methodology.

New objects of knowledge exceed and cannot be constrained or understood within the production of knowledge already operating. In so doing, epistemic disobedience can serve to disrupt the "episteme or fundamental arrangements of knowledge," insofar as knowledge practices perpetuate a specific worldview (Wynter 1987, 208). In addition, "for fundamental change to take place, it must take place both in the conception and in the pattern of relations" (Wynter 1992, 67).

A PLURI-CONCEPTUAL FRAMEWORK: MULTIPLICITY AND DIFFERENCE

Wynter's conception of the liminal exemplified by the Négritude movement and the function of epistemic disobedience provides the conditions for her theory of emancipation. That said, in order to further develop her theory of emancipation, we must develop what she calls a "pluri-conceptual framework." This framework is of particular importance to her theory of emancipation because it both demonstrates the importance of identities such as race for a theory of emancipation, and, in line with the role of the liminal articulated above, it also describes a component of her theory that is universal. Central to this framework is, thus, an articulation of emancipation that is dependent upon particularity *and* universality. Her conception of universality is developed in her discussion of what she calls "Jamesian poiesis."

In her essay titled "Beyond the Categories of the Master Conception: The Counterdoctrine of the Jamesian Poiesis" (1992), Wynter provides an analysis of the "deconstructive thrusts in [C. L. R.] James's works and the counterdoctrine that they produced" (63). Of interest to this project is her description of James's "pieza framework" that she describes as "pluri-conceptual" (63): "The pieza was the name given by the Portuguese, during the slave trade, to the African who functioned as the standard measure" or the equivalent of physical labor against which all the others could be measured" (81). The pieza was determined on the basis of the amount of labor an approximately twenty-five-year-old male in good health could produce. The values of slaves were thus determined on the basis of a pieza.

For Wynter, by way of James, the pieza can become a more general standard of measure "establishing equivalences between a wider variety of oppressed labor power" (81). In other words, the standard of slave labor is used to conceptualize oppressed labor power in general. The initial goal of the pieza framework is to displace normative Western conceptual frames, repositioning a labor conceptual framework such that it can incorporate the trade in African slaves (81). The starting point for this analysis of oppressed labor is the slave trade, thus emphasizing the importance of understanding the slave trade as foundational to a conception of labor. In addition, the pieza framework requires an analysis of the relation between modes of production and modes of domination (81). More specifically, "economic exploitation only follows on, and does not precede, the mode of domination set in motion by the *imaginaire social* of the bourgeoisie" (81, emphasis in original). Domination is thus not a product of economic exploitation, domination can be conceptually prior to economic exploitation, and a theory of labor must be able to account for this priority. James provides a theory of labor oppression that utilizes liminal positionalities and enacts epistemic disobedience.

Wynter's use of liminality for her theory of emancipation and her discussion of James's pieza framework also demonstrate the importance of identity for her theory of emancipation. Specifically, she states that "James was aided in the task of deconstructing these [master] conceptions by his identity as Negro. . . . It is because of the multiplicity of his consciousness" (68). Wynter's use of "Negro" in this instance is not merely an invocation of negative identity, whereby James's identity and existence are entirely constituted through the dominant (white supremacist) order. Rather, her description of James's deconstructing of master conceptions is meant to imply the critical capacity of the liminal position. James's marginalization and his critical interrogation of oppressive logics indicate that there is thus some knowledge or perspective that James has access to that aids in his ability to offer a critique of Western conceptions of labor.

It is important to note here that Wynter's reference to James's Black identity aiding in the development of his theory of emancipation is explicitly distinct from Badiou's theory of emancipation. Recall that Badiou considers minoritarian and identitarian logics that do "not hesitate to posit that this culture's constitutive elements are only fully comprehensible on the condition that one belongs to the subset in question" to be "genuinely barbaric" (2003, 12). By extension, as discussed in chapter 1, politics cannot adhere to identities if a politics is to be emancipatory. Instead, identities must be subtracted from the truth of politics. Badiou might then consider it "barbaric" or apolitical for James to utilize his Black identity for the purpose of augmenting his theory of emancipation. However, as should be evident at this point, it is indeed Badiou's project that is problematic and limited because of his failure to account for the role the liminal position can play in emancipatory movements. Furthermore, it is worth stating that the invocation of barbarity for prioritizing one's own experience of marginalization perpetuates harmful presuppositions of what counts and reinforces the supposed need for Eurocentric structures.

The question that remains, however, is as follows: In what way can Wynter offer a theory of universal emancipation that also emphasizes a role for identities? First and foremost, she stresses a multiplicity of identities in order to constitute one's lived reality. In speaking about James, she states, "These multiple permutations [color, levels of education, levels of wealth, and levels of 'culture'] gave rise to multiple identities: to the 'ecumenicism' then of being a Negro—of being Caliban" (1992, 68). The experience of "being a Negro" is not determined by any one particularity or essential characteristic. Instead there are multiplicities of identities that arise from a multiplicity of permutations. Similar to my description of race in chapter 3 through the work of Outlaw, race is conceived as "'a *cluster* concept' in which no single factor, like biological descent, is essential and thus the causal determinant of all the others" (Jeffers 2013, 406, emphasis in original).

Second, Wynter insists that "a system of color value existed side by side with capital value, education value, merit value, and labor value. To single out any of these factors was to negate the complex laws of the functioning of the social order, the multiple modes of coercion and power relations exiting at all levels of the social system" (1992, 69). It is thus imperative to provide an analysis of social systems and power relations through a pluralistic framework. In contradistinction to Sartre's emphasis on class over race, Wynter notes that the "factory model was only one of many models" (69). Furthermore, in contradistinction to Badiou, who subtracts particularity from his conception of the political, Wynter emphasizes "the multiple modes of coercion and of exploitation" (69). The pieza framework is an attempt to contain all modes of coercion and exploitation (69)—that is, a framework that aims to "constitute the multiple identities and competing subjective entry points of struggle particular for achieving Black self-determination" (Glick 2016, 161). In other words, there is no singular mode of oppression and exploitation that provides the conditions for theorizing Black liberation or the Negro question. Neither is it possible to conceive of emancipation by subtracting particularities such as race, class, or gender from its conception. Rather, the pieza framework requires that one address multiple modes of coercion. For example, as previously noted, a conception of economic exploitation ought not conceptually and materially center classism over racism and the trans-Atlantic slave trade.

Third, "Different Pieza groups means different sites, opportunities, and actors of resistance to domination" (161). Thus the implication is that political emancipation is a multifaceted approach. This means that there is no "mono-conceptual framework—no pure revolutionary subject, no single locus of the Great Refusal [of a social hierarchy], no single correct line" (Wynter 1992, 69). For Wynter the benefit of the pieza framework is that it names particular groups ("women, workers, dominated races, and other groups" [63]) in order to articulate a theory of emancipation that can address multiple forms of oppression. To subtract particularity and identity from a theory of emancipation would be to subsume all oppression under one general and generic framework, which would be problematic.

Wynter's emphasis on particularity can thus be juxtaposed with Badiou's conception of "the people." As discussed in chapter 1, the people, for the most part, must denote a generic set from which all particularity is subtracted. In order for "the people" to be constituted politically, they must be faithful to a political truth that transcends the logic of the current state. Furthermore, all identities and particularities (such as race and gender), insofar as they are determined by the logic of the state the subject aims to upend, cannot be utilized for the purpose of universal emancipation. In other words, the people cannot seek the emancipation of Black trans women, for instance. Identities are thus negative and cannot be utilized for the purpose of emancipation. The question that I am attempting to address through the pieza framework is as follows: What kind of oppression does such a theory of emancipation seek to upend? The problem that I have been attempting to make evident throughout this project is that, for Badiou, oppression itself seems to be conceived of along a single axis. In other words, there is little to no consideration of how different structures of oppression exist and how they need to be addressed in different ways. One might ask the following: In what way is the emancipation of Black people possible without considering the knowledge of those who have been oppressed on the basis of their Blackness, without addressing the structure through which oppression of Black people takes place (racism, sexism, classism, for example), and without the affirmation of Black people in particular?

Wynter's analysis and development of the pieza framework is an attempt to address such concerns regarding single-axis approaches to theories of emancipation. Yet the framework that she provides through James is not solely focused on individual particularities. Rather, the Pieza framework is pluralistic, emphasizing a multiplicity of identities at the same time, in order to address multiple faces of oppression. Her politics of emancipation emphasizes "the mode of being together in the polis, [which] is shaped by the struggle of groups and individuals to maintain or redefine the terms of their relations" (73). Universal emancipation thus takes the form of a multifaceted approach, through various identities, to approach all forms of oppression. "A pluri-conceptual theoretics, a universal based on the particular (Cesaire) is the logical result and outcome of the Jamesian poiesis . . . [that] leads necessarily to a praxis that is correspondingly plural in nature" (84). Thus, unlike Badiou for whom universality is juxtaposed against particularity, for Wynter, universality is based upon particularity. According to Wynter, it is possible to base universality on particularity if a theory of emancipation is pluralistic and intersectional and engages in what I would call a politics of solidarity. For instance, she states, "A relation in which the solidarity of the labor code, that is, of the world proletariat, must not negate the imperative solidarity of the African people. The road to the universal passes through the realization of the particular—at least in the popular conceptual frame" (87). Contra Sartre and Badiou, particularity must not be sublated in order to attain universality, as something that needs to be overcome. Rather, for Wynter, the realization of particularity is the source of universal emancipation whereby "black particularism . . . opens up the possibility of providing a transcultural perspective" (Wynter 1998, 281). The benefit of such a framework is that it remains open to a plurality of oppressions. This theory is inclusive of, for instance, poor rural whites in the U.S. South, and is sufficiently open to address systems of oppression that might not currently be addressed. It is important to note, however, that the experiences of oppression of poor rural whites will be distinct from poor Black people in the rural U.S. South.

The general mode of resistance offered by James is dependent upon the affirmation of marginalized and oppressed communities. Furthermore, for Wynter, emancipation is motivated by the lived experiences of those who experience a tension at the heart of their lived reality and who critically interrogate this tension—that is, those who exist in what she names the liminal sphere. For a theory to properly address the emancipation of all persons, it must not presume the mere contingency of racial identity. As Nick Nesbitt states:

> Césaire's brief article *"Conscience raciale et révolution sociale"* concisely refutes . . . the priority of proletarian class struggle, and the corresponding precedence of the vanguard Stalinist party (PCF), over anti-imperialism and anti-racism, to assert instead the imperative of black self-consciousness: "We must not be revolutionaries who accidentally happen to be black *[nègres]*, but truly revolutionary blacks *[nègres révo-*

lutionnaires]." The lived experience of racial subjection is in this view preeminent, and the recognition and assertion of the Martinican's negritude, the article asserts, must occur prior to any truly revolutionary politics. (2013, 104)[10]

In this instance it becomes apparent that race is not incidental to the revolution; rather it provides a central feature of it. As a result, the liminal is not something that is empty, nor ought we to endeavor to be indifferent to differences. Rather, the liminal is a position that, while unprivileged according to the norms and the structure of society, is privileged according to having the means to create new modes of existence. The liminal, as difference, is thus crucial for Wynter's theory of emancipation. This move is then further evidenced by her maintenance of "cultural movements," such as the Négritude movement, as having significant political import.

In many ways this is not only a cursory account of Wynter's project but also a cursory analysis of the relation between Badiou and Wynter. Wynter is deserving of significantly more attention and a more in-depth analysis of what I have called her political theory of solidarity. That said, the central feature of this project in its current iteration has been to analyze the role race plays in Badiou's and Wynter's respective theories in order to demonstrate that there are alternative and divergent framings of emancipatory movements. The previous chapters focused on Badiou's politics of indifference as providing the means for political universal emancipation. In this sense his position is easily juxtaposed to Wynter's uplifting of the liminal position (as difference) for whom identity can be constituted for the purposes of emancipation, whereby new objects of knowledge can be created for the purpose of a new emancipatory episteme and new conceptions of the subject. As such, I thought it appropriate to bring Badiou and Wynter into conversation, but one could have chosen any number of other theorists who engage in a similar mode of critique. What is perhaps most important to glean following this lengthy project is that theories of universality need not be emptied of particularities; rather, it is possible to conceive universal emancipation that is filled with particularities and which indeed also benefits significantly from what particularities (such as race and gender) have to offer. That said, there is much work left to be done.

Conclusion

This project aims to offer an analysis of the conception of race that operates in Alain Badiou's theory of the political, paying special attention to his conception of emancipation. Generally speaking, I have approached the problem of race with the following questions in mind: For whom is emancipation possible in Badiou's political theory? What counts as emancipation? And furthermore, what are the historical conditions that Badiou relies upon to decide what counts as politics and emancipation? Such questions have motivated the entirety of my project. Additionally, very few theorists have examined his conception of race in relation to francophone Black studies, and my project begins to take up that task as well. In what follows I first attend to historical connections within francophone political theory that link Badiou's work to authors of the Négritude movement. Second, I offer an overview of the project, and demonstrate the merits and relevance of such research today. Finally, I conclude by outlining several additional dimensions of scholarship to which my work on this project can contribute.

INTERVENTIONS IN FRANCOPHONE STUDIES

Francophone Black studies is a particularly pertinent and important area of study that ought to be brought into conversation with Badiou's project. As such, it will be important here to mention some biographical information about several of the authors that I have addressed in this project to highlight how their respective writings may be importantly put into conversation. As many readers may already know, Aimé Césaire was a Martinican politician and author. He attended the *École Normale Superieure* (passing the entrance exam in 1935) in Paris, and while he was there, he started a literary review journal titled *L'Étudian Noir* (The Black Student) with Léopold Sédar Senghor and Léon Dumas, both of whom were founding members of the Négritude movement alongside Césaire. Césaire was granted a state funeral in 2008, at which the president of France (then-president Sarkozy) was in attendance. Senghor, too, was reared in the shadow of French colonial dominance. He was born in French West Africa (what is present-day Senegal), studied at the Sorbonne, the *École Normale Superieure,* and graduated from the University of Paris in 1935.

Adding to this Black francophone history, Frantz Fanon was born and raised in the French colony of Martinique. Coming from a middle-class family, Fanon was well educated and studied under Césaire in Martinique, and then went on to study medicine and psychology in Lyons, France, where he also took classes with prominent French philosophers of the era, including Maurice Merleau-Ponty. Fanon was also close friends with Jean-Paul Sartre and Simone de Beauvoir.

Accordingly, Badiou's work as a French political theorist could be thought to fit well into this history of francophone theorists exploring conceptions of race and politics. Namely, Badiou was born in French Morocco and, like Césaire and Senghor, also attended the *École Normale Superieure* (from 1955 to 1960). As such, there are a number of geopolitical connections between Badiou, Césaire, Fanon, and Senghor that could be explored.

Moreover, such connections might warrant the assumption that there could be some acquaintance on Badiou's part of the work of these previous theorists. In this vein, it is apparent that Badiou should have, at the very least, a passing familiarity with these authors and their respective works. For instance, in *Black* he makes one reference to Césaire's writings, and in *Logics of Worlds* he refers to "the wretched of the earth" (2009, 53), an obvious reference to Fanon's *Wretched of the Earth.* Unfortunately, however, Badiou makes this statement without explicit reference to, or acknowledgement of, Fanon's work or projects. Accordingly, these disparate references in his corpus suggest that Badiou has not adequately done the work of engaging with these authors, nor with the literature and debates that surround these theorists, a limitation that I have addressed in this project and that future scholars in francophone political theory and Black studies can continue to explore.

ANALYZING BADIOU ON RACE

In offering a response to the kinds of questions presented in the opening paragraph of this conclusion, throughout the project I have brought Badiou's politics of indifference into conversation with a number of pertinent historical and philosophical debates regarding race.

First, I have drawn a correlation between Badiou's conception of Négritude and the 1948–52 debate between Jean-Paul Sartre and Fanon. As stated in chapter 2, the Fanon–Sartre debate is situated between Sartre's "Black Orpheus" (1948) and Fanon's *Black Skin, White Masks* (1952). Fanon's concern (according to Kathryn Sophia Belle and Robert Bernasconi) was that Sartre's "Black Orpheus" relinquished race to a moment in a dialectic that needed to be overcome in order to achieve universal emancipation. In Sartre's essay, race becomes an obstacle to emancipation, and thus is conceived as problematic. While there are notable differences between Badiou and Sartre, the similarities between their respective discussions of Négritude, and the role that Négritude can play in what they respectively call emancipation, is striking. I have argued that, like Sartre, Badiou construes race as an obstacle to universal emancipation. Fanon's concern regarding the denigration of race as a category for emancipation still haunts Badiou's 2017 book, *Black*. This comparative analysis between Sartre and Badiou is timely—given that *Black* was published so recently— and important, because the debate between Fanon and Sartre continues to be engaged by contemporary scholars of race in the twenty-first century.

The second debate that I have brought into conversation with Badiou's political theory of emancipation is located within the field of critical race studies, and I offered two approaches to understand critical approaches to race that are relevantly linked to Badiou's "politics of indifference." First, I addressed W. E. B. Du Bois's engagement with the question of whether "races" ought to be conserved. Second, I discussed two contrasting interpretations of the Haitian Revolution.

In Du Bois's 1897 essay titled "The Conservation of Races," the author proposes that there are conceptions of race that should persist despite considerable political gains for African Americans. This proposition presumes that there are conceptions of race that exist that are not reducible to what Fanon calls the "white gaze," or what might otherwise be named white supremacy or structural racism. While some figures, such as Anthony Appiah (2000), have critiqued Du Bois's argument for the conservation of races, other theorists such as Belle (Gines 2003), Chike Jeffers (2013), and Lucius T. Outlaw Jr. (1996) have not only engaged in a defense of Du Bois's argument but have extended it as well. Out of this rich debate regarding the conservation of races comes the necessity of distinguishing between positive and negative conceptions of race. As I argued in chapter 3, a negative conception of race maintains that race is reducible to oppressive structures and that in order to do away with racism one must also do away with race. This negative conception of race is consistent with my analysis of Sartre. For Du Bois, Belle, Jeffers, Césaire, Wynter, and Outlaw, however, there exist positive conceptions of race. A positive conception of race exists independently of racial oppression and affirms joy, life, and the value of Blackness (Césaire, Fanon, and Jeffers), as well as collective histories associated with Blackness (Belle, Jeffers, and Wynter). Accordingly, I endorse the claim that it is possible to think race independently of white supremacy, and that race ought not be reduced to an effect of white supremacy.

I thereby bring Badiou into conversation with these critical race theorists by way of my discussion of negative and positive conceptions of race. I argued that he fails to account for a positive conception of race that is consistent with this debate regarding the conservation of races. Badiou seems to propose that race can only be construed as a negative concept, bound up with notions of white supremacy (for instance) and, for this reason, that race is a concept that must be overcome in order to engage in political emancipation. His negative conception of race, I proposed, recenters whiteness as wholly determining. Furthermore, the presumption that race is antithetical to politics because it is divisive or essentialist offers a limited conception of race that fails to properly account for the many rich and diverse discussions available regarding positive conceptions of race. Contra Badiou, I proposed (alongside Wynter, Césaire, and Outlaw) that a positive conception of race can be political.

Within this vein of inquiry, in chapter 4 I situated a discussion of the Haitian Revolution as a hard problem for Badiou's theory of emancipation and his politics of indifference. In that chapter I offered two readings of the Haitian Revolution. First, Nesbitt, a prominent Badiou scholar, employs a Badiouian political framework in order to analyze the Haitian Revolution in *Universal Emancipation* (2008) and *Caribbean Critique* (2013). Nesbitt's articulation of the Haitian Revolution provides a mode through which one can apply Badiou's theory to a political movement that seeks the emancipation of racialized subjects. However, in Nesbitt's analysis, race does not have any political implications. The second (or alternative) reading that I offer emanates from David Geggus's *The Haitian Revolution* (2014) (a historian of the Haitian Revolution) and George Ciccariello-Maher's "So Much the Worse for the Whites" (2014) (a decolonial theorist). In their respective analyses of the Haitian Revolution, race takes on political significance. While one might ask why one should opt for the alternative reading of the Haitian Revolution rather than the one offered by scholars of Badiou, addressing this was not my primary concern. Rather, I aimed to shift the concern regarding this debate to ask instead, why should one opt for the Badiouian reading of the Haitian Revolution over the one that is concerned with race? Along this same line, what, then, would be the problem with race such that it must be excluded from a theory of emancipation? Moreover, in my analysis of the Haitian Revolution through the alternative readings offered by Geggus and Ciccariello-Maher, I outlined not only why the Haitian Revolution ought to be conceived of as a political event, and one that is emancipatory, but also how Badiou's conception of politics fails to properly take up this revolutionary moment. By way of a careful analysis of pivotal moments of the Haitian Revolution, it becomes apparent that race is a central proponent of this movement. Furthermore, attempts to devalue the role race plays for this revolution only seem to recenter a problematic conception of whiteness and Eurocentrism.

The third and last area of analysis that I brought Badiou's theory of emancipation into explicit conversation with is decolonial theory. Namely, I engaged with the work of Aníbal Quijano and (more extensively) Sylvia Wynter to examine their respective approaches to politics and race, and compared this to the position of Badiou. Wynter is a particularly relevant decolonial theorist to bring into conversation with Badiou in this project for two reasons. First, her use of Négritude as a theoretical and political concept—in "Ethno and Socio Poetics" (1976)—can be read alongside Badiou's description of Négritude as a cultural concept in *Black*. Wynter's interpretations of such authors as Césaire and Fanon also proved to be helpful in drawing a continuity between the Fanon–Sartre debate and her own writings. In this sense, inherent to Wynter's decolonial politics is an anti-essentialist conception of race whereby race is creative, changing, and productive.

Wynter's decolonial project drawing from C. L. R. James in "Beyond the Categories of the Master Conception" (1992) offers a model for universality (or universal emancipation) that can incorporate a positive conception of race. Once again, her reading of universal emancipation can be read alongside Badiou's theory of emancipation, and yet, as I argued in the last chapter, Wynter's conception of emancipation addresses the limitations of Badiou's project with respect to race outlined in chapters 2, 3, and 4. The critical comparative analysis performed in this project between these two authors is particularly illuminating because I engage in a debate about the relevancy of race and of particularity for a conception of emancipation. The debate in which I engaged is thus not one between conceptions of particularity over and against universality. Instead, much of my project concerns divergent conceptions of universality. Rather than propose that one must do away with all forms of particularity (like race) in the political realm in order to achieve something universal, Wynter calls for a politics of solidarity. According to such a view, particularities can coexist alongside other particularities when working toward converging goals. Or, as noted by Alcoff, "group interests sometimes coincide and at other times collide" (2016). Yet, for Wynter, universal emancipation requires that one address multiple forms of oppression through a multiplicity of forms of resistance.

FURTHER AVENUES FOR ANALYSIS

It is my hope that this project makes evident that more scholarship is needed that engages why it matters to examine race within Badiou's project and what the implications of his work are for theorists of race. One such potential line of research is to develop a response to the question, can Badiou be creolized? As briefly discussed in chapters 3 and 4, Jane Gordon's conception of "creolizing" in *Creolizing Political Theory* (2014) is described as a "particular approach to politics and to the engagement and construction of political ideas" (2) whereby "opposed, unequal groups [forge] mutually instantiating practices in contexts of historical rupture" (3). Just as Gordon brings Jean-Jacques Rousseau into conversation with Fanon, so too could one bring Badiou into conversation with a number of opposing and unequally situated political theorists. This method of creolization of Badiou's project could be a fruitful way to address some of the limitations of his project outlined in this book.

An additional potential area of investigation might be the implications of, and correlations between, Badiou's conception of race and his implementation of sexual difference throughout his writings. There are two reasons in particular why it is important to consider correlations between his conceptions of race and sexual difference. First and foremost, a properly intersectional account of race and sexual difference requires such analysis. The project as it currently stands, with its concentration on race to the exclusion of an account of sexual difference, runs the risk of effacing the position of Black women, for instance.

Second, 2011 marks a significant turn in Badiou's conception of sexual difference, according to Louise Burchill, a prominent Badiou scholar. In "Of a Universal No Longer Indifferent to Difference: Badiou (and Irigaray) on Woman, Truths and Philosophy" (2018), Burchill describes this radical turn:

> In a startling inflexion of his core tenet of truths' trans-particularity or the neutrality of the universal, Badiou's 2011 paper "Figures of Femininity in the Contemporary World" proclaims that truth processes can no longer be considered as indifferent to sexual difference, with it now necessary, thereby, to examine how sexuation functions in the domains of political, scientific, artistic and amorous truths. (2018, 1165)

As noted throughout this analysis, previously, Badiou called for the subtraction of all predicates from the subject. This means that the subject of truth could not retain any identity, including those pertaining to gender or sexuality. Consistent with the politics of indifference developed in chapter 1, politics must remain indifferent to differences (such as race and gender) in order to be emancipatory, and thereby political.

However, the turn that Burchill remarks as having taken place in Badiou's "Figures of Femininity" calls for a reconceptualization of what the subject of truth procedures can look like. One can now ask, for instance, "What is a woman involved in emancipatory politics"? (Burchill 2018,

1165). In other words, if the difference of sexual difference is pertinent to politics, then in what way does "woman," for instance, operate in that truth procedure? Furthermore, drawing on the title of Burchill's article, one might ask: What might a conception of the universal that is no longer indifferent to difference look like? As I have proposed throughout this project, I believe that Wynter offers us an analysis of what such an articulation of the universal might look like.

Regarding Badiou's political theory, considerable work must be done before an answer to this question is even possible, and theorists such as Burchill and Sigi Jöttkandt are already engaging in the implications of this radical change for his theory of sexual difference. That said, such an analysis requires that one understand why it is that sexual difference takes on a distinct role. Is Badiou unintentionally implementing a biological or essentialist conception of sexual difference? In addition, how are sexual difference and race constituted differently for him such that the turn in the relation between truth and sexual difference does not extend to race as well, evident in his most recent book about race, *Black*?

Whatever the case, this radical turn in Badiou's conception of sexual difference has significant implications for his conception of race as well as for his articulation of politics and emancipation. However, providing a response to such questions, and an analysis of the implication of this radical turn for his project, requires a considerable amount of additional work.

Lastly, regarding Wynter's political theory, I believe that much work is left to be done in order to demonstrate how it is that she is offering a new conception of humanism, one that is not indifferent to differences, for example. As I developed in chapter 5, Wynter is offering a critique of conceptions of "the human" that dominate various historical periods and the ways in which they are problematic. However, her attempt to critique and dismantle problematic conceptions of "the human" that operate for the purpose of oppression does not mean that she does not (or cannot) offer a robust and nuanced account of humanism. However, more work needs to be done in order to develop a clear analysis of her theory of humanism and draw out the differences between Wynter's and Badiou's humanisms.

Such questions are projects for another time. What I have offered here is an attempt to open further avenues for analysis within Badiou's work and engage with critical theorists of race and decolonial scholars to extend philosophical thinking about the questions of emancipation and universalism, race as a positive conception of identity and meaning, and the value of theorizing from the margins. Such questions, I hope, remain significant within political theory for many decades to come.

With that being said, with increasingly frequency I am asked whether one should continue to engage with the work of Alain Badiou. In light of this question, I am a bit hesitant to offer the above articulation of further avenues for analysis of his work. Perhaps one should ask whether it is possible to creolize Badiou's project, or whether the structural concerns that I have outlined in this book are sufficient to caution people that there are perhaps irreconcilable issues with Badiou's project. In response to all these questions, here is my response. First and foremost, it is important to recognize the important work done by Sylvia Wynter, as well as numerous other decolonial and critical race theorists. It is perhaps more pertinent to suggest that one turn to her work, among others, rather than attempt to stretch or complete Badiou. Furthermore, perhaps it is Badiou's responsibility to stretch or complete his own project in light of the critiques that I have outlined herein.

Second, one might ask why *I* have invested so much time and effort into Badiou's work. A considerable amount of my education was spent in a trajectory that led me to Badiou (notably by way of the work of Louis Althusser and Étienne Balibar). However, despite the seemingly progressive cloud that hovers around Badiou's theory of emancipation, I sought to understand how his project might be worked out in distinct social and political contexts. In a sense, the publication of *Black* provided me with the means to address concerns that I had suspected as underlying his political project. As such, I continued (and will likely continue) to engage with Badiou's work for two reasons. His work is not unlike other political projects that are circulating within a post-Marxist French political theory about which one should remain critical. Furthermore, there is a vast absence of critical analyses of Badiou's project, the lack of which allows for Badiou scholarship (and Badiou himself) to continue without any attention to the problematic structural aspects I have outlined throughout this book.

In conclusion, it is not my intention to save Badiou or compel others to engage with his political project. Rather, I aim to demonstrate the importance of reading decolonial theory writ large.

Acknowledgments

This book would not be possible without the ever-growing support I receive both in academia and beyond. I have been fortunate to have had my philosophical curiosity nurtured by various people over the years, and I am grateful to each and every one of them. I am indebted to more people than I have the opportunity to thank individually, however two people in particular have offered me guidance when it was most needed, calling me into philosophy through a shared interest in the writings of Simone de Beauvoir and encouraging me to push beyond those writings. My sincerest thanks to Emilia Angelova and Lorraine Code, for all their support.

I was provided institutional support from various universities and organizations while working on this manuscript. Foremost in my development were the resources made available at York University (Toronto) and the University of North Carolina at Charlotte. Notably, my colleagues heard various articulations of my project and offered me constructive feedback. Many thanks in particular to Shannon Sullivan, Eddy Souffrant, Danielle Boaz, Janaka Bowman Lewis, Robin James, Sonya Ramsey, Katie Hogan, Michael Kelly, Alice MacLachlan, Adriel M. Trott, and Antonio Calcagno.

The arguments that appear in this book have been reworked from material presented at various conferences and nourished by participation in a number of academic spaces, including the Historical Materialism Conference, the Caribbean Philosophical Association, Philosophy Born of Struggle, philoSOPHIA, the American Comparative Literature Association, the

Canadian Philosophical Association, the Pittsburgh Summer Symposium in Contemporary Philosophy, and the Feminist Decolonial Politics Workshops in Montreal and Charlotte.

To the wonderful editorial team at the University of Minnesota Press, especially Danielle Kasprzak, Anne Carter, and Leah Pennywark, I thank you. The comments I received from the external reviewers were tremendously helpful in reworking this project, and I am appreciative of the time and effort they put into helping me improve this project. My sincerest thanks to Sarah Kizuk for her tireless effort put toward producing the index. All errors are my own.

This work is also indebted to community members who offered invaluable wisdom regarding the connections between theory and praxis, and from whom I continue to learn. My heartfelt thanks go to Ash Williams, Jamie Marsicano, Myka Johnson, Aman Agah, and Sam Poler.

To my community in Charlotte, without whom this project would never have made it to fruition, I thank you. Danielle Boaz, Sarah Pollock, Janaka Bowman Lewis, Consuelo Salas, Daniela Recabarren, Tamara Johnson, Rachael Forester, and Erica Lennon, thank you for the faith you have in me. To Joseph Jordan, Alex Leferman, Dhruv Jain, and Amrit Mandzak-Heer, thank you for reading drafts of my earlier work and for your comments. To Karen Robertson and Suzanne McCullagh, our philosophical discussions over numerous cups of coffee were formative for this project. I appreciate you.

To my family, for the years of encouragement, for teaching me how to tend a garden and portage a canoe—there are not enough words to express how much your support means to me. My heartfelt thanks to my parents, Linda and Michel Paquette, and my siblings Dominique, Katrina, and David. And to all the strong women in my life who have provided me with strength, I thank you.

Most important, I thank my spouse, partner, and friend, Andrea. You opened up worlds to me that I had not known were even possible. You encouraged me through every step of this difficult process. This project would not have been possible without your feedback and your support. Thank you for joining me on this journey.

Appendix

A Timeline of the Haitian Revolution

This is a general timeline of the Haitian Revolution as outlined in David Geggus's *The Haitian Revolution* (2014). I included events that did not take place in Saint Domingue but are pertinent for our discussion of the revolution.

1789

The French Revolution begins and The Declaration of the Rights of Man and of the Citizen is signed in France.

1791

People who were enslaved in the northern regions of Saint Domingue and free people of color in the central region begin to revolt.

1792

The slave rebellion begins in the South. In April, free people of color are given full rights, the justification for which was to gain the support of free people of color against rebellious slaves (Geggus 2014, xx). In September, the monarchy is overthrown in France and two commissars arrive in Saint Domingue to enforce racial equality (xxi), one of whom is Léger-Félicité Sonthonax. Rebellions continue in Saint Domingue and "conservative officers considered disloyal to the new regime, and then autonomist Patriots who opposed their actions," are deported from the island (xxi).

1793

Slavery is declared abolished in Saint Domingue by Sonthonax. The justification for the abolition of slavery was primarily because the British–Spanish War made it very difficult for France to send troops to Saint Domingue and, additionally, for the purpose of defending Saint Domingue from foreign invasion. White and free people of color (i.e., the middle class and not the [recently] formerly enslaved) reject the abolition of slavery declared by Sonthonax and surrender large portions of land to the British and the Spanish in protest (xxii). Northern insurgents (composed primarily of free people of color) decide to fight against France and with the Spanish, alongside Jean-François and Biassou (xxii), who show no concern for the abolition of slavery. They were soon joined by Toussaint L'Ouverture (xxii), who was "born in slavery to African parents [and who] had been free for about twenty years" (xxiii).

1794

The Jacobin government abolishes slavery in all French colonies and declares the formerly enslaved to be citizens (Ibid., xxii). That said, in actuality, "Most former slaves remained subject to forced labor, as Sonthonax envisioned, and few were able to exercise political rights" (xxii). However, this declaration was useful for convincing various insurgent leaders to join the French against the Spanish, including Toussaint (xxii). In addition, by the end of this year, Jean-Jacques Dessalines, who was creole and an ex-slave, joins Toussaint's army.

1795

Spain withdraws from the war in Saint Domingue (xxiii), and Jean-François and Biassou are exiled to parts of the Spanish Empire (xxiv–xxv).

1797

Toussaint is named commander in chief of the Saint Domingue colonial army by Sonthonax (xxiv) and then orders the expulsion of Sonthonax. Also, due to the shifting of politics in France, many in French politics "regretted the abolition of slavery and criticized the new colonial regime" (xxv).

1798

British troops who remained in Saint Domingue and had been fighting against the French colonial troops are defeated this year and are evacuated from May to October, and sixty- to seventy-thousand slaves who were in the British-occupied area of Saint Domingue are finally free (xxv). Toussaint controls "all northern and central Saint Domingue" (xxv).

1799

Napoleon Bonaparte comes to power in France (xxvii).

1800

By August "the whole of Saint Domingue was under Toussaint's control. He could now extend the forced labor system Sonthonax had created in 1793. . . . Toussaint remained committed to the plantation system . . . because only the export of cash crops would generate the revenue that funded his army and administration. This policy alienated much of the ex-slave population" (xxvi).

1801

Bonaparte seeks the reinstitution of slavery in Saint Domingue and the capture of Toussaint. In August he "quietly canceled Toussaint's promotion to Captain-General and removed his name from the French army register." In July, Toussaint writes his own colonial constitution, the 1801

Constitution of Saint Domingue. As Geggus writes: "Remarkably bold, the constitution made Louverture governor for life, with the right to name his successor" (xxvii).

1802

Bonaparte sends Victoire Leclerc to Saint Domingue to "win over where possible the black generals, then disarm their soldiers, and eventually deport all black officers" (xxix), with the support of Britain, the United States, Spain, the Netherlands, and Cuba (xxix). Toussaint surrenders in May of this year and is deported to France (xxix). Other Black generals are incorporated into the French army and used to disarm rural masses (xxix). It now becomes apparent "that French policy was to reimpose slavery" (xxix) and racial discrimination (xxx). At this point, many of the Black generals and the formerly enslaved masses break with the French and decide that, "to maintain freedom and equality, they had to unite in a war for independence" (xxx). Dessalines becomes the leader of the independence movement (xxx).

1803

The last of the French troops withdraws from Haiti.

1804

Haiti is declared an independent nation by Dessalines. The massacre of remaining white colonists begins (xxx).

1805

The constitution of the free state of Hayti is written by Dessalines.

1806

The Republic of Haiti is founded after the assassination of Dessalines (xxxii).

Notes

INTRODUCTION

1. The list of approaches that I have outlined here are not exhaustive, nor are the approaches that I have outlined as simple or as straightforward as I have represented them. Regarding the former, one can engage in a critique on the basis of race that is not focused on a specific figure and/or a specific figure's work. Regarding the latter, one might also engage in any one of these critiques (which I have listed) simultaneously. As such, I offer these three approaches in order to provide a framework for my own project, while recognizing that it is somewhat of an over-simplification. These three approaches received significant influence from a talk given by Dilek Huseyinzadegan at the University of North Carolina at Charlotte in 2015.

2. It should be noted here that I am drawing a distinction between Badiou's discussion of "color" that composes the majority of his book *Black* and his discussion of "race" at the end of this same book. However, it is important to note that for Badiou race is only a color that has gained a series of "false 'objective' bases for oppressive classifications" (Badiou 2017, 104).

3. Similarly, one could also address his reference to "black gangsters" (Badiou 2011a, 292).

4. In a similar vein, Ciccariello-Maher notes his concern regarding the kind of universalism advanced by Badiou and figures like him (2017, 3).

5. See Sartre 1976, 2004a, 2004b; Kruks 1996; Marcano 2003.

6. See Fanon 1967, 2004, 2008; Bernasconi 1996, 2002, 2004; L. Gordon 1995, 2015; Nayar 2013.

7. See Césaire 1972, 1983, 2001, 2010.

1. INDIFFERENCE TO DIFFERENCE AND BADIOU'S THEORY OF EMANCIPATION

1. According to Badiou, "'Logic' and 'appearing' are . . . one and the same thing. 'Transcendental' names the crucial operators of this second identity" (Badiou 2009, 99).

2. For the sake of this example, it is important to note that appearance is not bound to consciousness or perception and that there are multiple worlds (as is evident in my discussion below). This means that it is not that the undercover police office must appear to the demonstrators for their existence to appear minimally. In other words, the world of the demonstration is not beholden to the perception of one individual group. That said, as I demonstrate below, for Badiou it is also that there can be multiple worlds operating in any one space simultaneously, each one organized by a different transcendental operator.

3. According to Adriel M. Trott, this point serves to situate Badiou's conception of world against, for instance, Hegel. She states, "For Badiou, Hegel's whole is not only morally and politically unjust [, but additionally] . . . the whole is not" (2015, 59). In other words, "Any claim to have achieved totality is false and irretrievably so because a totality of all that exists is impossible to maintain" (59–60). In this sense, contra Hegel, Badiou affirms the multiplicity of worlds.

4. According to Trott, Badiou is also particularly interested in conveying and understanding the role of contradiction for the construction of worlds in a manner that is distinguishable from that of Hegel. For instance, Hegel's dialectic aims to "resolve [a] contradiction into a whole" (Trott 2015, 60), whereby all identity is resolved into an absolute identity or completeness. However, for Badiou, completeness can never be achieved (61). Unlike Hegel, according to Trott, Badiou is not concerned with the resolution of contradictions, and, as a result, he maintains that there will always be a position that is beyond the whole that cannot be incorporated within it. For the purpose of this project, it is also important to keep in mind that these tensions or contradictions can be sites of violence. For an extended discussion of unity in Hegel beyond the work of Trott, see Maker 2007; Zambrana 2015; Hahn 2007.

5. This example is an oversimplification and in this sense it can be problematic. It is important to note that people who are undocumented are counted by the state in a variety of ways. For instance, they may pay income taxes, and are protected by antidiscrimination laws, and thus in these ways they would be counted by a particular branch of a state. That said, the function of this example is to demonstrate that there are multiple ways in which a state, in any given time and space, may recognize or count some folks but not others, and it can be done on the basis of nationality, citizenship, race, gender, sexuality, and ability, for instance. For the purpose of this example, we might consider a count on the basis of those who are excluded from participation in the democratic process of voting, to which we could include permanent residents, visitors to the state, people who are incarcerated (in some states), and people who are subject to racialized forms of voter disenfranchisement, for instance.

6. Alain Badiou's invocation of "all Africans" in this quote is sweeping and

clearly fallacious. Of course, there are many nation-states in which Africans do have a voice—especially within sovereign African nation-states. I imagine that the thrust of Badiou's claims are meant to be in reference to the marginalization of African and African-descended people who live in Europe (and particularly France) or the United States. These points will be taken up in my critique of Badiou in chapters 2 through 4.

7. Further evidence of why this is would require that I develop two points from Badiou's use of set theory—namely, the succession of ordinals and Gödel's incompleteness theory. Given that I have omitted a discussion of set theory in this book, it would not be helpful to introduce these concepts here.

8. There are (at least) four truth procedures for Badiou that, as a result, produce four distinct kinds of truths. For the purpose of this project, given that my concern is political emancipation, I focus on political truth procedures and thus political truths. The three other forms of truth procedures are love, art (or poetry), and science (or mathematics).

9. This is an oversimplification for a political situation that is arguably much more complicated.

10. There is a significant difference between Menon and Badiou and their respective critiques of identity politics. Menon focuses on the "truth of one's particularity" and the way in which identity and identity politics fail to properly account for this truth. Badiou, on the other hand, is not concerned with one's particularity or experience of the world in relation to identity. Rather, as previously noted, he rejects a kind of individuality and self-consciousness in his political theory and instead concentrates on collectivity as a site for political action. That said, both Menon and Badiou problematize the relation between identity and state power, and it is this relation that I am attempting to highlight in this instance.

11. It is extremely important to note that, for many people, the experience of crossing a border can be riddled with anxiety and can also make one subject to state violence. There exists a magnitude of exceptional scholars who engage this issue. For more information, see Rivera 1992, Ortega and Alcoff 2009, Walia 2013, and Mohanty 2003, to start. It is not my intention to minimize these experiences but rather to develop the implications of Menon's example for her articulation of a politics of indifference.

12. For an extended discussion of Fanon's articulation of violence, see chapter 1 of *The Wretched of the Earth* and L. Gordon 2008.

2. BADIOU ON RACE AND THE FANON–SARTRE DEBATE

1. Fanon states: "The concept of negritude for example was the affective if not logical antithesis of that insult which the white man had levelled at the rest of

humanity. This negritude, hurled against the contempt of the white man, has alone proved capable in some sectors of lifting taboos and maledictions" (2004, 150). Therein, Fanon seems to be describing Négritude as the direct opposite of the negative stereotypes construed and hurled by colonizers, which in effect did offer some successes. At the same time, however, Fanon also attributes to Négritude "naïveté, petulance, freedom, and indeed luxuriance. But also irresponsibility" (151). Similarly, in *What Fanon Said*, Lewis R. Gordon notes that Fanon "continues his meditations on negritude [in *The Wretched of the Earth*] on the grounds that in this instance it is more than a negative moment in a historical dialectic because of the misapplication it engenders through nationalism, racism, and all self-*interest*-laden models of group organizations instead of those premised on the common good" (2015, 121, emphasis in original). It would be incorrect to assume, or to assert, that Fanon's implementation and understanding of Négritude sits squarely within the project that I am proposing. As noted above, at various points in time Fanon is quite critical of Négritude in a manner that is not inconsistent with Sartre's articulation of Négritude in "Black Orpheus." While I address various differences of opinions on the focus and function of Négritude (which should also be understood as divergent and pluralistic at times), my focus in this chapter is to address Fanon's critique of Sartre's articulation of the relation between race and class.

2. One could draw a connection between Sartre's book titled *Anti-Semite and Jew* (1976) and Badiou's book titled *Reflections on Anti-Semitism* (2012). That said, such a discussion falls outside of the purview of this book.

3. Of course, one could also attend to his discussion of the black soul in relation to Senghor's discussion of the black soul, but that is not the foremost concern in this project.

4. See the *Critique of Dialectical Reason* for Sartre's extended discussion on race, notably the section titled "Racism and Colonialism as Praxis and Process." This later shift in Sartre's articulation of race and colonialism is worth an extended analysis. However, I have opted to postpone such an analysis. The function of my work on Sartre in this chapter is to draw a parallel between his work and the twenty-first-century work by Badiou, which falls into Sartre's earlier articulation of race.

5. It should also be noted that Sartre states the following: "I call this method 'objective poetry' *magic*, or charm" (1948, 30). Furthermore, he juxtaposes the myths of Négritude poetry with the epic poems of Medieval French poetry.

6. Put more concretely, Sartre seems to claiming that Négritude proposes the racial superiority of Black people over and against people of other races—including, one would assume, white people. Of course, such a line of argument fails to account for historical (and generational) harms from enslavement and/or marginalization through which the process of racialization takes place. Furthermore, it

also fails to adequately understand the goals and principles of the Négritude movement, as will be made evident below.

7. This chapter has also been translated as "The Fact of Blackness" in the 1967 Markmann translation. In the original French, the title of the fifth chapter is "*L'experience vécu du noir*," a title that makes explicit reference to lived experiences. As such, the Markmann translation is quite misleading and is a problematic translation.

8. Regarding the positive interchange between Fanon and Sartre, we can note their friendship and collegial exchanges. For instance, Sartre was asked to write the Preface to *Wretched of the Earth*. Furthermore, they met up at various points in time to discuss their respective theories. Sartre also visited Fanon when he was on his deathbed just after having arrived in the United States. These are just a few examples of the continuous dialogue, support, and respect that they held for each other. Simone de Beauvoir's *Force of Circumstance* (1965) provides descriptions of their various interactions. Additionally, "Fanon also admired Sartre, whose open position on the Algerian War, a position that endangered his life in France as the bombings of two of his apartments attests, redeemed him politically in Fanon's eyes" (L. Gordon 2015, 130–31).

9. Fanon also references these lines in *Black Skin, White Masks*. See Fanon 2008, 103.

10. Ciccariello-Maher argues that for Fanon "class was always an important but secondary phenomenon[,] ... [and] the central category of identification was first blackness, or negritude (in *Black Skin, White Masks*), and later the decolonial nation (in *Wretched of the Earth*)" (2017, 48).

11. While Fanon does not remain an avid supporter of Négritude throughout his entire, albeit cut far too short, life, it is a significant aspect of some of his earlier writings, in particular *Black Skin, White Masks*.

3. A CRITIQUE OF A POLITICS OF INDIFFERENCE

1. For more on the crises of Marxism, see Bosteels 2014.

2. The critique that I offer throughout this book might be confused with a liberal line of thought. In other words, one might assume that my project adheres to the liberal framework that argues for the inclusion of different identities in the political realm. However, it is important to note that my critique is firmly situated in a Marxist tradition, albeit often more prevalent in Black Marxist traditions.

3. For an analytic articulation of the relation between race and class, addressing also the Eurocentric structure of Marxism, see Charles W. Mills's *From Class to Race* (2003).

4. The reference to assimilation in this sentence is about assimilation to the

Communist Party. In other words, Césaire claims that one needed to assimilate to the Communist Party in order to participate in it. To assimilate in this instance is on the basis of race, that is, that Blackness or the Negro question was not a prominent concern for the party, resulting in an erasure of Blackness.

5. For an extended discussion of the negative conception of race, see Zack 1997.

6. See, for instance, these various texts for discussions on the correlations and disagreement between Fanon and Sartre: Kruks 1996; Bernasconi 1996; L. Gordon 2015.

7. Of course, the relationship between Fanon and Césaire is quite complicated. Much has been written about the influence of Césaire on Fanon, given that Fanon was a student of Césaire and, furthermore, that Césaire was a prominent theorist during Fanon's lifetime. See Abdel-Shehid and Kolia 2017; Bernasconi 2002; and my discussion of this text. One might also consider Sonia Kruks's claim that "it is through an examination of *négritude* that Fanon explores the dilemmas of the affirmation of black identity. *Négritude* is at once untenable and yet necessary" (1996, 130). That said, alongside Bernasconi, I am of the opinion that the presumption that Fanon wholly rejects Négritude and the writings of Césaire is misguided.

8. This letter culminates with the following statement: "Under these conditions, I ask you to accept my resignation as a member of the French Communist Party. *Paris, October 24, 1956*" (Césaire 2010).

9. George Ciccariello-Maher offers a very compelling critique of Sartre through the works of Fanon in *Decolonizing Dialectics*. He addresses not only the Eurocentric framework Sartre reinforces (50) and Fanon's reluctance to participate in the dialectic of Black identity (50), but also the imposition that was put on Fanon to embrace Black identity: "I had no choice" (53). Many aspects of the critique of Sartre that I utilize against Badiou have been drawn from Ciccariello-Maher's work, to which I am indebted.

10. One might ask how Badiou's critique of identity politics relates to the discussion of "the Algerian people" offered above. Additionally, one might ask: Is "the Algerian people" an example of a positive identity? While this example does provide an interesting caveat to the subtraction of identity and particularity from politics, this example is consistent with his critique of identity politics and does not assuage my concern regarding a lack of inclusion of identity. "The Algerian people" is consistent with his critique of identity politics for two reasons. First, it gains political legitimacy only because it is part of a political process, and second, it is not dependent upon the historical and epistemic situatedness of any particular group. As noted above, the predicate only receives political legitimacy if the state

is overthrown. Furthermore, once the state is overthrown, the predicate can no longer hold any political import. In other words, "the Algerian people" operates as a generic category, serving to name an evental site. Also, "the Algerian people" operates in name only and any particularity is subtracted from the predicate.

Badiou's politics of indifference is premised upon his critique of identity politics. As previously noted, he claims that identity is immanent to the logic of a particular state and serves to reproduce the power of that state. Identity cannot have any political or emancipatory import because emancipation and politics must transcend the logic and power of the state. As a result, he argues that identity must be subtracted from politics, and must be subtracted from a theory of emancipation insofar as it fails to be progressive. However, identities need not be thought of as merely negative—that is, as replicating an oppressive power structure. Badiou in his politics of indifference thus fails to address that a positive conception of identity is possible.

11. For an articulation of creolization that employs Jane Gordon's and Michael Monahan's respective work within the context of science fiction, see Mendoza 2018.

12. In a similar fashion, Jones critiques Nesbitt's description of Négritude in *Voicing Memory* for his dependence on Hegel's master/slave dialectic because of its reliance upon the recognition of the master race. She states, "The dialectic of reflection, by which self-consciousness is engendered, is inherently mutual for Hegel, yet the predication of self-esteem on the recognition of the master race is a tragically destructive act, an act sure to yield only shame and violence, internal and external" (2010, 167). In addition, she states, "it is absurd to think that slave labor of the New World plantations served any educative function [whereby the bondsman becomes conscious to his own meaning in the product of his labor] and that black intellectuals would embrace the fear and service that Hegel thought the bondsman must endure in order to become objective to himself. The Hegelian dialectic simply does not seem to fit the experience of African slaves in the New World" (167). One might also consider Fanon's critique of Hegel's master/slave dialectic in *Black Skin, White Masks*. However, this critique is not a central concern for this project.

4. POLITICS IS TO CULTURE AS CLASS IS TO RACE

1. It is important to note that Négritude was not an American phenomenon. There seems to be a bit of confusion between the Négritude movement (that was prevalent in Martinique, Senegal, and France) and the trans-Atlantic slave trade. Furthermore, his discussion of the trans-Atlantic slave trade refers specifically to America, to the exclusion of the Caribbean, an area to which over three million Africans were forcibly brought by the British between 1664 and 1807.

2. There is a third point that I address briefly here because it is relevant to Badiou's articulation of Négritude, even though it detracts from the argument in this section of the book—namely, his description of Black people as "more in tune with nature," as having "more rhythm," and as "more poetic" in particular. One might ask why Badiou has chosen to describe the Négritude movement according to these terms. Answers to this question reside in Frantz Fanon's *Black Skin, White Masks* (2008), paying special attention to pages 102, 104, and 108. In this text, Fanon problematizes such conceptualizations of Black people (as more natural, having more rhythm) insofar as it serves to resituate Black people and communities of color within a position of being less rational than white people. As noted in the first chapter, this was also Fanon's critique of Sartre.

3. It is also important to note, however, that it is problematic to draw a correlation between the color yellow (as is in the color of his underwear when he writes a mathematical theorem) and color that is racialized, such as being Black. Badiou, however, seems to argue that there is no difference between a racialized color (such as Blackness) and a nonracialized color (such as purple), because no "color" can be political—neither a racialized "color" such as Blackness nor the color purple. For further discussion of the practice of correlating race and "color," see Michael Monahan's "Race, Colorblindness, and Continental Philosophy" (2006) and Kelly Oliver's *Witnessing: Beyond Recognition* (2001).

4. See the appendix for a summary timeline of the Haitian Revolution.

5. It is also important to note the different forms of whiteness in this context. Carolyn E. Fick states that "this racial ideology did not produce a coherent and solid white bloc, either before or during the revolution" (1990, 18). Therein, she notes the distinctions made between the *grand blancs* (*Blancs-blancs,* i.e., "the great sugar planters . . . the real whites"), the *petit blancs* (*faux blanc* or *Blanchet,* i.e., "the small white who worked for a salary") (18).

6. For a more detailed account of the development of planation slavery in Saint Domingue from 1687 to 1790, see Dubois 2004, chapter 1; Fick 1990, chapter 1. Also, Fick notes that the number of free people of color jumps from 6,000 in 1770 (roughly equal to the number of white people) to 27,500 in 1789, which is "nearly twice the increase of the white population for the same period" (1990, 19).

7. In *Avengers of the New World,* Dubois avoids using the term "mulatto" because it "racializes and simplifies a complex reality, in favor of the term gens de couleur, which [he] translates as 'free people of color' or 'free-coloreds'" (2004, 6). I am following Dubois's lead and using the term "free people of color" throughout.

8. For an extended discussion, see Fick 1990, chapter 1.

9. For an overview of scholarship on the Haitian Revolution, see Fick 1990, introduction.

10. In *Anti-Semite and Jew,* Sartre notes a similar move. He states the following: "This universalism, this critical rationalism, is what one normally finds in the democrat. In his abstract liberalism, he affirms that Jews, Chinese, Negroes ought to have the same rights as other members of society, but he demands these rights for them as men, not as concrete individual products of history" (1976, 117).

11. Throughout this document, you will notice references to Toussaint, Toussaint L'Ouverture, and Toussaint Louverture. All are accepted names for the same person. I have chosen Toussaint L'Ouverture, in keeping with C. L. R. James's *The Black Jacobins,* but will also use Toussaint when appropriate. Toussaint Louverture appears in several quotes, which I have chosen not to alter.

12. Napoléon Bonaparte was first consul of France from 1799 to 1804 and emperor of the French from 1804 to 1814.

13. Or, as noted by Dubois, "Ultimately, while emancipation had been won through an alliance with the French Republic in 1794, it was preserved by the defeat of the French army in 1804" (2004, 4). Furthermore, he states that "the slaves of Saint-Domingue who had helped lay the foundation for the French Revolution would ultimately make it their own, and even surpass it, in their own struggle for liberty" (21). Interestingly, rather than the assumption that the Haitian Revolution was based on the French Revolution, Dubois is here suggesting what is effectively its opposite—that is, that the French Revolution was not only dependent upon the Black slaves of Saint Domingue but also that the Haitian Revolution surpassed the French Revolution.

14. For a more nuanced discussion on the topic of freedom and slavery, free people of color, and prisoners in Saint Domingue, see Joseph-Gabriel 2017. Therein she not only describes how freedom and unfreedom can be understood through mobility but also offers an articulation of slavery that is not limited to a plantation system.

15. Ciccariello-Maher refers to "biologically-white" and "politically-white" in this quote, a distinction that is worthy of a bit of clarification. First, it is important to note that he associates biologically-white with Buck-Morss's account of the Haitian Revolution, and "politically-white" with C. L. R. James's. Second, he argues that Buck-Morss centers whiteness and James decenters whiteness. While Ciccariello-Maher does not offer an explicit explication of what is inherent to these two conceptions of race, implicitly I believe that this distinction is dependent upon how they are conceived of operating in (or outside of) the political sphere. For instance, he uses "biologically-white" in reference to Buck-Morss because she presumes that race is not a political category but is instead something biological. Furthermore, as noted in this book, James argues that race is political (even whiteness), which justifies why Ciccariello-Maher uses "politically-white" in

reference to him. In summation, Ciccariello-Maher is noting not only that James's and Buck-Morss's objects of analysis (race or whiteness) are distinct but also that their respective approaches to their objects of analysis (to center or to decenter) are also distinct.

16. At various points you might notice that I make reference to Hayti and Haiti. The difference in spelling is intentional, each one corresponding to a particular moment in the history of what is currently called Haiti. Notably, the 1805 Constitution names the former French colony Saint Domingue as "Hayti." Following the death of Dessalines, the state becomes the Republic of Haiti. Thus, I use the "Hayti" spelling only in reference to the 1805 Constitution and the Declaration of Independence of that state in 1804 and the period therein.

17. Article 13 raises several questions regarding how women (Black, white, and mixed race, for instance) might be viewed in Haiti at the time of the revolution. However, there is insufficient time and space to address these questions here.

18. In this instance I am using Badiou's conception of "political."

19. It should be noted here that my use of "political" in this instance is *not* in reference to Badiou's conception of politics.

5. SYLVIA WYNTER'S THEORY OF EMANCIPATION

1. I use the term "New World" throughout this chapter in part because of Wynter's dependence upon it. That said, I also recognize that the presumption that the Americas is or was a new world fails to acknowledge that Indigenous communities were present on the continent prior to the arrival of European settlers. In addition, it risks perpetuating a narrative of the Americas as terra nullius, which is false but also central to arguments for settler colonialism.

2. True Christian Self, Man 1, and Man 2 (in addition to Man discussed prior to a distinction between its first and second form) as well as the Human, in this instance, are all technical terms that will be capitalized throughout.

3. Wynter's binding together of Judaism and Christianity in the concept "Judeo-Christian" has been criticized. For the remainder of this chapter, I refer to this period as the Christian conception of the subject, or the True Christian Self.

4. Spirit/Flesh is a technical term used by Sylvia Wynter.

5. In *The Avengers of the New World,* Laurent Dubois notes how "the 'devastation of the Indies' was chronicled by Bartolomé de Las Casas, who arrived in Hispaniola [the island which would later become Haiti and the Dominican Republic] as a young settler in 1502, and was transformed by what he saw. Within a decade he became the first priest ordained in the Americas, and a harsh critic of the brutal treatment of the Taino by the Spaniards" (2004, 14).

6. It is important to note that slavery was extremely violent and cruel, and

my use of "unjust methods" is not meant to distract from the violence that was enacted, and that has permeated generation after generation of those who were/ are negatively impacted. However, it is not entirely clear that Las Casas was concerned with the ways in which slaves from Africa were treated. Rather, as noted by Wynter in the quote above, he seems primarily concerned with how "just title" and "justice" are conceived within a particular worldview. As such, I have used the term "unjust methods" in this sentence to locate what seems to me to be the center around which Las Casas argument pivots. That said, as noted by Dubois, "Las Casas had, ironically, advocated the importation of African slaves to save the brutalized indigenous population. Soon imported slaves replaced the rapidly dying indigenous ones, serving as laborers in a new industry that supplemented that of mining" (2004, 15).

7. There seems to be some debate regarding the justifications used by Las Casas and Sepúlveda. While some times it seem apparent that Sepúlveda relies heavily on Aristotle to defend his claims, at other times it seems as though Las Casas "appears to accept that theory, or at least admit the possibility, that some men are by nature slaves" (Hanke 1959, 57), and yet he does not seek to defend that position in the context of the debate. Rather, "his argument tends to lead inevitably to the conclusion that no nation—or people—should be condemned as a whole to such an inferior position" (58).

8. It is important to note that Wynter explicitly references Fanon in this quote, indirectly citing the 1963 version of his *Wretched of the Earth*.

9. The lack of attention to race in Beauvoir's project is problematic. See Gines 2014 and Rivera Berruz 2016.

10. This selection of text refers to a specific era of Césaire's writings. There are various eras in his writings and (significantly) his political career, and there were various twists and turns throughout. That said, the quote that is used here most accurately reflects Wynter's use of his works.

Bibliography

Abdel-Shehid, Gamal and Zahir Kolia. 2017. "In Light of the Master: Re-reading Césaire and Fanon." *The CLR James Journal* 23, nos. 1–2, 175–92.

Alcoff, Linda Martín. 2006. *Visible Identities: Race, Gender, and the Self.* Oxford: Oxford University Press.

Alcoff, Linda Martín. 2016. *The Political Critique of Identity.* Accessed November 22, 2016. http://www.alcoff.com/content/chap2polcri.html.

Appiah, Kwame Anthony. 2000. "The Uncompleted Argument: Du Bois and the Illusion of Race." In *The Idea of Race,* ed. Robert Bernasconi and Tommy L. Lott, 118–35. Indianapolis: Hackett.

Badiou, Alain. 2001. *Ethics: An Essay on the Understanding of Evil.* Trans. Peter Hallward. London: Verso.

Badiou, Alain. 2003. *Saint Paul: The Foundation of Universalism.* Trans. Ray Brassier. Stanford, Calif.: Stanford University Press.

Badiou, Alain. 2005a. *Being and Event.* Trans. Oliver Feltham. London: Continuum.

Badiou, Alain. 2005b. *Infinite Thought: Truth and the Return to Philosophy.* Ed. and trans. Oliver Feltham and Justin Clemens. London: Continuum.

Badiou, Alain. 2008. *Conditions.* Trans. Steven Corcoran. London: Continuum.

Badiou, Alain. 2009. *Logics of Worlds.* Trans. Alberto Toscano. New York: Continuum.

Badiou, Alain. 2011a. *Polemics.* Trans. Steven Cocoran. London: Verso.

Badiou, Alain. 2011b. *Second Manifesto for Philosophy.* Trans. Louise Burchill. Cambridge: Polity Press.

Badiou, Alain. 2012a. *In Praise of Love.* New York: New Press.

Badiou, Alain. 2012b. *The Rebirth of History: Times of Riots and Uprisings*. Trans. Gregory Elliot. New York: Verso.

Badiou, Alain. 2016a. "La Frustration d'un désir d'Occident ouvre un espace à l'instinct de mort." Interview with Robert Maggiori and Anastasia. Vécrin. *Liberation*. https://www.liberation.fr/debats/2016/01/11/alain-badiou -la-frustration-d-un-desir-d-occident-ouvre-un-espace-a-l-instinct-de-mort _1425642.

Badiou, Alain. 2016b. "Twenty-Four Notes on the Uses of the Word 'People.'" In *What Is a People?* trans. Jody Gladding, 21–31. New York: Columbia University Press.

Badiou, Alain. 2017. *Black: The Brilliance of a Non-color*. Trans. Susan Spitzer. Cambridge: Polity Press.

Badiou, Alain, and Peter Hallward. 1998. "Politics and Philosophy: An Interview with Alain Badiou." *Angelaki: Journal of the Theoretical Humanities* 3, no. 3: 113–33.

Badiou, Alain, and Eric Hazen. 2013. "'Anti-Semitism Everywhere' in France Today." In *Reflections on Anti-Semitism*, trans. David Fernbach, 3–44. London: Verso.

Beauvoir, Simone de. 1965. *Force of Circumstance*. Trans. Richard Howard. Harmondsworth: Penguin Books.

Beauvoir, Simone de. 2011. *The Second Sex*. Trans. Constance Borde and Sheila Malovany-Chevallier. New York: Vintage Books.

Bernasconi, Robert. 1996. "Casting the Slough: Fanon's New Humanism for a New Humanity." In *Fanon: A Critical Reader*, ed. Lewis R. Gordon, T. Denean Sharpley-Whiting, and Renée T. White, 113–21. Oxford: Blackwell.

Bernasconi, Robert. 2002. "The Assumption of Négritude: Aimé Césaire, Frantz Fanon, and the Vicious Circle of Racial Politics." *Parallax* 9, no. 2: 69–83.

Bernasconi, Robert. 2004. "Identity and Agency in Frantz Fanon." *Sartre Studies International* 10, no. 2: 106–9.

Bernasconi Robert, Kathryn T. Gines, and Paul C. Taylor. 2013. "Letter from the Editors." *Critical Philosophy of Race* 1, no. 1: iv–v.

Bernasconi, Robert, and Tommy L. Lott, eds. 2000. *The Idea of Race*. Indianapolis: Hackett.

Bernasconi, Robert, and Anika Maaza Mann. 2005. "The Contradiction of Racism: Locke, Slavery, and the Two Treatises." In *Race and Racism in Modern Philosophy*, ed. Andrew Valls, 89–107. Ithaca: Cornell University Press.

Bosteels, Bruno. 2014. "The Fate of the Generic: Marx with Badiou." In *(Mis)readings of Marx in Continental Philosophy*, ed. Jernej Habjan and Jessica Whyte, 211–26. London: Palgrave MacMillan.

Bosteels, Bruno. 2016. "This People Which Is Not One." In *What Is a People?* trans. Jody Gladding, 1–20. New York: Columbia University Press.

Buck-Morss, Susan. 2000. "Hegel and Haiti." *Critical Inquiry* 26:821–56.

Buck-Morss, Susan. 2009. *Hegel, Haiti, and Universal History.* Pittsburgh: University of Pittsburgh Press.

Burchill, Louise. 2018. "Of a Universal No Longer Indifferent to Difference: Badiou (and Irigaray) on Woman, Truths, and Philosophy." *Philosophy Today* 62, no. 4: 1165–88.

Calcagno, Antonio. 2015. "Fidelity to the Political Event: Hegel, Badiou, and the Return of the Same." In *Badiou and Hegel: Infinity, Dialectics, Subjectivity,* ed. Jim Vernon and Antonio Calcagno, 177–92. Lanham, Md.: Lexington Books.

Cerdeiras, Raúl J. 2003. "Las politicas de emancipación." *Acontecimiento* 26. https://www.grupoacontecimiento.com.ar/las-politicas-de-emancipacion/.

Césaire, Aimé. 1972. *Discourse on Colonialism.* Trans. Joan Pinkham. New York: Monthly Review Press.

Césaire, Aimé. 1983. *The Collected Poetry of Aimé Césaire.* Trans. Clayton Eshleman and Annette Smith. Berkeley: University of California Press.

Césaire, Aimé. 2001. *Notebook of a Return to the Native Land.* Trans. Clayton Eshleman and Annette Smith. Middletown, Conn.: Wesleyan University Press.

Césaire, Aimé. 2010. "Letter to Maurice Thorez." *Social Text* 103 28, no. 2: 145–52.

Ciccariello-Maher, George. 2014. "'So Much the Worse for the Whites': Dialectics of the Haitian Revolution." *Journal of French and Francophone Philosophy* 12, no. 1: 19–39.

Ciccariello-Maher, George. 2017. *Decolonizing Dialectics.* Durham, N.C.: Duke University Press.

Corcoran, Steven, ed. 2015. *The Badiou Dictionary.* Edinburgh: Edinburgh University Press.

Coulthard, Glen Sean. 2014. *Red Skin, White Masks: Rejecting the Colonial Politics of Recognition.* Minneapolis: University of Minnesota Press.

Crenshaw, Kimberlé. 1989. "Demarginalizing the Intersection of Race and Sex: A Black Feminist Critique of Antidiscrimination Doctrine, Feminist Theory and Antiracist Politics." *University of Chicago Legal Forum* 140:139–67.

Crenshaw, Kimberlé. 1993. "Mapping the Margins: Intersectionality, Identity Politics, and Violence Against Women of Color." *Stanford Law Review* 43:1241–99.

Davis, Angela. 1972. "Reflections on the Black Woman's Role in the Community of Slaves." *Massachusetts Review* 13, nos. 1–2: 81–100.

Davis, Gregson. 1997. *Aimé Césaire.* Cambridge: Cambridge University Press.

Diagne, Souleymane Bachir. 2011. *African Art as Philosophy: Senghor, Bergson and the Idea of Négritude.* Trans. Chike Jeffers. London: Seagull Books.

Douglass, Frederick. 2013. *The Color Line.* Scotts Valley: CreateSpace Independent Publishing Platform.

Dubois, Laurent. 2004. *Avengers of the New World: The Story of the Haitian Revolution.* Cambridge, Mass.: Harvard University Press.

Du Bois, W. E. B. 1994. *The Souls of Black Folk.* Chicago: Dover.

Du Bois, W. E. B. 2000. "The Conservation of Race." In *The Idea of Race,* ed. Robert Bernasconi and Tommy L. Lott, 108–117. Indianapolis: Hackett.

Enderton, Herbert, and Robert R. Stoll. 2016. "Set Theory." https://www.britannica.com/topic/set-theory.

Eze, Emmanuel Chukwudi, ed. 1997. *Race and the Enlightenment: A Reader.* Malden, Mass.: Blackwell.

Fanon, Frantz. 1967. *Toward the African Revolution: Political Writings.* Trans. Haakon Chevalier. New York: Grove Press.

Fanon, Frantz. 2004. *The Wretched of the Earth.* Trans. Richard Philcox. New York: Grove Press.

Fanon, Frantz. 2008. *Black Skin, White Masks.* Trans. Richard Philcox. New York: Grove Press.

Farred, Grant. 2011. "Wretchedness." In *Living Fanon: Global Perspectives,* ed. Nigel C. Gibson, 159–172. New York: Palgrave MacMillan.

Farred, Grant. 2018. "The Fourth Spartacus." *Philosophy Today* 62, no. 4: 1115–38.

Fick, Carolyn E. 1990. *The Making of Haiti: The Saint Domingue Revolution from Below.* Knoxville: The University of Tennessee Press.

Geggus, David. 2014. *The Haitian Revolution: A Documentary History.* Indianapolis: Hackett.

Gines, Kathryn T. 2003. "Fanon and Sartre 50 Years Later: To Retain or to Reject the Concept of Race." *Sartre Studies International* 9, no. 2: 55–67.

Gines, Kathryn T. 2014. "Comparative and Competing Frameworks of Oppression in Simone de Beauvoir's *The Second Sex.*" *Graduate Faculty Philosophy Journal* 35, nos. 1–2: 251–73.

Glick, Jeremy Matthew. 2016. *The Black Radical Tragic: Performance, Aesthetics, and the Unfinished Haitian Revolution.* New York: New York University Press.

Gordon, Jane A. 2014. *Creolizing Political Theory: Reading Rousseau through Fanon.* New York: Fordham University Press.

Gordon, Jane A., and Neil Roberts, eds. 2015. *Creolizing Rousseau.* New York: Rowman and Littlefield.

Gordon, Lewis R. 1995. *Bad Faith and Antiblack Racism.* Atlantic Highlands, N.J.: Humanities Press International.

Gordon, Lewis R. 2008. *Fanon and the Crisis of European Man: An Essay on Philosophy and the Human Sciences*. New York: Routledge.

Gordon, Lewis R. 2015. *What Fanon Said: A Philosophical Introduction to His Life and Thought*. New York: Fordham University Press.

Gulick, Anne W. 2006. "We Are Not the People: The 1805 Haitian Constitution's Challenge to Political Legibility in the Age of Revolution." *American Literature* 78, no. 4: 799–820.

Hahn, Songsuk Susan. 2007. *Contradiction in Motion: Hegel's Organic Concept of Life and Value*. Ithaca, N.Y.: Cornell University Press.

Hall, Barbara. 2005. "Race in Hobbes." In *Race and Racism in Modern Philosophy*, ed. Andrew Valls, 43–56. Ithaca, N.Y.: Cornell University Press.

Hallward, Peter. 2001. *Absolutely Postcolonial: Writing between the Singular and the Specific*. Manchester: Manchester University Press.

Hallward, Peter. 2003. *Badiou: A Subject to Truth*. Minneapolis: University of Minnesota Press.

Hallward, Peter. 2007. *Damming the Flood: Haiti and the Politics of Containment*. London: Verso.

Hanke, Lewis. 1959. *Aristotle and the American Indians: A Study in Race Prejudice in the Modern World*. Bloomington: Indiana University Press.

Headley, Clevis B. 2019. "Bergson, Senghor and the Philosophical Foundations of Négritude: Intellect, Intuition, and Knowledge." In *Beyond Bergson: Race and Colonialism through the Writings of Henri Bergson*, ed. Andrea Pitts and Mark Westmoreland, 79–120. New York: State University of New York Press.

Hegel, G. W. F. 1997. "Geographical Basis of World History." In *Race and the Enlightenment: A Reader*, ed. Emmanuel Chukwudi Eze, 110–49. Oxford: Blackwell.

Henry, Paget. 2000. *Caliban's Reason: Introducing Afro-Caribbean Philosophy*. New York: Routledge.

hooks, bell. 2015. *Feminism Is for Everybody: Passionate Politics*. New York: Routledge.

James, C. L. R. 1989. *The Black Jacobins: Toussaint L'Ouverture and the San Domingo Revolution*. 2nd ed. New York: Vintage Books.

Jarosz, Lucy. 1992. "Constructing the Dark Continent: Metaphor as a Geographic Representation of Africa." *Geografiska Annaler* 74, no. 2: 105–15.

Jeffers, Chike. 2013. "The Cultural Theory of Race: Yet Another Look at Du Bois' 'The Conservation of Races.'" *Ethics* 123, no. 4: 403–26.

Jones, Donna V. 2010. *The Racial Discourses of Life Philosophy: Négritude, Vitalism, and Modernity*. New York: Columbia University Press.

Joseph-Gabriel, Annette. 2017. "Mobility and the Enunciation of Freedom in Urban Saint-Domingue." *Eighteenth-Century Studies* 50, no. 2: 213–29.

Jöttkandt, Sigi. 2010. *First Love: A Phenomenology of the One.* Melbourne: re.press.

Jöttkandt, Sigi. 2018. "'With a Lever . . .': Beckett, Badiou, and the Logics of Sexual Difference." *Philosophy Today* 62, no. 4: 1189–26.

Jules-Rosette, Bennetta. 1998. *Black Paris: The African Writers' Landscape.* Urbana: University of Illinois Press.

Kruks, Sonia. 1996. "Fanon, Sartre, and Identity Politics." In *Fanon: A Critical Reader,* ed. Lewis R. Gordon, T. Denean Sharpley-Whiting, and Renée T. White, 122–133. Oxford: Blackwell.

Laclau, Ernesto. 2005. *On Populist Reason.* New York: Verso.

Las Casas, Bartolomé de. 1971. *The History of the Indies.* Vol. 3. Trans. Andrée M. Collard. New York: Harper and Row.

Locke, John. 1993. *Two Treatises of Government.* Ed. Peter Laslett. Student edition. Cambridge: Cambridge University Press.

Love, Jeff, and Todd May. 2008. "From Universality to Equality: Badiou's Critique of Rancière." *Symposium: Canadian Journal of Continental Philosophy* 12, no. 2: 51–69.

Lumsden, Stephanie. 2016. "Reproductive Justice, Sovereignty, and Incarceration: Prison Abolition Politics and California Indians." *American Indian Culture and Research Journal* 40, no. 1: 33–46.

Maker, William. 2007. "Identity, Difference, and the Logic of Otherness." In *Identity and Difference: Studies in Hegel's Logic, Philosophy of Spirit, and Politics,* ed. Phillip T. Grier, 15–30. New York: State University of New York Press.

Marcano, Donna-Dale L. 2003. "Sartre and the Social Construction of Race." In *Race and Racism in Continental Philosophy,* ed. Robert Bernasconi and Sybol Cook, 214–26. Bloomington: Indiana University Press.

Marx, Karl, and Friedrich Engels. 1978. "Economic and Philosophic Manuscripts of 1844." In *The Marx-Engels Reader,* ed. Robert C. Tucker, trans. Martin Milligan, 66–125. 2nd ed. New York: W. W. Norton.

McKittrick, Katherine, ed. 2015. *Sylvia Wynter: On Being Human as Praxis.* Durham, N.C.: Duke University Press.

Mendoza, Bernabe S. 2018. "The Creolizing Genre of SF and the Nightmare of Whiteness in John W. Campbell's 'Who Goes There?'" *Journal of Science Fiction and Philosophy* 1:1–16.

Menon, Madhavi. 2015. *Indifference to Difference: On Queer Universalism.* Minneapolis: University of Minnesota Press.

Mentinis, Mihalis. 2006. *Zapatistas: The Chiapas Revolt and What It Means for Radical Politics.* London: Pluto Press.

Mignolo, Walter. 2015. "Sylvia Wynter: What Does It Mean to Be Human?" In *Sylvia Wynter: On Being Human as Praxis,* ed. Katherine McKittrick, 106–23. Durham, N.C.: Duke University Press.

Mills, Charles W. 1987. "Race and Class: Conflicting or Reconcilable Paradigms?" *Social and Economic Studies* 36, no. 2: 69–108.

Mills, Charles W. 1997. *The Racial Contract*. Ithaca, N.Y.: Cornell University Press.

Mills, Charles W. 2003. *From Class to Race: Essays in White Marxism and Black Radicalism*. Lanham, Md.: Rowman and Littlefield.

Mohanty, Chandra Talpade. 2003. *Feminism without Borders: Decolonizing Theory, Practicing Solidarity*. Durham, N.C.: Duke University Press.

Monahan, Michael. 2006. "Race, Colorblindness, and Continental Philosophy." *Philosophy Compass* 1, no. 6: 547–63.

Monahan, Michael. 2011. *The Creolizing Subject: Race, Reason, and the Politics of Purity*. New York: Fordham University Press.

Monahan, Michael. 2017. "Introduction: What Is Rational Is Creolizing." In *Creolizing Hegel*, ed. Michael Monahan, 1–22. London: Roman and Littlefield.

Nayar, Pramod K. 2013. *Frantz Fanon*. New York: Routledge.

Neocosmos, Michael. 2012. "Are Those-Who-Don't-Count Capable of Reason? Thinking Political Subjectivity in the (Neo-)Colonial World and the Limits of History." *Journal of Asian and African Studies* 47, no. 5: 530–47.

Neocosmos, Michael. 2016. *Thinking Freedom in Africa: Toward a Theory of Emancipatory Politics*. Johannesburg: Wits University Press.

Neocosmos, Michael. 2018. "Thinking Badiou's 'Immanent Exception': The Emancipatory Event of People's Power in 1980s South Africa." *Philosophy Today* 62, no. 4: 1089–114.

Nesbitt, Nick. 2003. *Voicing Memory: History and Subjectivity in French Caribbean Literature*. Charlottesville: University of Virginia Press.

Nesbitt, Nick. 2005. "Négritude." In *Africana: The Encyclopedia of the African and African American Experience,* ed. Kwame Anthony Appiah and Henry Louis Gates Jr., 193–99. 2nd ed. Vol. 4. Oxford: Oxford University Press.

Nesbitt, Nick. 2008. *Universal Emancipation: The Haitian Revolution and the Radical Enlightenment*. Charlottesville: University of Virginia Press.

Nesbitt, Nick. 2013. *Caribbean Critique: Antillean Critical Theory from Toussaint to Glissant*. Liverpool: Liverpool University Press.

Oliver, Kelly. 2001. *Witnessing: Beyond Recognition*. Minneapolis: University of Minnesota Press.

Ortega, Mariana, and Linda Martín Alcoff, eds. 2009. *Constructing the Nation: A Race and Nationalism Reader*. Albany: State University of New York Press.

Outlaw, Lucius T., Jr. 1996. *On Race and Philosophy*. New York: Routledge.

Paquette, Elisabeth. 2015. "Alain Badiou and the Feminine." *Badiou Studies* 4, no. 1: 47–71.

Paquette, Elisabeth. 2018. "Humanism at Its Limits: A Conversation between Alain Badiou and Sylvia Wynter." *Philosophy Today* 62, no. 4: 1069–88.

Quijano, Aníbal. 2007. "Coloniality of Modernity/Rationality." *Cultural Studies* 21, nos. 2–3: 168–78.

Rivera, Tomás. 1992. *. . . y no se lo tragó la tierra / . . . And the Earth Did Not Devour Him.* Houston: Arte Publico Press.

Rivera Berruz, Stephanie. 2016. "At the Crossroads: Latina Identity and Simone de Beauvoir's *The Second Sex.*" *Hypatia* 31, no. 2: 319–33.

Robinson, Cedric J. 2000. *Black Marxism: The Marking of the Black Radical Tradition.* Chapel Hill: University of North Carolina Press.

Ross, Luana. 2016. "Settler Colonialism and the Legislating of Criminality." *American Indian Culture and Research Journal* 40, no. 1: 1–18.

Sartre, Jean-Paul. 1948. "Black Orpheus." Trans. John MacCombie. *Massachusetts Review* 6, no. 1: 13–52.

Sartre, Jean-Paul. 1976. *Anti-Semite and Jew.* Trans. George J. Becker. New York: Schocken Books.

Sartre, Jean-Paul. 2004a. *Critique of Dialectical Reason.* Vol. 1. Ed. Jonathon Rée. Trans. Alan Sheridan-Smith. London: Verso.

Sartre, Jean-Paul. 2004b. "Preface." *Wretched of the Earth.* Trans. Richard Philcox. New York: Grove Press.

Senghor, Léopold Sédar. 2011. *Anthologie de la nouvelle poésie nègre et la malgache de langue Française.* Paris: Press Universitaires de France.

Smith, Barbara. 1999. "The Social Relations of Southern Women." In *Neither Separate nor Equal: Women, Race, and Class in the South,* ed. Barbara Smith, 13–33. Philadelphia: Temple University Press.

Srnicek, Nick. 2008. "What Is to Be Done? Alain Badiou and the Pre-Evental." *Symposium: Canadian Journal of Continental Philosophy* 12, no. 2: 110–26.

Stanley, Henry M. 2013. *Through the Dark Continent.* Vols. 1 and 2. New York: Dover.

Taylor, Paul C. 2004. *Race: A Philosophical Introduction.* Cambridge, UK: Polity Press.

Teran, Jackie. 2016. "The Violent Legacies of the California Missions: Mapping the Origins of Native Women's Mass Incarceration." *American Indian Culture and Research Journal* 40, no. 1: 185–94.

Trotsky, Leon. 1978. *On Black Nationalism & Self-Determination.* Ed. George Breitman. Toronto: Pathfinder Press.

Trott, Adriel M. 2011. "The Truth of Politics in Alain Badiou: 'There is Only One World.'" *Parrhesia* 12:82–93.

Trott, Adriel M. 2015. "Badiou contra Hegel: The Materialist Dialectic against the Myth of the Whole." In *Badiou and Hegel: Infinity, Dialectics, Subjectivity,* ed. Jim Vernon and Antonio Calcagno, 59–76. Lanham, Md.: Lexington Books.

Walia, Harsha. 2013. *Undoing Border Imperialism*. Oakland, Calif.: AK Press.

Wittig, Monique. 1992. *The Straight Mind and Other Essays*. Boston: Beacon Press.

Wright, Colin. 2009. "Badiou's Axiomatic Democracy against Cultural Politics: A Jamaican Counter-Example." *Culture, Theory and Critique* 50, no. 1: 77–91.

Wright, Colin. 2013. *Badiou in Jamaica: The Politics of Conflict*. Melbourne: re.press.

Wright, Colin. 2018. "Color Intensities: Logics of Race and Resistance in Jamaica." *Philosophy Today* 62, no. 4: 1049–68.

Wynter, Sylvia. 1976. "Ethno or Socio Poetics." *Alcheringa* 2:78–94.

Wynter, Sylvia. 1982. "Beyond Liberal and Marxist Leninist Feminisms: Towards an Autonomous Frame of Reference." Prepared for the session "Feminist Theory at the Crossroads" held at the Annual Conference of the American Sociological Association, San Francisco.

Wynter, Sylvia. 1984. "The Ceremony Must Be Found: After Humanism." *Boundary 2* 12 and 13, nos. 3 and 1: 19–70.

Wynter, Sylvia. 1987. "On Disenchanting Discourse: 'Minority' Literary Criticism and Beyond." *Cultural Critique* 7:207–44.

Wynter, Sylvia. 1992. "Beyond the Categories of the Master Conception: The Counterdoctrine of the Jamesian Poiesis." In *C. L. R. James's Caribbean*, ed. Paget Henry and Paul Buhle, 63–91. Durham, N.C.: Duke University Press.

Wynter, Sylvia. 1995. "1492: A New World View." In *Race, Discourse, and the Origin of the Americas: A New World View*, ed. Vera Lawrence Nettleford and Rex Nettleford, 5–57. Washington, D.C.: Smithsonian Institution Press.

Wynter, Sylvia. 1998. "Black Aesthetic." In *Encyclopedia of Aesthetics*, Vol. 1, ed. Michael Kelly, 273–81. New York: Oxford University Press.

Wynter, Sylvia. 2003. "Unsettling the Coloniality of Being/Power/Truth/Freedom: Towards the Human, after Man, Its Overrepresentation—an Argument." *CR: The New Centennial Review* 3, no. 3: 257–337.

Zack, Naomi. 1997. "Race, Life, Death, Identity, Tragedy, and Good Faith." In *Existence in Black: An Anthology of Black Existential Philosophy*, ed. Lewis R. Gordon, 99–110. New York: Routledge.

Zambrana, Rocío. 2015. *Hegel's Theory of Intelligibility*. Chicago: University of Chicago Press.

Index

Africa: colonization of, 42, 43, 126; Négritude and, 50–52, 60, 62, 99; Valladolid debate and, 135–38

Alcoff, Linda Martín, 10; emancipation and, 87, 122, 162; identity politics and, 67–68, 97, 117–18, 121–22; race and class and, 71, 123; racial eliminativism and, 34

Algerian Revolution: event as, 23, 26–27; people and, 38–40, 178n10; race and, 45

Althusser, Louis, 1

American Revolutionary War, 106

Americas: colonization of, 126; Haiti and, 105; "New World," 182n1

anti-Négritude, 59–60. See also Badiou, Alain; Sartre, Jean-Paul

Anti-Semite and Jew (Sartre), 41, 47–48, 68, 98, 104

appearance: maximal, 16, 23, 29; minimal, 16, 23, 95, 174n2; presentation, 18–19; world and, 15–16, 22, 120, 174n2

Appiah, Anthony, 76, 102, 160

Aristotle, 137, 183n7

assimilation, 71, 79, 177n4

Badiou, Alain: additive politics and, 13, 21, 36, 100; anti-historicism and, 117–18; capitalism and, 20, 30–31; dialectic and, 46–47, 63, 104, 121; generic and, 7, 36–37, 65–69, 119–20, 153; language and, 22–25, 29, 96, 98; Marxism and, 65–69, 165; materialist dialectic and, 22, 25–27; militant and, 26–28; name and, 24–26, 29, 39–40, 91, 96; negative conception of race and, 75, 92, 98–99, 101–2, 118, 160; Négritude and, 43, 46–47, 96–105, 116–17, 119, 159, 180n2; political emancipation, 6–9, 23–24, 32–34, 37–40, 62, 116–23; power and, 18–21, 24, 31–33, 100, 175n10, 178n10; set theory and, 1; sexual difference and, 5–6, 163–64

Beauvoir, Simone de, 2, 56, 143, 158

Bell, Kathryn Sophia (Gines): collective memory and, 10, 92–93, 118–19, 160; conservation of race and, 73, 76–77, 80, 160; Fanon and, 61, 73–74, 84, 119, 159; negative identity and, 75, 81, 104, 145, 160;

Négritude and, 62, 68, 98, 145; positive conception of race and, 66, 73–76, 81, 84, 89, 104, 111–19, 145; race and class and, 58, 68; Sartre and, 53, 68, 73–74, 98, 119, 159

Bernasconi, Robert: Négritude and, 9, 55, 57, 61–62, 159, 178n7; preservation of race and, 74, 76, 89

Biassou, Georges, 111

Black: aesthetics, 3, 50–51, 77–78, 145–46; history, 10, 77–78, 93, 118–19; joy, 77–78, 160; liberation, 47, 72–73, 79, 83, 99, 152; lived experience, 55, 62, 72, 154, 177n7; men, 4–5, 39, 50, 52, 83–84; nature, 56, 99, 180n2; peoples, 52, 56–57, 72, 85, 134, 140; poetry, 50–51, 176n5; political category, 62, 79–80, 115–16, 181n15; positive value of, 58–59, 63, 77–78, 160; pride, 86; resistance, 58, 78, 93, 122; rhythm, 56, 97–99, 180n2; women, 8, 31, 122. See also Black consciousness; Black identity

Black (Badiou): affirmation of Blackness, 99; dialectic, 46–47, 121; Fanon, 158–59; nonrealist conception of race, 102–3; particularity, 101–2; sexual difference, 164–65; social construction of race, 43–44; Wynter, 161

Black consciousness: antiracist racism, 52–54; conservation of race, 57–58, 74, 119; dialectic, 56–59, 63, 82; Négritude, 42–43, 50–52, 57, 73, 82, 119; racial self-consciousness, 42–43, 51, 154; subjective–objective method, 51–52, 56

Black identity, 9; affirming, 98, 178n7; communism, 69–74; dynamic, 61, 86; emancipation, 151; essentialism, 56; product of oppressive structures, 31, 75; racial dialectic, 46, 56–59; revolutionary, 51, 63, 82; subjectivity, 48–54

Black Marxism, 69–74

"Black Orpheus" (Sartre): dialectic, 159; Fanon, 41, 55, 81; Négritude, 52, 61, 82, 175n1; race consciousness, 49, 53, 74; socialism, 68

Black Panther Party, 46

Black Skin, White Masks (Fanon), 41, 54–55, 81, 84, 159

blanchitude, 144–46

body: individuals, 25–26; schema, 56; subject-body, 22; subjectivated-body, 25–26

Bosteels, Bruno, 26

Buck-Morss, Susan, 108–12, 181n15

Burchill, Louise, 5, 164

Calcagno, Antonio, 34, 95

Canada: Indigenous communities and, 141; Pride and, 30; Québec and, 17–19; race in, 32

Cantor, Georg, 1

capitalism: identity and, 30–31; liberal-capitalist state, 20; Négritude and, 50, 71, 84; Western capitalism, 135

Caribbean, 96–97, 105, 179n1; coloniality and, 147–48; critique, 37; Marxism, 70–71

Cerdeiras, Raúl, 5

Césaire, Aimé: communism and, 70–74, 83–84, 154, 177n4; emancipation and, 10, 62–63, 82–85;

Fanon and, 9, 162, 178n7; history and, 72–73; Négritude and, 40, 42–43, 50–51, 57–63, 97–98, 144; politics, 71–73, 84–86; universal, 61, 72, 74, 84–86, 153–54

Christian subject, 129–32; Valladolid Debate and, 135–36

Ciccariello-Maher, George, 10, 108–13, 115, 161, 181n15

class: Black bourgeoisie, 45; bourgeoisie, 70–71; consciousness, 48, 57, 84; Marx, 65–67; objective, 54; struggle, 53, 118, universal, 67–68. *See also* Marxism; race to class relationship

collective memory, 10, 93, 118–19, 160, identity and, 93, 118–19

colonialism: conception of Man and, 84, 127–28, 134; French, 40, 49–50, 52, 105–6, 110–11, 158; Marxism and, 49, 67, 71; *terra nullius,* 136

coloniality, 127–28, 147

color line, 140–41

communism. *See* Marxism

conservation of race, 66, 73–74, 76–81, 102, 159–60

Copernican Revolution, 131. *See also* rational political subject

Copernicus, 130–33

Corcoran, Steven, 15

Coulthard, Sean Glen, 148

Crenshaw, Kimberlé, 8, 45

creolization: Badiou and, 89–92, 162–63, 165; emancipation and, 87–88, 91; Fanon and, 88–92; Jane Gordon and, 60, 87–92, 148, 162; Monahan and, 88–90; Négritude and, 89; Rousseau and, 88, 89, 92

culture: distinction from politics, 10,

95–97, 121, 151; Haitian Revolution and, 115; identity and, 35–36, 103, 117, 121; immanence and, 9, 21, 96, 100, 108; Négritude movement as, 96–105, 116, 145–46, 155, 161; positive conception of race and, 76–79, 145–46; transcendental index and, 100; universal and, 145–46, 154–55

damné (damned), 114, 139–40

Darwin, Charles, 139–40

Davis, Angela, 122

Davis, Gregson, 61–62, 86

decolonial theory, 41, 91, 161, 164–65; Ciccariello-Maher and, 108, 161; Fanon and, 44–45; Mignolo and, 147–48; Quijano and, 127, 148; Wynter and, 8, 10, 127–28, 147, 161–62, 165

delinking, 147–49

Depestre, René, 71–72

Derrida, Jacques, 2

Dessalines, Jean-Jacques, 110, 112, 115

Diagne, Souleymane Bachir, 61–62

dialectic: Badiou and, 22, 25–27, 46–47, 63, 104, 121; Fanon and, 44–45, 55–58, 60, 90; Haitian Revolution and, 108, 115, 117–18; racism and, 43, 57, 72–74, 78, 80–84, 87; Sartre and, 49, 53–55, 57, 82; Wynter and, 144–46

difference. *See* politics of indifference

difference/deference organizing principle, 143. *See also* liminal position

domination: coloniality and, 127; modes of, 150; white domination, 46; Wynter and, 117, 126, 138, 152

Douglass, Frederick, 140–41

Dubois, Laurent, 110

Du Bois, W. E. B.: "Conservation of Races," 74, 76, 79, 102, 159; double consciousness and, 140–43, 144; historical memory and, 77; negative conception of race and, 76; positive conception of race and, 76–77, 79, 84, 86, 89, 92; *Souls of Black Folk,* 140, 143

Dumas, Léon, 158

economic and biological man, 138–42; Darwin and, 139–40

Egypt, 28

Enderton, Herbert, 1

Engels, Friedrich, 66

epistemic disobedience, 146–49, 155

ethnicity: coloniality and, 127; conservation of race and, 79; Négritude and, 52–53

Eurocentrism, 66, 71, 78–79, 81, 87, 116

event: emancipation and, 23, 35, 37, 161; evental site, 24, 28–29, 35–36, 69, 121; excess and, 23–26; inexistent and, 23, 95; naming and, 22, 25, 96; particularity and, 26, 67, 69, 90, 118–20; the people and, 26–28; political event, 25, 37, 95–96, 117–18, 120–22; productive of truth and, 22, 24, 27–28, 35, 67, 96

evental situation. *See* event

faithful subject, 27, 119–20

Fanon, Frantz: conception of race and, 74–75, 82–84, 118–19, 160, 175n2; emancipation, 57–58, 72, 74, 81–82; history and, 56–60, 118–19; Marxism and, 70, 72; Négritude and, 54–66, 82–84, 89,
159, 175n1, 178n7; politics, 58, 81; racial consciousness and, 45, 57–59, 73, 82; reason and, 54–57; schema and, 56; universal, 57–59, 63, 81–82; violence and, 39; white gaze and, 55–56, 160. *See also* Fanon–Sartre debate

Fanon–Sartre debate, 10, 14, 62–63, 152, 159, 160; class consciousness and, 52; emancipation and, 53; identity and, 48–49, 54–55; Négritude and, 42–43, 50, 59, 61, 82–84; race consciousness and, 50–52, 58–59; rationality/irrationality and, 55–57; subjective–objective and, 51, 54–56

Farred, Grant, 5, 44–45, 122

feminism, 2, 5–6, 8, 143, 163–64

Fick, Carolyn E., 105

Foucault, Michel, 1

francophone studies, 157–59

French Revolution, 1, 7; as event, 25; group identity and, 45, 107, 116, 121–22; Haitian Revolution and, 105–7, 109, 111, 116, 121–22

Geggus, David, 105, 108, 112

Genet, Jean, 43

Gines, Kathryn T. *See* Bell, Kathryn Sophia

Glick, Jeremy Matthew, 152

Gordon, Jane A.: Badiou and, 89–93; creolization and, 87–92, 148, 162–63; Fanon and, 88–92, 148, 163; Négritude and, 60–61, 89

Gordon, Lewis R., 9, 39, 41

Gulick, Anne W., 113–15

Haitian Revolution, 7–8, 37; American Revolution and, 107; as cultural movement, 115–16; emancipation and, 96–97, 109–10; as event, 105–8, 115, 161; French Revolution and, 106, 107, 109; as political movement, 105–8, 161; race and, 108–17, 161; universal, 96, 105–12, 115–17

Hall, Barbara, 2–3

Hallward, Peter: Haitian Revolution and, 105, 108; liberal-capitalist state and, 20; negative conception of race and, 75; Négritude and, 98, 101; politics and, 14; production of truth and, 120

Hanke, Lewis, 137

Hazen, Eric, 43

Headley, Clevis B., 42, 59–61

Hegel, G. W. F., 2, 3; creolization and, 88; Haiti and, 108; master/slave dialectic and, 179n12; Négritude and, 53; world and, 174nn3–4

Henry, Paget, 91

history: Blackness and, 34–35, 56–58, 72, 117–20, 160; collective memory and, 10, 77–78, 93, 118–19; Négritude and, 47–49, 57, 72–73, 76, 79

Hobbes, Thomas, 2–3

hooks, bell, 45

human, the. See Christian subject; humanism

humanism: abstract, 36–37, 54, 72, 145; economic and biological man and, 138–42; generic humanity, 7, 36–37, 65, 69, 120, 153; the human, 129–32; liberal humanism, 138; rational political subject and, 132–38; universal humanism, 123, 164

identity, 16–17, 30–42; constructed by state power, 30–31, 33, 35–36;

cultural identities, 104; difference and, 16, 32; politics of indifference and, 8–9, 14, 37; racial identity, 31, 48, 58, 75, 86–87, 108, 110

identity politics, 13–14; Alcoff and, 67, 97; emancipation and, 47, 65–69; Fraser and, 67–68, 121; Gitlin and, 67–68, 121; Menon and, 31–33, 37; universality and, 43–47

inexistent: emancipation and, 33, 35, 39, 69, 106, 120–21; event and, 27–29; negation of, 125, 127, 138; recognition and, 20, 23, 37, 95

intersectionality, 8, 45, 154, 163

Iraq, 33

Jamaica, 25

James, C. L. R.: Black identity and, 31, 151–52; pieza framework and, 127, 150–51, 153–54

Jarosz, Lucy, 4

Jean-François (Papillon), 110

Jeffers, Chike: cluster conception of race and, 152; conservation of race and, 77–80, 84, 89, 160; positive conception of race and, 77–80, 86, 92, 160

Jones, Donna V., 61–62, 83, 86, 179n12

Jöttkandt, Sigi, 5, 164

Judeo-Christian subject. See Christian subject

Jules-Rosette, Benetta, 59–60

justice: Haitian Revolution in, 107–8, 116; injustice and, 143; political truth and, 24, 28, 67, 96, 120; universal, 29–30, 37, 103

Kant, Immanuel, 3, 14

Lacan, Jacques, 1, 6

Laclau, Ernesto, 26

Las Casas, Bartolomé de, 135–38, 182n5

Legesse, Asmaran, 143

LGBTQ: gay, 68, 143; homosexuality, 30–31, 37, 38, 103; identity and, 68; medical and, 31; Menon and, 5, 9, 14, 32; Pride, 30; queer, 17, 38

liminal position, 142–47; consciousness and, 142, 144; emancipation and, 149–51; knowledge and, 146, 155

Locke, John, 3

L'Ouverture, Toussaint, 107, 109–10

Love, Jeff, 19

Lumsden, Stephanie, 141

Man 1. See humanism; rational political subject

Man 2. See economic and biological man; humanism

Maoist Revolution, 1, 14

Marcano, Donna-Dale L., 47–49, 104

Marx, Karl, 1

Marxism: Black, 69–70, 177n2; Césaire and, 70–73, 83–85; Communist Party, 14, 85; Fanon–Sartre debate and, 65, 68, 72; identity politics and, 67–69; race and, 63, 65–67, 69–74; universal emancipation and, 65, 66–69

May, Todd, 19

McKittrick, Katherine, 125

Menon, Madhavi: identity and, 31, 36–37, 101; politics of indifference and, 32–33; queer universalism and, 9, 14, 32; universalism and, 35, 101

Mentinis, Mihalis, 5

Merleau-Ponty, Maurice, 158

Mignolo, Walter, 137, 147–49

militant, 26, 28

Mills, Charles W., 70–71, 75

minority discourse, 143

Moïse, Hyacinthe, 110

Monahan, Michael, 10, 34, 88–90; Fanon, 88–92, 148, 163

naming, 25–27, 29, 39–40, 91

nature: natural law, 133; race and, 56, 99, 137, 143, 180n2

Nayar, Pramond, 60

negative conception of race: anti-racist racism as, 55, 57–58, 160; antirealist approach and, 76; as dialectical, 53–54, 57–58, 145–46; emancipation and, 78, 153; Haitian Revolution and, 107–8; Negro/blanchitude and, 145–46; negative group identity as, 47–49, 55–56, 73–74, 101, 104, 118; oppression and, 78; overcoming and, 62–63, 74, 75–76; as rationality–irrationality, 55–59; social constructivist model and, 75. See also Badiou, Alain; Sartre, Jean-Paul

Négritude: class and, 50–52, 58, 68, 71, 83; culture and, 10, 97–105; debates in, 59–63; dialectic and, 53–55, 57–59, 82; emancipation, 52–54, 57–59, 62–63, 70–74, 76–78, 81–86; essentialism and, 59–60, 61; liminality and, 142–47; pluralism and, 61, 73; poetry and, 50–51, 176n5; politics, 79, 84; positive conception of race as, 82–84, 86; self-consciousness and, 42–43, 50–53, 58, 59, 82; as subjective movement, 51–54; universal, 57–63, 68–69, 72, 74, 78, 80–86

Neocosmos, Michael, 122
Nesbitt, Nick: Haitian Revolution, 37, 96, 105–12, 115–16, 121, 161; Marx and, 66; Négritude and, 42–43, 179n12; racial identity and, 154
nominalism. *See* racial eliminativism
nonexistent. *See* inexistent

oppression: identity and, 32–33; systemic forms of, 1–2, 6, 76. *See also* racism
Outlaw, Lucius T., Jr., 66; cluster concept of race and, 152; conservation of races and, 89, 160; politics of difference and, 79–81; positive conception of race and, 79–80, 84, 86–87, 89, 92, 160

particularity: difference as, 33–34, 47, 100–101, 115; emancipation and, 10–11, 52–54, 62, 67–69, 85, 126–27; Haitian Revolution and, 113–16; immanence and, 101; Négritude and, 52–54, 57, 72, 85, 97–105, 126; pluri-conceptual and, 152–55, 162; politics and, 100–104, 115; race and, 7–8, 30–32, 54, 85, 102, 113–14; subtraction of, 26, 126, 152–53; universality and, 7–8, 37–39, 67–69, 116, 150, 153
people, the: Algeria and, 23, 26, 38–40, 178n10; identity and, 26, 38–39; nationality and, 26; nonexistent and, 23, 39–40; particular and, 26, 36, 38, 69; subject and, 26, 28, 32, 38, 39
pieza framework. *See under* pluri-conceptual framework
Plato, 2

pluri-conceptual framework, 149–55; emancipation and, 127, 142, 149; pieza framework and, 8, 150–51; universal and, 153–54
poetry: Négritude and, 50–51, 176n5; race consciousness and, 50–51
political subject. *See* people, the
politics of indifference: critique of, 65–66, 69–74; faithful subject and, 119–20; generic humanity and, 36–37; group history and, 117; identity and, 118; indifference to difference, 8–9, 11, 13–14, 30, 47; Marxist critique of, 66; method of abstraction and, 36; revolutionary change and, 35; subtraction and, 36, 103
positive conception of race, 9, 81, 119; Badiou and, 86–87, 98–99, 102, 118; conservation of race and, 74, 77–78, 80; culture as, 77–79; emancipation and, 81–85, 120–21; memory and, 98, 118; as political, 78–81, 160; as value, 58–59, 62, 74–77, 160; Wynter and, 62, 144–46. *See also* Bell, Kathryn Sophia; Césaire, Aimé; Du Bois, W. E. B.; Fanon, Frantz; Jeffers, Chike; Outlaw, Lucius T., Jr.
power: Black, 47; colonialism and, 49, 106, 109, 127; identity and, 31–33, 175n10; labor and, 150, 152; oppression and, 10, 16, 44; state and, 18–22, 24, 27, 32–33, 100, 178n10
preservation of race. *See* conservation of race
proletariat. *See* class; Marxism; race to class relationship

Québec, 17–19
queer theory, 5, 32
queer universalism, 9, 14
Quijano, Aníbal, 127–28, 137, 161

race: biological conception of, 34–35,
    76, 102; colonialism and, 126,
    127–29, 134–38; essentialism and,
    42, 50–52, 56; Europe and, 43–44,
    49, 71, 92, 116–17, 121–23; Haitian
    Revolution and, 96, 107, 108–17,
    121; identity and, 45–51, 55–58,
    61, 66, 74–81, 86–87; particular
    and, 49, 52–54, 57, 72, 77–78, 85;
    social construction of, 2, 43–44, 47,
    75. See also Black; Black conscious-
    ness; Black identity; Césaire, Aimé;
    conservation of race; Fanon–Sartre
    debate; Marxism; negative concep-
    tion of race; Négritude; positive
    conception of race; race to class
    relationship; racism; Sartre,
    Jean-Paul
race to class relationship: Black Marx-
    ism and, 69–73; emancipation and,
    83–85, 122–23, 153; Négritude–
    class dichotomy, 52, 54, 58, 154,
    175n1, 177n10; race and class func-
    tion together, 62–63; subtraction of
    race from class, 55, 57, 66–68, 90,
    119, 152
racial consciousness. See race
racial eliminativism, 34, 37, 76, 102,
    160
racial realism, 76
racism: Négritude and, 50, 53–55, 57,
    60, 72, 82, 98; preservation of race
    and, 73–74, 76; race product of,
    43–46, 49, 53–54, 78, 81–82, 84,
    87; resistance to, 58, 80, 99, 101,

118–19; white gaze and, 55–56, 73,
    160; white supremacy and, 46, 63,
    75, 77–79, 110, 160
Rastafari movement, 25, 122
rational/irrational organizing prin-
    ciple, 132, 140. See also rational
    political subject
rationality: dichotomy with irratio-
    nality, 56, 58, 140, 144; irrational
    (opposite), 56, 132, 134, 135,
    137–40; Négritude and, 55–58;
    rational subject, 126, 129, 132–38,
    141, 147; subrational, 134–35, 137,
    144; universal, 133
rational political subject (Man 1),
    132–38
Robinson, Cedric J., 69–71
Ross, Luana, 141
Rousseau, Jean-Jacques, 26, 88–89, 92,
    148, 163

Sartre, Jean-Paul: anti-racist racism
    and, 52–53; Black consciousness
    and, 50–54, 57–59; class and, 48,
    53–54, 57, 63, 72; emancipation,
    53–54, 57–58, 68–69, 84; gaze
    and, 47–49; Négritude and, 47–54,
    159, 176n6; politics, 49–50; social
    construction of race and, 47–49, 53;
    subjective–objective method and,
    51; subject/object dichotomy and,
    56; universal, 53–54, 57–58. See
    also Fanon–Sartre debate
self–other master code, 130–32, 136,
    138, 141. See also Christian subject;
    economic and biological man;
    rational political subject
Senghor, Léopold Sédar, 42, 50, 57, 61,
    97, 158
Sepúlveda, Juan Ginés de, 135–38

social constructivist model of race, 44, 47–49, 53, 75, 76, 79

socialism. *See* Marxism

solidarity: Alcoff and, 88, 122, 162; identity and, 52–53, 79, 81, 116, 122; Wynter and, 154–55, 162

Sonthonax, Léger-Félicité, 109

soul: Badiou and, 46, 99; Du Bois and, 140; Fanon and, 56; Sartre and, 50–52, 73

South Africa, 5, 28, 34–35, 122

Spirit/Flesh organizing principle, 130–32, 135, 140. *See also* Christian subject

Srnicek, Nick, 27–29

Stanley, Henry M., 4

state, 14–41; identity and, 14, 16, 31–38; immanent practices of, 15, 24, 29, 96, 100–101, 178n10; inexistent and, 19–20, 23, 32–33, 35, 37, 125; justice and, 24, 28–29, 36–37; language, 23–25, 29; logic of the state, 16–18, 21–29, 30–31, 35–40, 100–101, 103–4; necessity of, 20; representation, 13, 18–21, 23, 31–33, 70; state power, 16, 18–21, 24, 27, 31–33, 95

Still, Robert R., 1

subject: event and, 25, 27–29, 38, 90, 96, 119–21; as obscure, 27; as reactive, 27

subjectivation, 25–26

subject–other, 127–29. *See also* Christian subject; economic and biological man; rational political subject

subtractive theory of politics, 13, 21–22, 36–38, 104, 120, 178n10

Taylor, Paul C., 74, 76

Teran, Jackie, 141

transatlantic slave trade, 42, 53, 105, 136, 150, 152

transcendental operator/index, 15–18, 22–23, 95, 100, 129

Trotsky, Leon, 72

Trott, Adriel M., 19–21, 174nn2–3

truth, 13, 22–30; adaptive truth-for, 133; bodies and language and, 22, 24–25; emancipation, 104; immanent, 24; indifference to difference and, 30, 102; justice and, 95; production of truth, 24, 27, 120; singular and, 35; subject of, 22; universal and, 24, 29–30, 69, 101, 126

truth procedures: as art/poetry, 22, 23, 175n8; event and, 23–29, 36; evental site and, 28–29, 35–36; faithful subject and, 27–28; language and, 24–25, 29; as love, 175n8; name and, 24–27, 29, 39–40; politics, 22–24, 29, as science/mathematics, 175n8

United States: Haitian Revolution and, 113; homosexuality and, 31; Indigenous communities and, 141; Pride and, 30; race in, 7, 32, 34, 63, 98, 140; same-sex marriage and, 21

Valladolid debate, 135–38

violence: Fanon and, 39; freedom from, 68; as political process, 39

white: gaze, 55–56, 73–74, 104, 145, 160; political whiteness, 181n15

Wittig, Monique, 143

world: appearance and, 15–19, 22–23, 28–29, 100, 120, 141–42; bodies and, 24–26, 56; emancipation and, 116–17, 121; language and, 24;

logics of, 120, 125–26, 128–29, 131, 134, 135; multiplicity of, 17, 174nn2–3; race, 51, 59, 70

Wretched of the Earth (Fanon), 39, 44–45, 49, 158

Wright, Colin: culture and, 10, 99–100; history and, 118; inexistent and, 20, 32; political truth and, 10, 22, 24–25, 67; subtractive theory and, 21–22

Wynter, Sylvia: aesthetics and, 146; difference, 138, 143–44, 149–55; emancipation, 126–27, 144, 149–55, 161–62; enchantment and, 127–28, 145; epochal rupture and, 130–32, 136–37; Négritude and, 126, 127, 144, 147, 155; politics, 126–27, 132–38, 146–47, 152–55; selection and, 139–40; social imaginary and, 127–28; Torrid Zone and, 130–31; universal humanism and, 123; universality, 132–34, 150–55; worldview and, 125–26, 131, 134, 141–44, 147–49

ELISABETH PAQUETTE is assistant professor of philosophy and women's and gender studies at the University of North Carolina at Charlotte.